Words of the World

Words of the World

Abram de Swaan

Polity

First published in 2001 by Polity Press in association with Blackwell Publishers Ltd

Editorial office:
Polity Press
65 Bridge Street
Cambridge CB2 1UR, UK

Marketing and production:
Blackwell Publishers Ltd
108 Cowley Road
Oxford OX4 1JF, UK

Published in the USA by
Blackwell Publishers Inc.
350 Main Street
Malden, MA 02148, USA

A catalogue record for this book is available from the British Library.

Library of Congress Cataloging-in-Publication Data

Swaan, A. de.
    Words of the world : the global language system / Abram de Swaan.
        p. cm.
    Includes bibliographical references and index.
    ISBN 0-7456-2747-1—ISBN 0-7456-2748-X (pbk.)
        1. Language and languages—Philosophy. 2. Language policy. 3. English language—Foreign countries. I. Title.

P107 .S93 2001
401—dc21

                                                                          2001036802

Typeset in 10 ½ on 12 pt Sabon
by Kolam Information Services Pvt. Ltd., Pondicherry, India
Printed in Great Britain by TJ International, Padstow, Cornwall

This book is printed on acid-free paper.

Contents

Preface

This book is much more a product of the global language system than its author ever intended it to be. I began work on it in 1993, in the hospitable, anglophone environment of Cornell University, NY, where I held the Luigi Einaudi chair of international studies. Once I returned to the familiar and increasingly bilingual setting of the University of Amsterdam, I continued to write in English, using Netherlandish mostly for essays and columns in Dutch newspapers, much as one might take a plane to remote destinations and ride one's bike on nearby trips. In the autumn of 1995, I found myself abroad once again, this time in Budapest, where I occupied the European Union chair of social policy at the Eötvös Loránd University. This time I was surrounded by Hungarians who had such facility in English (and German, and French and Russian) that I never had a chance to pick up more Magyar than the most indispensable: *nagyon szépen köszönöm*, many thanks to my colleagues there, and most of all to Professor Zsuzsa Ferge, my thoughtful hostess and longtime friend. The decisive spurt in writing this book came in the academic year 1997/8, when I was elected to the *chaire européenne* of the Collège de France at the initiative of Pierre Bourdieu, who thus contributed much to the completion of this project. The professors of the Collège are expected to present thirteen *conférences* each year, and write them up, in French, of course. I made the best of my predicament and told the students that my halting French was an apt demonstration of the realities of the world language system. They were duly impressed, by the realities. Indeed, I did write the first complete version of this book entirely in French: 'Oops, wrong language!' I rewrote the text, once again, in English: the version that lies before you. Finally, Leonoor Broeder translated it most competently into Dutch. Reading one's own writings in translation feels like being impersonated by an actor. But seeing the translation into my own native tongue, I felt as though I were being confronted with a Doppelgänger, who to everyone else appears perfectly indistinguishable, but to me can never be the same.

In this edition, too, there is a slight sense of alienation: English is not the language of my childhood years (although it was my parents' secret language which therefore had to be urgently deciphered).

Native speakers of English have the great fortune that their language has become *the* lingua franca of the world, which saves them much effort and yields them great opportunities. On the other hand, many hundreds of millions have appropriated this global vehicular as a foreign language, with considerable exertion, and much to their advantage.

A variety of Englishes has emerged in different parts of the world, but so far they have all remained mutually intelligible. The more peripheral and the more recent varieties command less prestige and attention than the established usage of educated native speakers in the UK and the US. Moreover, for a long time to come, American and British media will remain in control of the worldwide distribution of texts and performances in English. For all those who learned English after their childhood years, I hope that the privileged position of its native users will gradually erode. But that is not likely to happen soon. In the meantime, even the foreign speakers, underprivileged as they are, still share in the advantages of the one global language.

Among the pleasures of working on this book was the collaboration with a sequence of research assistants: Jannes Hartkamp in Budapest, Jeanne Kouta and Florence Colas in Paris, Jeroen Starrenburg and Jacek Magala in Amsterdam. For some reason they all turned out to be both gifted and devoted, a surprising combination that put me much into their debt.

The Royal Netherlands Academy of Science, the European Cultural Foundation and the Brouwers Stichting provided me with grants. Numerous colleagues from different disciplines and countries helped me with facts, references and critical comments. My intellectual debt to them should be apparent from the notes and citations in the book. One among them is mentioned here: David Laitin, who was an early companion in the political sociology of language.

I took the world as my research area, compared five different language constellations, and combined notions from economics, linguistics, history, political science and sociology in a synthetic perspective. A huge topic is not necessarily more difficult than a small one, nor is a multidisciplinary approach more learned than a specialist view, but they can be a bit more intimidating. I was encouraged throughout by my friends Johan Goudsblom and Kitty Roukens, who read each chapter as a draft and gave me their views with insight, generosity and tact.

This is in English, not in French, or Dutch, or Swahili (and the preceding phrase is absolutely untranslatable). Why it should be in this language rather than another can be explained from the dynamics of the global language constellation, and that is what this book is about.

Abram de Swaan

Introduction: the global language system

The human species is divided into more than five thousand groups each of which speaks a different language and does not understand any of the others. With this multitude of languages, humankind has brought upon itself a great confusion of tongues. But nevertheless, the entire human species remains connected: the division is overcome by people who speak more than one language and thus ensure communication between different groups. It is multilingualism that has kept humanity, separated by so many languages, together. The multilingual connections between language groups do not occur haphazardly, but, on the contrary, they constitute a surprisingly strong and efficient network that ties together – directly or indirectly – the six billion inhabitants of the earth. It is this ingenious pattern of connections between language groups that constitutes the global language system. That is the subject of this book.

This worldwide constellation of languages is an integral part of the 'world system'. The population of the earth is organized into almost two hundred states and a network of international organizations – the political dimension of the world system; it is coordinated through a concatenation of markets and corporations – the economic dimension; it is linked by electronic media in an encompassing, global culture; and, in its 'metabolism with nature', it also constitutes an ecological system. The idea of a global human society which indeed constitutes a system on a world scale has regained much attention in recent years. However, the fact that humanity, divided by a multitude of languages, but connected by a lattice of multilingual speakers, also constitutes a coherent language constellation, as one more dimension of the world system, has so far remained unnoticed. Yet, as soon as it has been pointed out, the observation seems obvious.[1]

The global language constellation will be discussed in this book as an integral part of the world system. This implies that language constellations are considered as a – very special – social phenomenon, which can be understood in terms of social science theories. This, too, is new, albeit not entirely without precedent.[2] Rivalry and accommodation between language groups will be explained with the aid of the political sociology of language and the political economy of language. The former focuses on the structure of the language system and its subsystems, and looks at 'language jealousies' between groups, at elite monopolization of the official language, at the exclusion of the unschooled, and at the uses of language to achieve upward mobility; the latter approach analyses how people try to maximize their opportunities for communication, how this confronts them with dilemmas of collective action that may even provoke stampedes towards another language and the abandonment of their native tongue, and what occurs in the unequal relations of exchange between small and large language groups. Many of these notions from sociology and economics have never before been applied to languages or language groups.[3] Together they constitute a coherent theoretical framework that can explain events in such disparate language constellations as India and Indonesia, Sub-Saharan Africa and South Africa, or the European Union.

That language has emerged at all is a cause for marvel; its evolution into innumerable, mutually unintelligible languages is an equally amazing testimony to human ingenuity. As languages grew apart in the course of collective transmission and transformation, new forms of pronunciation must have emerged, thousands of new words appeared and hundreds of grammatical and syntactical rules (and as many exceptions) evolved. All of this was the result of human action and almost none of it was the outcome of human intention.

It seems increasingly likely that all languages that are currently spoken on earth are related and have developed from a common predecessor, roughly following the evolutionary path of present human beings from a common genetic stock in the course of some hundred and twenty thousand years. Evolutionary genetics, comparative linguistics and archaeology are now producing a quickly growing body of evidence for this shared origin.[4] But even if it turns out to be the case that the human species and its languages come from several, diverse origins, there is no doubt that at present all human groups constitute a single interdependent whole, and that their languages together form a global constellation that represents one dimension of the modern world system.

Five or six thousand languages are spoken on earth. The number cannot be specified more exactly, because languages are not always countable. In this respect they resemble clouds: it is hard to tell where one begins and the other ends, and yet most clouds and languages are obviously distinct, with a clear expanse separating them.

In their inexhaustible variety and almost impenetrable complexity, languages are best compared to that other most complex and variegated phenomenon, life itself. Much as a biological species is defined by the capacity of pairs of male and female members to reproduce, a language may be defined by the capacity of any two speakers to understand one another. Two languages are considered distinct if the speakers of one and the other are mutually unintelligible. Just as species are subdivided into many varieties that can indeed interbreed, within languages various mutually intelligible dialects are discerned. Biological varieties of one species shade into one another as do dialects of the same languages, and that is why, in both fields, classification is so often controversial.[5] Indeed, cognate languages can be very hard to tell apart. Where in biology the proof is in the mating, in linguistics it is in the understanding. But mutual intelligibility is not simply a characteristic of the two languages involved; not entirely unlike interbreeding, it also depends on the individuals involved. They may have greater or lesser skills in understanding strangers, they may be more or less eager to communicate with one another, and the context of their encounter may be so structured as to facilitate mutual comprehension or hinder it.

There is no doubt that Chinese and Dutch are two entirely different languages, but it is a matter of controversy whether German and Dutch are indeed distinct languages,[6] while almost everybody would agree that Flemish and Dutch are two varieties of the same language (since their respective speakers would have no trouble at all explaining to one another, each in their own idiom, how insuperable the differences between the two are). Granting the cloudy nature of languages, nevertheless most of the time they are discussed here as if they were distinct entities, separated by barriers of incomprehensibility.

1.1 The global language system: a galaxy of languages

Mutually unintelligible languages are connected by multilingual speakers, but not at all in random fashion. In fact, the scheme of all the world's languages and of the multilinguals that connect them displays a strongly ordered, hierarchical pattern, quite similar to those reversed tree-structures that the French call 'organigrammes', charts used to depict the organization of armies or large bureaucracies.

The vast majority of the languages in the world of today, some 98 per cent of them, are situated in the lower part of this chart: these are the 'peripheral languages' and although there are thousands of them, all together they are used by less than 10 per cent of humankind. Very little of what has been said in all these languages has ever been recorded, be it on clay, stone, papyrus, paper, tape or disk. They are the languages of memory, and whatever was uttered in these languages could only endure because it was heard and remembered, repeated, understood and memorized again.[7] Rather than being defined by what they are not, as 'unwritten' or 'scriptless' languages, these languages deserve to be identified by what constitutes their strength: they are the languages of conversation and narration rather than reading and writing, of memory and remembrance rather than record.

Any two peripheral groups are mutually connected through members that speak the languages of both. But on the whole such ties tend to be scarce. Or rather, they are becoming scarcer since communication between the inhabitants of adjacent villages has become less important, as they increasingly come to deal with traders and administrators in the district capital. As a result, members of the various peripheral groups are more likely to acquire one and the same second language, one that is therefore 'central' to these groups. All or most communication between the peripheral groups occurs through this central language. The peripheral languages, grouped around the central language, may be compared to moons circling a planet. There may be about one hundred languages that occupy a central or 'planetary' position in the global language system.[8] Together they are used by some 95 per cent of humankind. The central languages are used in elementary education and usually also at the level of secondary and higher education. They appear in print, in newspapers, in textbooks and in fiction, they are spoken on radio, on cassettes and increasingly on television. Most of them are used in politics, in the bureaucracy and in the courts. They are usually 'national' languages, and quite often the official languages of the state that rules the area. These are the languages of record: much of what has been said and written in those languages is saved in newspaper reports, minutes and proceedings, stored in archives, included in history books, collections of the 'classics', of folk tales and folkways, increasingly recorded on electronic media, and thus conserved for posterity.

Many of the speakers of a central language are multilingual: first of all, there are those whose native speech is one of the satellite, peripheral languages, and who have later acquired the central language. In fact, everywhere in the world the number of this type of bilinguals is on the increase because of the spread of elementary education and the printed word, and through the impact of radio broadcasting. The second type, on the other hand, that of the native speakers of the central language who have learned one of the peripheral languages, is much less common. Apparently, language learning occurs mostly upward, in a 'centripetal' mode: people usually prefer to learn a language that is at a higher level in the hierarchy. This again reinforces the hierarchical nature of the world language system.

If the mother-tongue speakers of a central language acquire another language, it is usually one that is more widely spread and higher up in the hierarchy. At this next level, a number of central languages are connected through their multilingual speakers to one very large language group that occupies a 'supercentral' position within the system. It serves purposes of long-distance and international communication. Quite often this is a language that was once imposed by a colonial power and after independence continued to be used in politics, administration, law, big business, technology and higher education. There are about a dozen of these supercentral languages. Their position in the global language system resembles that of so many suns surrounded by their planets, the central languages, which, in turn, are encircled by their respective satellites, the peripheral languages. The supercentral languages are Arabic, Chinese, English, French, German, Hindi, Japanese, Malay, Portuguese, Russian, Spanish and Swahili. All these languages, except Swahili, have more than one hundred million speakers and each serves to connect the speakers of a series of central languages. In subsequent chapters a number of regional constellations will be discussed, each centring on one or more of these supercentral languages, such as the Indian constellation around Hindi and English; the Indonesian constellation around Malay (*bahasa Indonesia*); the French-centred constellation of 'francophone' West Africa and the East African constellation that hinges upon English;

the South African constellation, where English and Afrikaans compete; and, finally, the constellation of the European Union, where a dozen national languages are increasingly linked by English, less and less by French and hardly any more by German.

If an Arab and a Chinese, a Russian and a Spaniard, or a Japanese and a German meet, they will almost certainly make themselves understood in one and the same language, one that connects the supercentral languages with one another and that therefore constitutes the pivot of the world language system. This 'hypercentral' language that holds the entire constellation together is, of course, English.

In the present world, English is the language of global communication. It is so to speak at the centre of the twelve solar language systems, at the hub of the linguistic galaxy.[9] English has not always held that position. On the contrary, it has now done so for only half a century or so and one day it may lose its hypercentral functions again, but in the next decades it is only likely to reinforce its position even further.

If the origins of language correspond closely to the origins of the human species, the spread of languages across the globe is intimately connected with the history of humanity. For scores of millennia, languages spread with demographic expansion and migration. In historical times, they followed in the wake of conquest, commerce and conversion. It is only since a century ago at most that languages spread more frequently through formal schooling than in any other way. But the educational system certainly does not operate independently of the political, economic and cultural context, which continues to shape the patterns of language acquisition.

1.2   A historical atlas of the world as a language system

The best way to visualize the evolving global language constellation is through a series of maps of the world.[10] Quite probably, in prehistoric times, as the human species scattered across the continents, small bands must time and again have left their main group, crossed mountains and seas, to settle in areas that were quite distant from the next human population. There, in isolation, and in the absence of any written texts, their languages may have changed rather quickly, reaching unintelligibility with respect to the original language in the span of a few dozen generations.[11] Encounters with other human groups and the ensuing language contacts produced new amalgamations. Thus an imaginary map of the prehistoric distribution of languages would render language areas as fairly small circles, extending and elongating as language groups spread and trekked across new territory, stretching to the breaking point, when a separate circle would indicate the emergence of a 'new' language in that location.

Thus, the hypothesis of 'monogenesis', the evolution of all languages from a single predecessor, does not at all contradict the existence of a great many, mutually unintelligible, languages, once the human species had scattered across the continents. The early distribution of human languages was much more fragmented than the present world language system. Yet it is quite likely that bands in adjacent territories traded and intermarried and some people learned the language of the next group. The circles, no matter how small, may have shown some overlap in the more densely populated areas. As people settled and began to work the land, they must have developed a language for communication between adjoining villages: an early lingua franca, which appears on the map as a dotted line, enclosing the entire area where the linking language is used. That is where the pattern of language distribution is regaining some coherence.

The early 'military-agrarian' regimes, based on military conquest of agrarian communities, demanded the payment of tribute for protection (against other warriors and themselves).[12] With their dominion, they also usually imposed their religion, and their language. Thus the first 'central' languages emerged, linking the peripheral languages of the conquered communities through bilingual speakers to the language of the victors: the language of conquest, conversion and commerce. On the language map, the territory of such regimes would be rendered in a solid but rather pale colour, indicating its wide extension and relatively low density. The circles of the peripheral languages would still clearly show through in their respective areas.

The next stage of integration of the language system occurred with the formation of empires. Marching armies laid one people after another under tribute, maintained roads and harbours, and protected trading routes across the territory. The map of the language constellation in the year 1 shows several such 'world empires'. Not much is known about the western hemisphere or Africa, in that period, but on the Eurasian continent plenty of written records have survived. At least three languages had already spread along very long, but very thin lines. First of all, Latin, emanating from Rome all along the Mediterranean coast, stretched across the southern half of Europe and, more sparsely, further to the north, into the Germanic and Celtic lands. Latin was a spoken and a written language; it served to administer the conquered areas, to carry out diplomatic missions and trading ventures, and to spread new knowledge and technology. Soon, moreover, it was to be the vehicle of Christian expansion. After the fall of the Roman Empire, Latin served for another fifteen hundred years as a major European linking language. But in all the many language groups of Christendom there were only a few individuals, clergy usually, who had learned the language of the church and hence could communicate with their peers all over the continent. They served as translators and mediators to connect their communities with the continental network. Until the Renaissance, Latin hardly had competitors as the language of learning and long-distance communication. The connecting web may have been extremely tenuous, the Latin speakers very few in number, but in the domains of scholarship, law and religion it held together until the nineteenth century. Thus, Europe, with Latin as its supercentral language, already constituted a coherent, if precarious, language system more than two thousand years ago. The language map of the era would have displayed the supercentral presence of Latin by a pattern of rays in a single colour, extending from Rome in ever thinner lines across the continent and overlaying the solid patches of central languages with the circles of the peripheral languages still visible underneath.

The second imperial language of that era was of course Chinese. In the core area of contemporary China, a 'pre-classical' version of Han Chinese already functioned as the language of long-distance communication, spoken and written by clerics and scholars, and used in court as the language of rule and administration. In South Asia, learned and religious men used Sanskrit for the same purposes and an equally fine and extended grid overlaid the language map of that subcontinent. If they had strictly limited their encounters to their peers, clergy and courtiers, at the time, might have travelled all across the Eurasian landmass, using only Chinese, Sanskrit and Latin (and maybe some Persian or Greek). But with the common people, the innkeepers and the traders, let alone peasants and soldiers, these languages would have been quite useless.

One thousand years later, the great classical languages had spawned vernacular versions all over their respective regions. Yet they continued to serve for long-distance communication in the fields of administration, diplomacy, religion, science, literature and trade over an area that had grown even larger in the meantime. Right at the centre of the Afro-Eurasian land mass, a fourth language had been spreading for some time: Arabic, originating in the Arabic peninsula and extending its lines across northern Africa to the southern tip of Spain, along the East African coast and deep into Central Asia.

Clearly, the regions of the classical languages more or less coincided with the areas of the great religions, Islam, Christendom, Hinduism, Confucianism and Buddhism (the last of which overlaps with the preceding two). The supercentral networks were vast, but still very thin, as so few people could understand, and even fewer could read or write, the corresponding languages.

Another five hundred years later, at the 'dawn of the Modern Era', around 1500, the pattern of long-distance communication had begun to change perceptibly. First of all, the vernaculars that had sprouted from the great classical languages were coming into their own: they were crafted into standard versions by poets, writers and scholars, increasingly used in trade, science, law, administration and, in the West, also in religion and at princely courts.[13] In Europe, among the many popular languages that derived from Latin, Italian became a literary language early in the fourteenth century. It soon developed into a language of scholars, courtiers, politicians, artists, scientists and the military.[14] From the flourishing Italian city states it spread over southwestern Europe as a vehicular language of diplomacy and learning.

The other vernaculars that derived from Latin each also spread over broad territories of their own, helped by a vast increase in the circulation of their written versions through the new printing presses. Increasingly, they were used at the royal court and in the courts of law, in parliament, in the schools and academies. As will appear later, they succeeded in driving out the peripheral languages (or the marginalized, formerly central languages of conquered territories), in the process each becoming the hegemonic language of its realm.[15] A similar development rendered Russian and German hegemonic in their respective territories. The language maps of the epoch for Europe increasingly show closed, single-coloured areas of a more and more intense hue, while the patches of the peripheral languages slowly fade away. These processes of national language unification that occurred throughout Europe represent another stage in the integration process, this time on a smaller scale but with much greater density than in the preceding empires.

The new European vernaculars travelled overseas with the explorers to Africa, Asia and America, where they initially found a tiny niche near estuaries or on islands near the coast. Thus began their long career on distant continents as the languages of rule, trade and conversion.

Around this time, Arabic reached its zenith as a world language. But the language of the Koran was to be conserved in its unadulterated form; any divergence could only spell degeneration. Hence, the vernaculars it engendered never developed into distinct, acknowledged languages as did the descendants of Han, Sanskrit and Latin.

The overseas expansion of Chinese was brought to a halt, once the Ming rulers suspended maritime trade and exploration in the early sixteenth century. As a result, henceforth their language could only spread over land, albeit across a vast expanse. In India, in the course of the sixteenth and seventeenth centuries, the Mughal kings extended their rule ever southward, at a time when the vernacular languages (the *prakrits* in the north, Dravidian languages in the south) had established themselves, each in its own area. One of those, the version of Hindi that was current in the Delhi region, finally became the vernacular and the vehicular of the Mughal realm.

The Russians had conquered a good part of what is known today as 'Russia' in the seventeenth century and were laying the groundwork for an expansion towards the east that would continue for centuries, until all of Siberia, and most of central Asia, had been conquered. Throughout this vast area, Russian functioned as the supercentral language, taught increasingly in the schools as the first 'foreign' language.

The Modern Era was very much the period of the expansion and imposition of European vernaculars across the globe. Portuguese, Spanish and English between them almost entirely covered the western hemisphere; English became the dominant language of the Australian continent; French prevailed side by side with Arabic in northern Africa. Russian came to dominate all of northern Asia. All these new territories were settled in large numbers by colonists from the European 'mother' country.

In Sub-Saharan Africa and in most of South and South-East Asia, English, French and Portuguese had spread with colonial conquest, and functioned increasingly as media of administration, trade, higher education and long-distance communication, but they never eliminated the indigenous languages. One reason was that Europeans migrated to those lands in much smaller numbers. But in almost all the former colonies, the European language continued to serve key functions, even after the departure of the colonizers, and still do after half a century of independence. The end of this worldwide presence of European languages is not yet in sight. And one of these vernaculars, English, is still increasing its hypercentral prominence almost everywhere on the globe.

A map of the present global language system looks quite like a composite of political maps from the eighteenth, nineteenth and twentieth centuries. It shows how much language constellations are determined by political events, but also how they often survive long after this political base has disappeared. Thus, Spanish and Portuguese came to the southern part of the western hemisphere as colonial languages, and so did English and French in North America. And although almost the entire continent became independent of the European mother countries between the end of the eighteenth and the middle of the nineteenth century, the languages of the former colonizers, English, Spanish and Portuguese, still prevail there.

Equally, by the end of the nineteenth century almost all of Africa had been divided between the West European powers. After World War I, Germany was divested of its African possessions. Today, three or four decades after independence, the former colonial languages, English, French and Portuguese, still function throughout Africa; the linguistic map does not look very different from the political map of, say, 1920.

Nor has the map of European languages changed much when compared to the political map of, say, a century ago. The central languages of many European countries coincide with the state borders (although a more detailed map would reveal incongruities in almost every country). But this apparent stability hides great upheavals that occurred in the twentieth century.[16] German spread with the Nazi conquerors, and receded as soon as they were defeated. Russian was imposed on the countries of Central and Eastern Europe and swiftly abolished after the Transition. Likewise, Japan expanded in the past century from Manchuria to New Guinea, and Japanese followed the paths of conquest, only to disappear almost entirely after the defeat of Japan.

In Asia also, the military conquests of preceding centuries very much determine the present distribution of languages. The most notable exception is Indonesia, where after Independence Dutch disappeared completely, while Malay spread all over the archipelago. But the language constellations of China and India, the Philippines, Thailand and Malaysia still coincide rather closely with the political patterns of a century ago. In Vietnam, Laos and Cambodia, French had to make room for English in the wake of more recent wars.

1.3   Supercentral constellations in the present language system

The supercentral languages mostly spread in two ways: over land and over sea. German, Russian, Arabic, Hindi, Chinese and Japanese each cover a large contiguous area, more or less coterminous with the territory once or still controlled by a major empire: these are the 'land-bound' languages that spread with marching empires.[17] English, French, Portuguese and Spanish, on the contrary, spread with the conquest of territories overseas. Swahili and Malay initially functioned as regional vehicular lingua francas and became national languages after Independence.

The Chinese language constellation covers mainland China and Taiwan. The vast majority of continental Chinese are by now able to read the most current Chinese characters and speak or at least understand *putonghua*, a standardized version of the Mandarin variety from Beijing that has been taught in the schools all over China since 1948. Mandarin differs considerably from the other varieties of Han Chinese that are spoken mostly south of the Yangtse. Of the 1.2 billion mainland Chinese, 96 per cent use one of the varieties of Han, 93 per cent are native Han speakers and 63 per cent are mother-tongue speakers of its most important variety, Mandarin.[18] The largest non-Han language spoken in China is Zhuang, with 13 million speakers.[19] Abroad, varieties of Han Chinese continue to be used by many millions of emigrants, mostly at home and on social occasions, and in newspapers for the local immigrant community. The supercentral position of Mandarin *putonghua* in mainland China is illustrated by the fact that the lion's share of 'minority' members who did acquire a second language (18 million) learned a Han variety (almost all of them Mandarin) and only a tiny fraction (0.9 million) learned other 'minority languages', whereas very few Han speakers (1.2 million) learned one of the peripheral languages. Yet, for its huge numbers and ancient tradition, Han Chinese in its several versions plays a rather minor role in communication beyond China's borders, except for the many millions of emigrants.

Unlike China, India was occupied by a Western colonial power for almost a century and a half. Once again, the language map reproduces features of earlier political maps: English, more than half a century after independence, is still very much present as a second language, in stiff competition with Hindi. The presence of the Dravidian languages in the south very much complicates the Indian constellation. This is the subject of a separate chapter (chapter 4).

German, Russian and Japanese nowadays are barely supercentral languages, confined as they are to the remaining state territories. In the wake of centuries of conquest and rule each of these languages became established as the official language, the vernacular and the predominant mother tongue in a vast and contiguous area. In the course of the twentieth century, as a result of military expansion all three of them spread far beyond their former limits, and receded again once the defeated conquerors had to surrender their territorial gains.

Since the early 1990s, the Russian language constellation has been rapidly coming apart. The Central and East European satellite states have regained their full autonomy and quickly did away with Russian as the first foreign language, turning instead to English or German. The former autonomous republics of the Soviet Union became 'independent states' and likewise discarded obligatory Russian, reverting to their regional languages, from Latvian, Lithuanian and Estonian on the Baltic Sea, to Armenian and Georgian on the Kaspic shores, or Kazakh, Kirghiz, Turkmen and Uzbek, and Tadhzik in Central Asia. Siberia retains Russian, although indigenous peripheral languages remain current locally.

But even in the core area of the Soviet empire, the speakers of Belorussian and Ukrainian increasingly came to see their languages as essentially different from Russian and abandoned the idea of complete mutual intelligibility that had prevailed without much controversy during the Soviet era.[20] As a result, Russian began to lose many of its supercentral functions in the former Soviet empire. English took over these linking tasks almost everywhere, Turkish grew in importance in the Central Asian republics and German plays a modest linking role in Central and Eastern Europe.

Just as Russian was discarded by its European vassal states immediately after the transition, some forty years earlier German had been uprooted and abolished in the same region, while in East and South East Asia, Japanese was 'forgotten' just as quickly.[21] On the other hand, in the respective core territories, where political rule by the central state had already been consolidated during the nineteenth century, these languages have conserved all their functions and are still spoken by practically all citizens, almost without competition from smaller indigenous languages. Apparently, in the twentieth century imperial conquest did not pay in terms of enduring language expansion. Maybe national languages had already taken hold too deeply in the newly conquered territories to be eradicated definitively; possibly also the foreign occupation did not last long enough to establish the conqueror's language for good.

In Europe, German has the most numerous native speakers covering an area that comprises present-day Germany, Austria, the northern part of Switzerland (where it coexists with the Schweitzerdeutsch variety) and Luxembourg (where the local variety is Letzeburgesch). Moreover, as Alsatian it is spoken by most inhabitants of Alsace-Lorraine, an area that became German in 1871, only to revert to France in 1919. By the end of the nineteenth century, German had become one of the most important commercial and scientific languages, almost on a par with English and French.[22] Had Germany not been dispossessed of its overseas territories by the League of Nations after its defeat in the Great War of 1914–18, those parts of Africa that were once German colonies, Tanganyika, Rwanda, Burundi and Namibia (and also Eastern Papua New Guinea), would almost certainly have adopted German as their official language. In Central and Eastern Europe, German was the native tongue in communities of German settlers (*Volksdeutsche*), many of whom had lived in the area for centuries. Until 1945, it was the most important language of long-distance communication in that part of the continent (it had of course been the language of the Austrian empire and – with Hungarian – of the Austro-Hungarian monarchy). During World War II, German became a major foreign language throughout the occupied areas of Europe and many people made an effort to learn and use it. Immediately after the end of the war the language was abandoned in the liberated territories, and as most *Volksdeutsche* were driven out of Eastern and Central Europe, the language lost its strongholds in that part of Europe, too. Yet, to some degree, German continues to function as a supercentral language of science, commerce and arts in contemporary Central and Eastern Europe.[23] It may still gain in importance in the language constellation of the European Union (see chapter 8).

Very much the same applies to the brief expansion of Japan and Japanese in North and South East Asia: the defeat at the end of World War II also undid the gains of Japanese as a supercentral language in the territories it had occupied since the end of the nineteenth century: Taiwan (1895), Korea (1910), Manchuria (1931) and large parts of Mongolia on the eve of World War II. During the war years Japan wrested large parts of South East Asia from European colonial rule, including Indonesia. In all the occupied territories it made an effort to instil Japanese language and culture, while often ferociously repressing the indigenous heritage. As a result, after the defeat of Japan the newly liberated countries strongly rejected Japanese influence and the language disappeared almost completely. At present, in Japan, Japanese is used by practically everybody for every domain. Here or there local languages are spoken, mostly at home, in Okinawa for example. Abroad, Japanese plays a very limited role as a transnational language of science and business.

The foregoing supercentral languages cover a contiguous area that corresponds to the territories once conquered by military might. Arabic, too, spread through conquest and commerce, mostly over land. More than other languages it also spread by conversion, even overseas. The Arabic language constellation roughly covers the world of Islam. It is widely spoken as a first language in North Africa and the Middle East, but elsewhere it has continued to function in competition with other supercentral languages, remaining mostly confined to the domain of religion: on the Indian subcontinent, in South-East Asia (most notably Indonesia), and also in parts of Sub-Saharan Africa. More recently, Muslim immigrants to the European Union brought Arabic with them, as a liturgical language and for many North Africans as the home language, too. The vast expansion of Arabic is a relic of a long succession of explorations and conquests. The fact that, subsequently, Arabic in many areas was relegated to liturgical functions mostly bespeaks the growing might of succeeding conquerors: the European powers.

English, French, Portuguese and Spanish all originated on the shores of the Atlantic ocean and their expansion beyond their core area was mostly maritime. These languages became predominant wherever European settlers succeeded in colonizing relatively thinly inhabited areas with a moderate climate and could oust the aboriginals (greatly helped by the more virulent microparasites[24] and the more resistant plant and animal species they – unwittingly or wittingly – brought with them).[25]

Thus, Spanish and the Spanish conquered and colonized almost all of South and Central America, pushing the indigenous peoples and their languages into peripheral positions. The Portuguese did the same in Brazil. As a result, Portuguese and Spanish have remained true 'world languages' that number a hundred and twenty-five million and two hundred and fifty million speakers respectively, even though their 'metropolitan' versions, spoken on the Iberian peninsula, count roughly ten million in the case of Portuguese, and some forty million in the Spanish case (the two languages are moreover quite closely related, although not mutually intelligible without some learning effort). Brazilians and Portuguese can still understand each other, and so can mainland Spaniards and the hispanophone inhabitants of South and Central America. Lisbon and Madrid (or Barcelona) have remained important centres of the book-publishing industry for their former colonies.

The northern half of the western hemisphere was first colonized by English settlers, and they succeeded in maintaining English as the predominant, well-nigh exclusive language of North America, in the end ceding only Quebec to French. Hesitant attempts to claim a position for other immigrant languages, such as German, were quickly abandoned, until massive Spanish immigration in the last part of the twentieth century secured strong local footholds for Spanish in some US cities, and may yet result in urban enclaves of Hispanic-English bilingualism.[26]

As British colonists settled the Australian continent and established their language there, the indigenous, Aboriginal languages withered away. Later cohorts of immigrants who came with other mother tongues were never numerous or determined enough to make a dent in the hegemony of the language that the first, English, colonizers had brought with them. In South Africa, a settler colony initially populated by 'Boers' (immigrants from Dutch stock), British rulers introduced English, which to this day competes with Afrikaans, a descendant of Dutch, for the central position in the area. (The South African language constellation will be the subject of chapter 7.) English also remained the official language in the former British colonies in Africa, with the partial exception of Tanzania (see chapter 6 on Sub-Saharan Africa).

French, too, spread with overseas colonial conquest. But the French were much less successful than the British in establishing and maintaining settler colonies. Only Quebec, after much strife, succeeded in conserving French as its first language, and even there it must weather stiff competition from English.[27] The great francophone settler communities in Morocco, Algeria and Tunisia disbanded when these countries regained their independence and the '*pieds noirs*' left en masse for the mother country. French nevertheless remains the 'high' medium in North Africa, but it must confront the re-emergence of Arabic in a nationalist and religious revival of 'Arabisation'.[28]

In the former possessions in Sub-Saharan Africa, French continues to serve as the supercentral language par excellence, and within each of these countries it remains the language of politics, administration, law and education. Recently, French has been losing ground to English in Rwanda, after exiles educated in Uganda took over the government there in 1995. In the rest of 'francophone' Africa, individual intellectuals and scholars are gradually turning more to English. What occurred in the former French colonies in South East Asia, where English almost entirely replaced French, may yet occur in francophone Africa (see also chapter 6 on Sub-Saharan Africa).

Closer to home, on the European subcontinent, French claimed its greatest triumphs: by the seventeenth century, it had emerged as a European vehicular language, emanating like Italian from courtly circles. In the course of the eighteenth century it was adopted at courts all over the continent, by royalty, courtiers and diplomats, and by men and women of taste and learning. French thus became the pre-eminent vehicular language in Europe and anyone who pretended to some refinement and education had to master it. By the nineteenth century it was current as a second language in bourgeois circles from the Netherlands to Russia, especially in more formal settings. Until the mid-twentieth century it remained the language of diplomacy par excellence and the main transnational language of literature and the arts, centred as they were on Paris as a global hub of culture.[29]

At present, the most important transnational functions of French are played out in the European Union, where it is still a major language in everyday administration and politics, once again next to English, which has consistently been making inroads on its hegemony since the United Kingdom joined the European Community in 1973.

English, Portuguese and French have remained supercentral languages in the conquered territories of Asia and Africa, even in those areas that never became settler colonies, and even after colonial rule was abolished. Why the former colonial languages have persisted so tenaciously in these countries after Independence is one of the recurrent questions in this book.

There are, however, domestic languages that have weathered the competition with the language of the colonizer and at present fulfil most supercentral functions in their area: Hindi in northern India, Malay in Malaysia and Indonesia (*bahasa Indonesia*), and Swahili in Tanzania and Kenya. Each of these language constellations is the subject of a separate chapter or section (4, 5 and 6.3.2 respectively).

English is the hypercentral language that holds the entire world language system together. This has not always been the case. It is in fact a very recent phenomenon. Only after 1945 did primacy, also in global diplomacy, radically shift to English. This may not always remain so; the 'end of history' is not yet in sight and hegemony, even global hegemony, may still wane. But even if the economic and political power of the English-speaking nations, the United States foremost among them, were to dwindle, most probably English would continue to function as the pivot of the global language constellation for a long time. It takes, after all, a major effort to acquire a new foreign language, and a language once learned is not all that easily forgotten or abandoned. That is one cause of 'linguistic inertia', one reason why the language constellation tends to lag behind when the political constellation changes.

1.4   Scope and approach of this book

This is a book about languages and the people who speak them in groups. It is a book about competition and compromise between language groups. It looks at these rivalries and accommodations from a global perspective. The languages of the world constitute a global language system, the linguistic dimension of the world system, on a par with its political, economic, cultural and ecological dimensions. The present global constellation of languages is very much the product of prior conquest and dominion and of ongoing relations of power and exchange.

The subject matter of social science is history, conventionally recent history. Hence, the empirical material for this study comes from accounts of language politics in specific constellations in the past half-century or so. This material is approached from a theoretical perspective that combines a political sociology of language with a political economy of language. The twofold theoretical approach allows us to compare the separate language constellations within a common conceptual framework.

The notion of a world system, with a periphery, a semi-periphery and a core, is central to contemporary political macro-sociology.[30] Here, the task is to identify the linguistic dimension of this evolving system: the global language constellation.[31] State, nation and citizenship, with their interconnections, constitute another central theme of political sociology and it is in this context that specific language constellations are situated in the present approach. At this level, the focus is on bilingual elite groups who may attempt to monopolize opportunities for mediation between their monolingual clientele and the central state apparatus. In a later phase, administrative elites may exploit an official language to monopolize access to government and the administration and to the higher echelons of commercial employment. This presupposes that established and outsider groups can communicate in a shared vernacular, but that the excluded groups lack basic literacy skills that might enable them to learn the written version of the central or supercentral language so as to join the competition for the more rewarding jobs.

The second perspective is that of the political economy of language. Here, the focus is on the preferences people have for learning one language rather than another. It is assumed that – given half a chance – people will learn the language that provides them with the greater communication advantage, the greater 'Q-value'. In an economic perspective, languages are defined as 'hypercollective goods'. This helps to explain the accelerating spread of a language that is expected to gain speakers, and the abandonment of one that appears to be endangered by desertion. It also provides an economic explanation of ethnic and cultural movements for the conservation of the language: the threatened language alone can provide access to the collective cultural capital of its speakers, to the totality of all texts recorded and remembered in that language.

These notions derive from rational choice theory and welfare economics. That does not imply that the economic paradigm is adopted in its entirety. Rather, the concepts are treated here as central intellectual ideas, current in contemporary social science, and to be used when and as needed, in a pragmatic and eclectic manner.

The theoretical structure of the book is based on the ideas of language groups in unequal competition in a global context, on different levels. From 'world system' theory comes the notion of a 'core', an intermediate level (a 'semi-periphery') and a 'periphery'. These levels correspond partly to those of the hypercentral and supercentral languages, of the central languages, and of the peripheral languages. As in the world system in general, the global language system displays strong oligopolistic features. Generally, exchange between language groups proceeds on very unequal terms.

From the viewpoint of sociology, the world system constitutes a transnational society. The first task for the social sciences is to take up again the thread from Adam Smith via Auguste Comte to Karl Marx and reconceptualize 'society', not as coextensive with the nation-state, but as an entity that transcends national and state borders and by now covers the entire globe. Political scientists (and students of international relations and international organizations), economists and ecologists have all carved out their own speciality in this global context. In this division of labour, sociologists, who study human beings in their social context, should concentrate on the connections between people that transcend national borders. These connections may be direct, as between emigrants and their families and friends at home, or between tourists and native inhabitants, or they may be mediated by states, corporations, organizations, social movements and media.

It goes without saying that these connections proceed through language. Surprisingly, this simple and stark fact is not mentioned much: it is taken for granted and left implicit in studies of transnational society or world system, and it is certainly not a topic that has earned discussion in economics.

Of course, linguists have studied language, and with great profit. Sociolinguists have focused on language groups. It is from the field of sociolinguistics that most of the data and many of the ideas in this book have been taken. Applied macro-sociolinguists (and political scientists interested in language conflict) have been studying language policies for over half a century now, and in the process they have produced a vast amount of empirical documentation and policy analysis. But sociolinguists have focused their investigations on the national and subnational level (in fact, a considerable amount of work has been devoted to the so-called 'smaller languages'). Having entered the field as an outsider, I have been able to apply economic and sociological theory to material collected by sociolinguists or analysts of language policy and come up with new insights. That is the profit in the risky venture of crossing boundaries between disciplines.

In many respects, this book is a continuation of an earlier work of mine on the sociogenesis of the welfare state in the West in the course of the past five centuries.[32] That book demonstrated the spread of 'care arrangements' from the parish level to big city policies at the regional level, and beyond towards the scope of the nation-state, which became the carrier of the welfare state in its contemporary shape. There, too, 'figurational' historical sociology provided the overall scheme, supported by an eclectic application of notions from game theory and welfare economics. Finally, the rise of elementary education was discussed in that book very much in terms of language conflict and the attempt to impose a common code for national communication.

The present book takes off from there. It looks at a long-term and global process of integration: the emergence of language constellations held together by a 'central language', linked in turn to a higher level through individuals competent in a supercentral language that, finally, is connected to the hypercentral language. The integration of transnational society proceeds in terms of 'globalization' of markets and media, but also very much through the spread of connecting languages that give the people who have learned them access to the next-highest level of the world system.

1.5 Plan of the book

The next two chapters continue the theoretical discussion. In chapter 2 languages are characterized from an economic perspective as a very special kind of good, possessing the characteristics of a 'collective good' and also displaying 'external network effects': a 'hypercollective good'. These properties may cause stampedes towards one language and desertions from another. Whether a language gains or loses speakers very much depends on its position within the language constellation. It is this more or less strategic position that determines the communication value of the language and decides whether outsiders will choose to learn it. The 'Q-value' of a language is the product of the proportion of those who speak it among all speakers in the constellation *and* the proportion of multilingual speakers whose repertoire includes the language among all multilingual speakers in the constellation. People will prefer to learn the language that most increases the Q-value of their repertoire.

The relations between language groups can be quite asymmetric. Chapter 3 deals with the unequal exchange of texts. Anything that has been memorized or recorded in a language constitutes a text. The unequal terms of exchange are very much determined by the relative Q-values of the languages involved. Producers and consumers of texts in languages with high or low Q-values have very divergent interests in the exchange. Apart from their individual preference for learning a language with a high Q-value, they share a collective interest in the survival of their original language, irrespective of its Q-value: it provides access to the accumulated texts in that language, which constitute their collective cultural capital. The theory can deal with matters of transnational cultural exchange (in so far as it applies to 'language-bound' culture) and with the dynamics of movements in defence of ethnic or regional language and culture.

The theory of free exchange and the theory of collective goods both revolve around a dilemma. Under conditions of free exchange there is a choice for authors between being a small fish in a big pond or a big fish in a small pond. When the collective good of language conservation is at stake, there is a choice whether or not to join one's peers in an effort to maintain the language as a separate small pond. The final section of chapter 3 discusses what happens when authors switch to the dominant language, while competence in that language spreads among speakers of the original, domestic language: at some point the latter may begin to be abandoned and the collective, accumulated stock of texts in that language will become increasingly inaccessible. Under these conditions, 'hypercollectivity' operates against the survival of the language community and its collective cultural capital, resulting in a stampede towards the dominant language at the expense of the domestic idiom.

The following chapters discuss distinct language constellations, in postcolonial societies, and in the postnational context of the European Union. India is the subject of the fourth chapter: there, Hindi, by far the most widely spread language on the subcontinent, English, the language of the former colonizers, and a number of Dravidian languages, spoken mostly in the south, have achieved a somewhat uneasy equilibrium. The southern language groups play off English against Hindi. The educated elites in administration and government have an interest in maintaining the advantage that their competence in English grants them. Hindi speakers insist on gaining for their language the position that their numbers warrant. A rearrangement of state frontiers, designed to make them coincide with language borders, increased homogeneity within states, and thus considerably mitigated language conflicts.

Indonesia took an entirely different path, as chapter 5 demonstrates: the colonial language disappeared almost without trace. The language with the greatest number of speakers by far, and also the language of the dominant group, Javanese, was discarded in favour of Malay, which before independence had mostly functioned as a bazaar language, familiar to about 10 per cent of the population. Standardized as '*bahasa Indonesia*' it became in fact the vehicular language of the new republic – a rare case of victory for a domestic language in postcolonial society.

Independence did not do much to change the predominance of the colonial language in Sub-Saharan Africa. Thus, as chapter 6 shows, French prevails from Rwanda to Senegal and Zaire/Congo, even though the respective constellations are very unlike one another: in the first country a domestic language is spoken by almost everyone, in the second country several regional languages coexist, one of which also functions as a lingua franca and covers at least three-quarters of the population, and in the third, a plethora of languages is held together by a quartet of popular lingua francas. Nevertheless, in all these countries, French continues to dominate the domains of politics, business, learning, the media and entertainment. Yet only a small minority of schoolchildren end up with a modicum of competence in the language.

Similar dynamics operate in the survival of English on the African continent. Again three language constellations are compared, among themselves and with the francophone triad. In Botswana the vast majority of citizens speak a domestic language, Tswana, and yet English maintains its position as the language of government, business, science and the media. The same is true of Nigeria, where among a multitude of domestic languages four stand out as especially important, Hausa, Ibo, Yoruba, and a fourth, a vehicular English-based creole, known as 'Pidgin'. In the third country, Tanzania, on the contrary, a domestic language was adopted as the official medium of the state, and now functions as the national language for the vast majority of the population: Swahili, which in neighbouring Kenya competes with English as the vehicular and the official language, while it functions as a popular lingua franca from Uganda to the eastern part of Congo/Zaire and even further south.

Since the abolition of Apartheid, South Africa – the subject of chapter 7 – has adopted a constitution that grants equal place to eleven languages. In fact, however, English, and to a lesser degree Afrikaans, continue as the official languages and the medium of business, education and the media. Among the other nine regional languages, four might conveniently be grouped under the heading of 'Nguni', three others as 'Sutu', thus creating two much more numerous language groups that each might stand a chance of being adopted in all fields of contemporary communication. So far, much as in India, the recognition of these numerous 'scheduled' languages is mostly ceremonial.

The fact that up to half a century after independence the ex-colonial languages have maintained their dominant role in so many postcolonial societies is in part explained by the insufficiencies of elementary education. Where so many children never learn to read and write, they are effectively prevented from acquiring written languages (they may learn to speak new languages in the street, in the market or at work). Since people can apparently be excluded from learning the official language, in this case it cannot be considered a collective good; an exception to the general definition. Under these conditions the educated elite may continue to reap group monopoly profits from its competence in the official language and has every interest in prolonging that situation. The second reason for the predominance of the former colonial language may be sought in 'language jealousy'. Whenever the decision is about to be implemented, a choice must be made between them; no language group is ready to accept the predominance of another, even if it means continuing with the language of the former oppressors.

Chapter 8 discusses the language constellation of the European Union. There are four different levels of communication in the Union, and each requires a different language regime. First of all, there is the level of domestic, civil society in each member country. European languages are especially robust as a result of the long process of language unification at the national level. This 'robustness' and the continued support of the state preclude the emergence of pidgins or an amalgamation of languages. Rather, the national language will coexist in a situation of 'diglossia' with English, as the super- and hypercentral languages. These national languages are 'robust' by dint of the support provided them by the state. Yet they must confront English, the international language of high prestige, which may in the long run erode their position in their own 'home society'.

The next level is that of transnational civil society in the Union. At this level, English is paramount, facing some competition from French in southern Europe and some rivalry from German in the countries of Central and Eastern Europe that may before long join the Union. Survey data reveal the distribution of language skills among Europeans in the Union. More than 80 per cent of secondary school students learn English, less than 40 per cent French, not even 20 per cent German, and just under 10 per cent Spanish. The available statistics allow us to calculate the Q-values of the respective languages. These figures, in turn, permit us to predict the course of the European language constellation with some confidence.

The third and fourth level concern the institutions of the European Union. At the public, ceremonial level, and whenever decisions have an external, legal effect, democratic principle and treaty obligations require that all official languages of the member states be treated on an equal footing. This principle underlies the language regime for the European Parliament, the Council of Ministers and the external correspondence and publications of the Commission. It turns out that the language preferences of the member states on the basis of the Q-values together define an implicit voting cycle that prevents any decision that would alter the status quo.

The final level concerns internal communication within the European institutions, in the Commission bureaucracy and also in the corridors of the Parliament. When it comes to the day-to-day deliberations and messages between officials or representatives, then French, and increasingly English, are the actual working languages.

Chapter 9 provides a summary, discusses the findings and raises some questions of language policy. Language experts, of old the champions of language standardization and unification, have changed sides en masse; they now defend the rights of the smaller languages and advocate the use of indigenous languages. Many of their arguments are spurious. As a matter of course, they are all phrased in English or one of the other supercentral languages that the experts command. On their part, those who are illiterate and know only their local languages would dearly love to understand the pleas made so eloquently on their behalf.

The political economy of language constellations

The languages of the world form a coherent and strongly ordered system. This constellation of language groups has evolved and continues to change. Some groups have grown in numbers and passed on their language to their children, others have seen their ranks shrink through famine, disease or defeat. As migrants spread to new lands, they took their language with them. But much more rapid change comes to the system as people acquire new languages, beyond their mother tongue. Of old, such learning efforts have reflected unequal relations: when the defeated and the dominated adopted the language of their conquerors and rulers, with or without coercion, or when weaker, poorer groups engaged in trade with a mightier, wealthier nation and had to learn its languages. Languages are learned 'upwards': from the small to the large language, from the little to the great tradition, from the poor to the rich language group, from the subjugated to the dominant nation.

In more recent times, formal education has greatly accelerated the spread of a few world languages which are taught to the quickly growing numbers of schoolchildren and students. Even if no actual compulsion is at work, there are usually constraints on language acquisition. Yet there also is an element of choice, and the interaction of these choices provides language spread with a dynamics of its own.

Preferences for learning one language rather than another are very much shaped by perceptions and expectations of other people's language acquisition. These impressions and estimates ricochet to and fro between people, reinforcing mutual perceptions and raising expectations that then tend to fulfil themselves. Such reverberations are a feature of the very particular character of languages in social interaction. They are best understood by adopting an economic perspective, as a special version of a social science approach.

In order to explain the dynamics of the global constellation, this chapter sets out at the opposite pole, with the preferences of individuals and the behaviour of groups. But these groups and individuals function within the larger context of regional, national and even global language constellations.

The first section deals with the general characteristics of languages in the strategic interaction among large numbers of users. In this respect, they share many characteristics with networks on the one hand, and public goods on the other. Languages can indeed be considered as 'goods', but of a very particular kind. It is this peculiar character of languages in an economic sense that clarifies a good part of the dynamics of language spread and decline.

The second section takes as its point of departure the micro-sociology and the micro-economics of language constellations: why do people decide to learn one language rather than another, how do these decisions influence the choices of other people and what are the overall consequences of the individual choices? In this section, the utility or 'communication potential' of a language to its individual users is defined in terms of the numbers of its speakers, especially its multilingual speakers. This allows us to explain the choices that individuals make in learning one language rather than another. The perception of other people's choices very much determines one's own decision, and vice versa.

From the outset, economic theory has dealt with issues of preference and choice, and it is from economics that some core concepts will be taken. But when economic theory is applied beyond its proper realm – markets, firms, households – it loses much of its precision.[1] Languages do not come with a price tag. Yet what is the relative value of competence in a given language rather than in another for its actual and prospective users? How are we to determine the costs of learning a language? Economic concepts applied within a sociological framework can clarify issues in the acquisition and distribution of languages, even if these do not come with a price tag. And as the empirical chapters will demonstrate, a model based on simple and parsimonious assumptions can indeed render the dynamics of specific, historical language constellations.

2.1   Languages as 'hypercollective goods'

What kind of goods are languages, in an economic sense? Languages are not exactly scarce, they are abundant all over the world. People only need to learn a language that is current in their immediate environment and, once they have mastered it to some degree, they are free to use it as often and as verbosely as they wish. It costs no more to be talkative than to be sparse with words, except in terms of other people's patience. Clearly, language is not used up in using it, rather the opposite. With practice an ever larger part of its potential becomes available to the speaker. Moreover, the more people use a language, the more valuable it is to each one of them. This again is a remarkable characteristic of languages that sets them apart from most economic goods, which are 'consumed' as they are used.

Although language can be used freely and without cost, a prior investment is required. Children learn their mother tongue apparently with very little conscious effort,[2] and even adults often pick up a new language in their environment as they go, but mastering a foreign language that is not current in one's habitat usually requires hard work, no matter how rewarding in itself – an investment of time, attention, memory and, as the case may be, tuition money. Thus, for any given individual, languages are there, available for anyone who wishes to learn them, much as lakes and rivers are there for anyone wishing (or, nowadays, daring) to drink from them. But, in order to quench one's thirst, one needs some minimal investment in getting there and bringing a cup or a bucket. Learning a new language requires at the very least exposure to it, that is proximity to people who speak it, or else books, teachers, audiovisual learning aids and all the other paraphernalia of language study. And, although readers might almost forget it, learning a language at a more formal level requires literacy. This will turn out to be a major threshold for language learning among the less privileged in the less wealthy societies of the world.

Thus, the languages one already knows, adopted effortlessly and at a young age as a mother tongue, or acquired with considerable exertion at a later age, are in many respects free goods: anyone who knows one may use it without limit, without added cost, like breathing air. Since no one can learn an unlimited number of languages, choices must be made. If efforts are equal, people will choose to learn the language that they expect will benefit them more than another language.

From an economic point of view, languages may be compared with standards, and with networks. Standards are conventions, rules for measuring time or space or value, or procedures for operating machines, or protocols for coordinating actions, or recipes for manufacturing appliances. What matters is their conventional character; possibly, other rules could have been selected with equally good reason, but any set of rules must be broadly adopted to be effective at all. Networks are systems of nodes and connections, like pipelines that deliver water and gas or remove sewerage, cables that supply electricity or carry telephone and TV signals, and railways or roads. Economists have written extensively about standards, especially industrial standards, and also about supply and transport networks.

But somehow, when economists write about standards and networks, they overlook the most obvious instance: language.[3] And when linguists write about the economics of language, they dwell upon the costs of instruction and translation, but never realize the very extraordinary nature of language as an economic good.[4]

When consumers make a choice between appliances that conform to one among several competing standards, such as televisions that use PAL or SECAM, they acquire a stake in one such standard by the very act of buying, say, a TV. When people subscribe to a newspaper, or connect to a telephone company, they acquire a vested interest in that particular service network. Their commitment to one standard or network depends in the first place on the net benefits they expect from the one they have opted for, minus the expected net benefits of the next-best option, plus the costs of switching to that alternative. Changing newspapers hardly involves any costs; switching banks may cause some expense; opting for a new word processor requires considerable retraining; adopting a different language demands major learning efforts. And, of course, any change in familiar habits is a mental sacrifice in itself. Language loyalty is an extreme case of consumer loyalty.

Whenever people opt for appliances with a specific standard, subscribe to a particular supply network or learn a given language, by doing so they increase the utility of that standard, network or language for all other consumers, subscribers or speakers who are already using it. There are several reasons for this: in supply networks the constant costs of the infrastructure are shared by a greater number of users. Of course, the same effect occurs with all commodities that can be manufactured at a lower cost per unit as production volume increases: these are straightforward economies of scale. When prices are decreased accordingly, these benefits accrue to new purchasers, and in the case of networks, in the course of time, they profit the old subscribers too. In the case of languages, however, no such effect is at work. They are not produced by anyone: they are simply there, freely available in live conversations or written, printed and recorded. Of course, in so far as languages are learned in courses and from books, which may be supplied with decreasing marginal costs to growing audiences, the spread of languages indirectly generates economies of scale.

Since they necessarily acquire a stake in the standard, or the language of their choice, people will opt for the alternative that is most likely to survive in a competitive environment. This will guarantee them the availability of spare parts, accessories and repair facilities, of programs and software in the future, and, in the case of languages, the continued supply of conversation partners and reading materials in the particular idiom.

For similar reasons, people prefer large brands with an established reputation: they assume that large suppliers will manage the manufacturing process more carefully and will be more willing to take back defective products or compensate for damages than the owners of smaller brands are wont to do, precisely because the good reputation of the famous brand is such a valuable asset to the supplier. But it is irrelevant for the spread and maintenance of languages. However, a commodity with a grand reputation confers prestige on its users. Many brand names are designed and manipulated to do just that. The languages of the great powers, or of the 'great traditions', likewise shed some of their glory upon their speakers.

Another effect occurs with consumer appliances that function with specific kinds of information carriers ('software'), such as personal computers, televisions, record players, CD, CD-I or CD-ROM players, recorders for tape, cassette, DAT, DCC, DVD and video, and so on. The larger the market share of a given standard, such as PAL or SECAM in television, the greater the number and variety of programs and recordings supplied for machines conforming to that standard. And this in turn increases the value of these appliances to their users. In this case there is a close correspondence with languages: the more speakers there are, the more readers, and therefore the more authors that supply all the more texts.

The features mentioned so far are known in the economics literature as 'external network effects' and they operate in every kind of network as a special sort of economy of scale.[5] But there is an additional reason why the value of certain networks may increase for its users as new subscribers join them – a reason that applies directly to languages. In some networks, such as telephone systems, every individual user can communicate with a larger number of other subscribers as the number of connections grows. This does not apply to all supply networks. It is not the case with sewage, gas, electricity or cable TV systems, which deliver a centrally supplied commodity or service to their users, but do not also directly connect them with one another. On the other hand, that is just what road and railway systems, telephone networks or postal delivery services do. *This special external effect is typical of those networks that serve the function of connecting the users with one another: that is, transport and communication networks.*[6] In these cases every new extension increases the number of potential connections for all existing users. For this reason, too, every user stands to profit from the participation of all other users.

Precisely this effect operates in the case of languages as they gain new speakers: for every actual speaker of the language, the number and variety of possible conversation partners or correspondents increases with each new speaker added. However, there is a critical difference between mutually connecting transport and communication networks, on the one hand, and languages on the other. Road and railway networks, telephone systems and postal services are 'excludable': they are accessible only for a fee – a tax, a toll, a ticket, a subscription, a stamp and so forth. Languages, on the contrary, are not produced, owned or marketed by any particular agent; they exist as free goods.[7] The same applies to standards for measuring time, distance, temperature and so forth. The most recent and spectacular instance of a non-excludable network is the internet. Although the use of a telephone line and a 'server' is indispensable for connecting to the world-wide web, no servers are excluded from the net and anyone who has access to such a machine can enter the network and move about freely.

Yet the external network effects occur independently of the fact that languages are free and non-excludable goods: all mutual communication and transport networks produce the same effects, even though they are excludable, being someone's property and accessible only for a fee. The non-excludable character of languages will, however, turn out to be highly relevant in their definition as collective goods.

Languages exist, they are the product of human creativity, but they are the creation of no one in particular and they are nobody's property. Anyone making the effort to learn them is free to speak or write them. This raises another question: does that make languages collective goods?

The question cannot be answered without defining the collectivity with respect to which languages may or may not be collective.[8] This collectivity can be no other than the category of people who are actual or potential users of the language, that is, all those persons who belong to the wider language system or subsystem (constellation) under consideration. If a language is to be considered a collective good in the strict sense, four conditions must be satisfied:

1   It is impossible, on technical or economic grounds, to exclude anyone from enjoying a collective good.[9] On the whole, natural languages are completely accessible for anyone making the effort to find a textbook or an instructor (or, for that matter, a patient conversation partner). Even the most secluded regimes, like Albania during the Cold War or North Korea long afterwards, did not attempt to prevent outsiders from learning their language, although they obstructed any attempt to practise it by denying entry to visitors.[10]
2   The collaboration of many but not of all concerned is required to bring about and maintain the collective good. Since natural languages already exist, what matters here is maintenance: a language can survive defection by some speakers, and therefore the survival of a language is not in jeopardy when any particular speaker defects; that is, no one has a veto on the survival of a language.
3   For the collective good to be brought into existence or maintained, the efforts of a single person are not sufficient. No one can create or salvage a language on his or her own.[11] (If one person could decide, this would again make the language's fate dependent on a single person's veto.)
4   Finally, the collective good's utility to its users does not diminish as new users are added.[12] For languages, an even stronger property applies: a language's utility does not just remain *equal* as its speakers increase in number. It actually *increases*. This is due to the operation of external network effects. Since languages both satisfy the definition of a collective good and display external network effects, they constitute a very special category; they are '*hypercollective*' goods. All non-excludable transport and communication networks that are also collective goods share this property of hypercollectivity.

Transport and communication networks, such as road, rail, telephone and computer networks, do allow the imposition of a user's fee for connection, hence they are 'excludable'. As potential or actual users can be excluded from these networks, they do not constitute collective goods, but rather 'joint' or 'common' goods; accordingly, they may be called '*hypercommon*' goods.

Since in the case of hypercollective goods neither entry nor exit can be controlled, stampedes may occur, either towards or away from the goods. As the number of their users grows, so does their utility. In the case of a language, its communication value increases, and at each higher-value level new categories of users may find it profitable to join, when their particular 'tipping point' has been reached.[13] This moment occurs for a language in a given (sub)system whenever the speakers of a different language find that they can increase the communication value of their repertoire by a greater amount by learning that language rather than another and when they find the gain worth the learning effort. Each new round would make the expanding language more attractive to the speakers of yet another repertoire, until every speaker in the system would be better off by adding this language rather than some other. At this point, it would become part of the repertoire of every speaker in the (sub) system. Since, in actual fact, multilanguage systems are quite stable, there must be some force working for inertia, namely the costs of expanding one's repertoire, that is, the expense and the effort of learning an additional language in relation to the expected benefits.[14]

Conversely, an outward stampede, the cumulative desertion from a language, may occur when an increasing number of speakers become fluent in another language and the number of speakers that can be reached in the former language only decreases: at some point it seems no longer worthwhile to teach it to one's children and it is abandoned entirely. Of course, the two processes – the stampede towards the expanding language and the stampede away from the imploding language – may reinforce one another, especially when expectations about the numbers of converts to the one language and deserters from the other begin to play a part in the choices of language learners. The costs of language acquisition can slow down these cumulative effects. Moreover, people may neglect to use their language, but they cannot so easily erase it from their memories. Definitive desertion occurs only when the next generation no longer learns the parental language. Finally, collective measures may be adopted to discourage people from abandoning their language, but such initiatives evoke all the dilemmas of collective action. This theme will come up again in the next chapter, which deals with the choices that present themselves to the users of the smaller languages, especially those who specialize in producing texts: the authors. Should they favour free exchange of texts, either in the original or a translated version, or should they favour protectionist policies? should they learn to read and even write in foreign languages, or should they pay for translation? should they abandon their mother tongue or maintain it, so that their collective cultural capital will remain accessible? Will these dynamics result in the conservation of the original language, produce a stable equilibrium of diglossia, or lead to the transition from one language to the other?

Much depends, of course, on the perceptions of prospective language learners. How do they estimate the gains to be made from adding a new language to their repertoire? What role, if any, do their expectations of the learning behaviour of others in their constellation play in their own choices? These questions may be answered by defining a measure for the communication potential of a language in a given (sub)system.

2.2   The communication potential of a language: the Q-value

What role, in effect, do individual language choices (if such choices are available at all) play in the dynamics of the language constellation? What is the aggregate result of these individual choices?

Suppose that someone intends to learn an additional language in order to increase the possibilities of communication. The larger the number of its speakers, the more attractive the language. Imagine a language called 'λ_i'. The 'prevalence', p_i, of this language is defined as the proportion of speakers of λ_i in the overall language constellation.

But the prospective language student will also assess the way this language is connected through multilingual speakers to other language groups in the constellation. This is measured by the 'centrality', c_i, of the language: the larger the number of speakers of λ_i that are *also competent* in some other language(s), the more connected the language is and the higher its centrality.

The 'centrality', c_i, of a language λ_i is accordingly defined by the proportion of *multilingual* speakers that are also competent in λ_i. Language students will choose the language which appears to be the most useful, the one which offers the greatest possibilities of communication, either directly, or *indirectly*, through the mediation of interpreters or translators. A language is more likely to be selected the more prevalent or the more central it is in the relevant language constellation. The prevalence of a language is an indicator of the opportunities it has to offer for direct communication with other persons in the constellation. The centrality of that language provides an indication of its connectedness to other languages and, as the case may be, of the chances for indirect communication it provides. The communication value or 'Q-value' of a language is the product of its prevalence and its centrality.

> The communication value of a language λ_i for a speaker in a constellation (S) can now be expressed in terms of its Q-value, Q_i^S, indicating the potential of λ_i to link this speaker with other speakers in S, directly or indirectly. The prevalence (p_i) of language λ_i is defined by the number of speakers (P_i) that are competent in λ_i, divided by all the speakers (N^S) in constellation S. This measures the proportion of persons with whom direct contact through language λ_i is possible. The centrality (c_i) is defined by the number (C_i) of *multilingual* speakers who are also competent in language λ_i, divided by all the *multilingual* speakers (M^S) in constellation S. This provides an indication of the connections between language λ_i and the other languages in constellation S. The communication value or Q-value equals the product of the prevalence (p_i) and the centrality (c_i) of language λ_i in constellation S:
>
> $$Q_i^S = p_i \cdot c_i = \frac{P_i}{N^S} \cdot \frac{C_i}{M^S}$$

This expression for the Q-value provides an adequate indication of the position of a language in the overall constellation. The current scarcity and unreliability of statistics on the distribution of language skills do not permit a more elaborate measure.[15] Moreover, since the Q-value is used to infer the preferences and choices of prospective language learners, it should roughly reflect their perceptions of the communication opportunities that the various languages in the constellation have to offer. Such perceptions can only be based on rather broad impressions and simple considerations. That rules out more complexity. Yet an even simpler measure would lack validity.

In those cases where reliable data on mother-tongue and second-language skills are available, the Q-value yields results that correspond with an informed assessment of the constellation. Most probably, prospective language learners choose on the basis of an – intuitive – estimate of the proportion of speakers of the language (p_i), weighted by a second factor, a rough estimate of the number of multilingual speakers competent in the language.

For the sake of simplicity, the discussion so far has proceeded in terms of single languages. But the argument can and should be couched in more general terms. Prospective speakers are more likely to compare language *repertoires*. How much would a speaker with a single-language repertoire, say, only German, stand to gain in Q-value by extending it to a two-language repertoire by learning French and how much by learning English instead?

The unit of analysis is no longer an individual language λ_i (with i ranging from 1 to n in a constellation with n different languages), but a language repertoire ρ_j (with j ranging from 1 to 2^n, for all possible combinations of languages). In this case, the number of French speakers is found by adding the speakers of all repertoires that contain French: French only, plus French and German, plus French, German and English, plus French and Spanish, and so forth. The prevalence p_j of a repertoire ρ_j is now defined as the proportion of speakers who are competent in one, or more, of the languages contained in the repertoire ρ_j and who can therefore be contacted directly by a speaker with that repertoire ρ_j.

The number of speakers of a particular repertoire ρ_j is written as f_j. In order to calculate the prevalence p_j of a repertoire ρ_j the number of speakers f_k of every repertoire ρ_k who have at least one language in common with ρ_j must be added (since this is the sum total of speakers who can be addressed directly in one of the languages in ρ_j) and this sum (P_j) must be divided by the number of all speakers, N^S. The requirement that two repertoires, say ρ_j and ρ_k, have at least one language in common is equivalent to the requirement that the set of languages that are an element of both the set ρ_j and the set ρ_k is not 'empty' ($\varnothing$): $\rho_j \cap \rho_k \neq \varnothing$.

The sum of the frequencies of all repertoires in S equals N^S, the number of all speakers in the constellation: $\sum f_i = N^S$ for $i = 1, \ldots 2^n$.

The prevalence p_j of a repertoire ρ_j may now be written as:

$$p_j = \sum f_k / N^S \text{ for all } f_k \text{ such that } \rho_j \cap \rho_k \neq \varnothing; k = 1, \ldots j, \ldots 2^n.$$

Likewise, the centrality c_j of a repertoire ρ_j is found by adding all the frequencies of multilingual repertoires (i.e. that *contain more than one language*) and that have at least one language in common with repertoire ρ_j and by dividing this sum by the total of the frequencies of all multilingual repertoires, M^S. If the number of languages in a repertoire ρ_j is defined as n_j, multilingual repertoires are defined by $n_j \geq 2$, and M^S is the sum of the frequencies f_j of all repertoires ρ_j in S, such that $n_j \geq 2$.

The centrality c_j of a repertoire ρ_j can now be expressed as:

$$C_j = \sum f_1/M^S \text{ for all } f_1 \text{ such that } \rho_j \cap \rho_1 \neq \varnothing \text{ and } n_1 \geq 2; 1 = 1, \dots j, \dots 2^n$$

Accordingly, the Q-value Q_j^S of a repertoire in constellation S is now rendered as:

$$Q_j^S = p_j \cdot c_j = \left(\sum f_k/N^S\right) \cdot \left(\sum f_1/M^S\right)$$

for all f_k such that $\rho_j \cap \rho_k \neq \varnothing$; $k = 1, \dots j, \dots 2^n$
for all f_1 such that $\rho_j \cap \rho_1 \neq \varnothing$ and $n_1 \geq 2$; $1 = 1, \dots j, \dots 2^n$.

The Q-value of a single language λ_i is identical to the Q-value of the one-language repertoire ρ_i that contains λ_i as its – only – element ($n_i = 1, \lambda \in \rho_i$).

The interpretation of the Q-value is quite straightforward. The first component, the prevalence, is the proportion of speakers in a constellation that can be directly contacted with the languages in a given repertoire. The second factor, the centrality, indicates the number of connections, or multilingual speakers, that link the languages in this repertoire with all others, as a proportion of all connections between languages in the constellation. This definition produces satisfactory results when used to calculate the Q-value of language repertoires in the European Union, the best-documented case, and in several other constellations. As an example, take a fictitious case with four languages, A, B, C and D (table 2.1).

The upper half of table 2.1 shows in each row the number of native speakers of the language. The 'Sole or second language' columns show those speaking only their native language (the figures on the diagonal) and those that speak that language plus a second one. There are also trilingual speakers, whose numbers appear in the 'Third language' columns. The total number of native speakers of, say, language A appears in the rightmost column. The total number of speakers of a language is obtained by adding the numbers in the row for that language (i.e. the total number of native speakers) to those in the columns for that language (i.e. foreign speakers of the language as a second or third language), avoiding counting the number of monolingual speakers on the diagonal twice.

The lower half of the table contains the Q-values. It has been 'folded over the diagonal'. Since the native speakers of A who speak C as a second language and the native speakers of C who speak A as their second language all possess the same repertoire A&C, they have been added in the cell A/C, while the cell C/A is left empty.

Table 2.1 An example of the calculation of Q-values

Native language	Sole or second language				Third language		Native speakers
	A	B	C	D	A&B&C	A&C&D	
A	50	4	3	0	1	0	58
B	8	60	2	0	1	0	71
C	4	2	30	0	0	0	36
D	0	0	0	15	0	1	16
Q-value:							
A	0.34	0.75	0.59	0.40	0.92	0.67	
B		0.30	0.64	0.38			
C			0.13	0.18			
D				(0.003)			

N^S (i.e. total speakers in S) = 181.
M^S (i.e. total multilingual speakers in S) = 26.
Greenberg's A = 0.60 (see below).

In this example, B is the language with the greatest number of native speakers: 71. The same language B also has the largest number of speakers (including the seven foreign speakers):[16] 78. Accordingly, its prevalence, p_B, that is, the total number of its speakers, P_B, divided by the total N^S, of speakers in the constellation S is: $p_B = P_B/N^S = 78/181 = 0.43$.

The centrality, C_B, is calculated likewise, dividing C_B, the number of multilingual speakers of language B, by M^S, the total number of multilingual speakers in constellation S:

$$C_B = C_B/M^S = 18/26 = 0.69.$$

The Q-value of B is obtained from:

$$Q_B = p_B \cdot c_B = (0.43) \cdot (0.69) = 0.30.$$

In this example the language A has fewer native speakers (58) than B, and fewer native plus foreign speakers (58 + 14 = 72) than B. However, all in all the number of multilinguals who also speak A is $C_A = 22$; larger than $C_B (= 18)$. As a consequence, although the prevalence, p_A, of A is lower than p_B, the centrality, c_A, of A is so much higher than c_B that their product, the Q-value, Q_A, ends up higher than Q_B. Accordingly:

$$Q_A = p_A \cdot c_A = (72/181) \cdot (22/26) = (0.40) \cdot (0.85) = 0.34$$

(whereas $Q_B = 0.30$). Thus, a language that counts fewer speakers can still end up with a higher Q-value than one with more speakers, on account of the former's greater centrality.

The language D, with a relatively small number of speakers (15 + 1), has an almost negligible Q-value, $Q_D = 0.003$, because its centrality is minimal: $c_D = 1/26$. Apparently, language group D has a small but well-educated trilingual elite. But no outsiders have bothered to learn language D, and its connection to the rest of the constellation is tenuous.

An outsider wanting to gain entrance to this constellation would obviously do best to learn A, as it has the largest Q-value. Within the constellation, the speakers of A prefer B as their second language, because the repertoire (A&B) has a higher Q-value than (A&C) or (A&D); the speakers of B would rather learn A; C-speakers, however, will opt for B rather than A; speakers of D would be best off with A as their second language. Depending on the rate of second-language learning in each group, either A or B may gain more new speakers and the final state of the constellation cannot be determined beforehand.

In the chapters on the respective language constellations, tables for Q-values will be presented whenever the data on language skills allow it. The most elaborate tables appear in chapter 8, on the European Union.

Every table of Q-values also presents a value for 'Greenberg's A'. This is a measure for 'language diversity'. The first quantitative research on language constellations dates back to 1956, when the famous linguist Joseph H. Greenberg[17] introduced his 'diversity index', A. This measure was later elaborated by Stanley Lieberson[18] and based on the odds that a randomly selected pair of speakers in a given constellation would *not* have a language in common.[19] Greenberg's indices define the degree of fragmentation ('diversity') of the *constellation*. The Q-value, by contrast, characterizes the position of a specific *language* (or repertoire) within the constellation.

The Q-value serves as a rough-and-ready measure for the communication value of a language in a given constellation. Even this simple indicator cannot be calculated for some constellations, for lack of the necessary statistics on language skills. A more complicated construct would have to be based on pure guesses or remain without factual underpinnings. An even simpler measure, for example the straight figures for the number of speakers of a language, ignoring multilingual skills, would do no justice to the dynamics of the constellation.

The Q-value is an indicator of the communication value of a language. But it also purports to reconstruct the 'value' that speakers attribute to that language, an evaluation that guides their choices of foreign languages to learn. In fact, no one has ever before calculated Q-values, and certainly not the many millions of prospective language students in the constellations under study. And yet in many cases they have weighed one option against another and let themselves be guided by impressions, intuitions and third-party advice grounded on similar perceptions: their idea of the spread of a language must have played a role, and so must their notion of its connectedness to other languages in the constellation where they sought to make themselves understood. The Q-value conveys these considerations. It is an approximate quantity. And that is how the scores should be read. Within one and the same constellation Q-values may be compared as 'greater' or 'smaller', qualified as 'much' or 'barely' greater. But no more can be said. This agrees with the highly approximate quality of the choices that are made by the people who must make up their minds in an actual language constellation. The Q-value is grounded in the theoretical concept of a world language system with its hierarchically organized pattern of connections between languages at four different levels. Whether it is also an empirically valid construct will appear from subsequent chapters that discuss factual language constellations. If it works, it is real.

Language, culture and the unequal exchange of texts

Languages define areas of communication. Beyond these limits, cultural practices and products travel with greater ease the less they depend on language: the visual arts cross much more easily than, say, poetry. For language-bound culture to transcend linguistic barriers requires the services of specialized bilinguals, that is, translators, or a foreign audience that has learned the language of the original version.

Language both insulates and protects the language-bound cultural elites in its domain. On the one hand, what they produce does not on its own transpire to the outside world. On the other hand, the cultural production in other languages cannot penetrate and compete directly; it requires local competence in these foreign languages, or translation into the domestic language.

This insulation operates more intensely for the less widely spread languages. As a result, the cultural elites concerned are faced with a dilemma: adopt a more widely spread second language and compete with many more producers in a much larger market – the 'cosmopolitan strategy'; or stick to the less widely spread language and compete with only a few others for a much more restricted public – the 'local' strategy.

Thus, say, Surinamese, Frisian or Antillian authors face a dilemma between Sranan, Frisian or Papiamento on the one hand, and

Netherlandish[1] on the other. On the next system level, Dutch authors, in turn, have had to confront the choice between publishing in Netherlandish and English.

The case for remaining with the smaller language is usually better argued and advanced more explicitly than its opposite, the choice for the large language. The arguments most commonly presented in the first case are threefold. First, the small idiom is threatened: it may even disappear eventually as people abandon it in increasing numbers and it finally meets 'language death'.[2] Next, this argument may be generalized from language to all indigenous cultural practices and products, bound to disappear unless the language in which they are embedded continues to be spoken and understood. This will erode the sense of personal identity and of identification with the community. Finally, linguistic imperialism and the pursuit of global cultural hegemony are only abetted by defectors from the smaller language group who adopt the most widely spread language.[3]

The case for choosing the larger language, on the other hand, remains mostly implicit and the choice often appears like tacit desertion of one's cultural heritage. And yet it is not all that hard to mobilize not just the apologias of self-interest but also the canons of universalism in its support.[4] The widely spread language will not just improve career prospects for its new practitioners, it will also open up a larger world, with broader knowledge, richer culture, more varied lifestyles and moral options.

In this chapter, these dilemmas between the local and the cosmopolitan position will be placed in the perspective of the world language system, of the particular, hypercollective, character of languages and of the Q-value of language repertoires. By introducing the concept of 'collective cultural capital', that is, the totality of available texts in a given language, a case can be made for its conservation in terms of the present approach. Without invoking such values as 'identity' or 'solidarity', the argument demonstrates the dilemmas of collective action that are involved in the effort to conserve the cultural heritage, embedded as it is in language.

3.1   Texts as commodities in international exchange

Now that a measure for the value of a language, its Q-value, has been defined, and the distinctive, hypercollective character of languages has been established, two new and related issues present themselves. Under what conditions do authors and speakers prefer free exchange of language-bound products, or texts, and when will they choose to protect their community from the linguistic encroachments that may well result from the free exchange of texts with a larger language community? And, second, under what conditions will they resort to collective measures to protect their common language? In other words, how does the theory of free trade vs. protectionism apply to language-bound cultural exchange, and what can be said on the collective aspects of the dilemmas of language loyalty vs. language defection? The first issue is discussed in this section, the second in the next.

In the international exchange of language-bound culture goods, that is, texts, transport costs play a minor role, decreasing to almost zero for electronic transmission. In this respect, texts are the international commodity par excellence. What can make foreign texts costly is the expense of translation. Interpreters or translators produce a version of a foreign text in the domestic idiom. The costs of their specialist services may in many respects be compared with those of transportation. Even the concept of distance has some relevance: 'distant' languages are generally harder to learn, requiring greater effort on the part of translators.

But there are many members of the domestic public who need no translation services, being themselves competent in the foreign language. Such skills did not come without cost, in terms of time and effort spent on foreign language learning. The learning effort is in some respects comparable to purchasing a second home in another country or opening a branch office there.[5] It allows one to operate in two national markets, saving transport costs and duties while residing abroad, just as polyglots can save themselves translation costs, once they have made themselves at home in the foreign language by investing in its acquisition.[6]

Very much like transportation costs and excise duties, the costs of translation or foreign language learning also function as a barrier protecting indigenous authors, that is, domestic producers of texts in the local language. As a consequence, a community where competence in a foreign language (especially one with higher Q-value) is relatively scarce provides authors with a natural 'protective' barrier. Their captive audience finds itself restricted to domestic or translated texts, very much like consumers who must either buy goods produced domestically or pay transport costs and import duties. A somewhat chauvinistic public may not mind too much, preferring texts with a strong *couleur locale*, just as it prefers the flavour of domestic bread, wine or beer to outlandish alternatives.[7]

Let us pursue the argument by concentrating on one kind of – highly specialized – language users: the authors. Their most advanced language skills, and for literary authors, moreover, their 'style', represent their major, if not their only, investment capital.[8] They may be thought of as single-minded entrepreneurs, out to maximize their audience, or at the very least conquer a niche in the market, a readership of their own among the public at large.

Authors who grew up with a rather peripheral language (i.e. with a low Q-value) may find it to their advantage to write in it, if their public is mostly monolingual. In that case, they need not make the costly investment of learning another language to such perfection that they can publish in it. They are assured of a public that cannot turn elsewhere, while their foreign competitors find themselves hampered by the costs of translation, quite forbidding for small language communities. Probably, native authors are best protected in societies where most people can understand and read the standard version of the domestic language; that is, where elementary education is widespread, while few citizens have attended secondary school and therefore fluency in other, larger, languages is rare. There is thus a wide audience for texts in the domestic language and only a small public has access to alternatives in foreign languages. This is probably the case in China, in the Hindi part of India (even though illiteracy rates are well over 60 per cent),[9] in Egypt, in Indonesia and in the Philippines. Indeed domestic-language newspapers, indigenous radio or television programmes and popular songs with lyrics in the local idiom flourish in these countries.

The consumers of language-dependent culture, on their part, are best served by the most varied supply of texts, accessible at the lowest cost. Understanding a text in their native language for them requires neither translation nor foreign language skills. But in the smaller language communities, the supply of domestic texts is necessarily limited. Even much larger societies often cannot produce textual genres that require an extensive infrastructure, a very high investment or a mass audience, such as scientific publications or spectacular films.[10] Domestic authors on their own cannot satisfy local demand for such texts, as such genres require a very costly, extensive and finely branched production network: academic departments, or a film and music industry. Thus, if the consumers wish to extend their options in these genres, they must gain access to foreign texts, in translation, or they must learn the relevant language, to have access to the original.

The authors, on their part, are faced with a restricted market for their texts: the local audience that reads the domestic language. Especially in the smaller language communities, demand may not be sufficient to sustain more than a few authors in the specialized genres, such as novels, poetry, and literary and historical essays. Unless the authors accept that they must diversify their activities – for example take a job on the side, as most literary writers in the smaller language communities find themselves compelled to do – they will be prompted to seek access to larger markets and try to publish in a more widespread language. The author then has two options: (1) learn a foreign tongue with high Q-value well enough to compose texts in it, a major and high-risk investment; (2) find a foreign publisher who will commission a translation into the high-Q language; this, too, requires a considerable and risky investment – on the part of the publisher. But the potential gains are proportional: a chance of large circulation in a much bigger market.[11]

Mastering a foreign language to such perfection that one can compete with native authors requires a major effort, but it has been accomplished, not only by Conrad and Nabokov, or Ionesco, Cioran and more recently Kundera, but also by Jan de Hartog, and, in the unstylish realm of social science, by quite a few scholars, me among them. The other option, that of having the texts translated, comes at considerable cost. Translation of, say, a 300-page book at present rates costs approximately $US 15,000. The median first printing of a novel on the English-language market is not much larger than that of a novel on the Dutch market. For an expected circulation of 2000 copies – certainly not too conservative an estimate – translation accounts for $US7.50 of an average shop price of, say, $US25 per copy. This makes translation costs three times as high as customary royalties (say, 10 per cent on the list price). For films, translation costs tend to be much lower, but dubbing is again quite costly: it is routinely required by audiences in large countries who tend to despise subtitles, which are almost proverbial for the snob appeal of exotic movies.[12]

To sum up, for authors whose native language is understood by a relatively restricted audience, there is the low-risk, low-gain strategy of publishing in the mother tongue for a domestic public, and the high-risk, high-profit strategy of seeking publication in a widespread language. The two, however, are not mutually exclusive; authors can aim for the global market in translation, all the while maintaining a hold on the home market in the original version. The cosmopolitan strategy demands making an effort and taking a risk, and more often than not it requires good connections with foreign publishers and literati; that is, it takes transnational social capital.[13]

The users of texts in the more peripheral languages who want to transcend the limitations of domestic supply equally face two options:

pay for translation, or learn the language with the higher Q-value. The first option implies continual payment of the current costs of translation. The second represents an investment in learning the more widespread language, a considerable investment in terms of time, effort and money, which, moreover, requires some maintenance, that is, regular reading and viewing of products in the foreign language.

Once a text is translated, however, the expense does not increase with the size of the text's circulation. Marginal costs are nil. Therefore, translation costs of texts that achieve a very large circulation, or that remain in demand for a long time, tend to become insignificant. Products of mass culture and products of classic culture, such as a TV soap like Dallas or a volume of the complete works of Shakespeare, may be translated at very low cost per consumer.

Readers and listeners with specialized interests, be it in science, high literature, or any other specific field of language-bound culture, will find that translations may appear with much delay, in erratic fashion, of low quality or at high prices, if at all. They may find it more useful to invest in learning the high-Q language, thus avoiding paying for translation and increasing their access to products in that language. Interestingly enough, the rarer translations of foreign texts are, the more it pays for consumers to invest in learning the larger language. Moreover, the smaller the peripheral language in question, the more likely it is that translations from the larger language will remain rare and inadequate.

Finally, in Western Europe and the US almost all foreign-language learning occurs in secondary school and the vast majority of the relevant age cohort does indeed attend full daytime education at that level.[14] As a result, the investment is compulsory and the effort is made at the very start of one's career as a consumer of language-bound cultural goods. In other parts of the world, secondary school attendance is much lower. It is left to the parents who can afford it to send their child to a school where foreign languages are offered, or it depends on the adult individual's decision to take private language courses.

Whether a foreign language is compulsory in school or not, the motivation for learning it increases when attractive cultural products are unavailable in translation into one's own, peripheral language. On the other hand, the incentive for publishers to translate texts into the more peripheral language decreases if more potential readers and spectators are also fluent in the more central language.[15]

In conclusion, restrictions on the translation and dissemination of foreign-language-bound products paradoxically will increase motivation among the public for learning a foreign language, an effect that may be much reinforced by the increased prestige of such foreign products.

3.2   Protectionism and free trade in cultural exchange

There is, however, one caveat: authors in small languages have some reason to be worried by foreign competition, but so do their readers, who may come to fear that eventually their indigenous authors will be forced out of the field through the impact of translated and imported texts. Concern may grow that in the end this will lead to a general erosion of the mother tongue and of domestic culture in general; that is, in the terms of this analysis, to an overall depreciation of the original investment in mastery of the mother tongue. In other words, the short-term preferences of individual consumers may damage their collect-ively accumulated cultural capital in the long run. This is of course a very familiar argument, both in the debate on the protection of na-tional cultures and in the discussion on the protection of domestic 'infant' and 'essential' industries, such as nutrition or armaments. Moreover, given the low marginal costs of translation of foreign texts, the familiar arguments from international trade theory about 'dumping' may well apply in the case of cultural exchange also.[16] Television and film conglomerates in the very large language commu-nities can afford to export comedy series and old films at negligible rates, preventing the small countries at the receiving end from develop-ing a domestic entertainment industry that can compete – even if only internally – with foreign imports. American film and TV producers, especially, have dumped their products abroad.

In the realm of the arts and sciences, moreover, a vast proportion of products exported abroad have been subsidized at home by govern-ment or foundation grants to artists or to academic scholars. Under the terms of classic trade theory this might justify protective tariffs against 'cheap' imports in the receiving country,[17] but the argument is rarely invoked in the case of high art and science, as they appeal to a quite restricted, highly educated public in a society that does not itself produce these high cultural goods, anyway.

However, producers in the small and not so small language areas do at times advocate protectionist policies against cultural imports from abroad. In fact, the proposal has come up time and again during the former GATT and present WTO negotiations between the US and the

European Union.[18] Producers petitioned the Commission to impose
tariffs or quotas on imported films, a practice that has been adopted
by the French government for television, films and popular music
broadcasts. Once again, the case is built on arguments against
'dumping'.

Although most of these arguments have some substance, in the case
of quotas and outright prohibition, limits are imposed on consumers'
freedom of choice, an especially contested practice in the realm of
culture, where freedom of expression and information is a core issue.
The less invasive policy of imposing tariffs on foreign imports still
taxes consumers in the sensitive realm of cultural participation. Moreover, these policies are commonly justified as protecting especially
valuable assets, in this case, products of high culture. Thus, the French
campaign for a quota on American cultural imports into the European Union (mainly films and TV series) equated 'European' cinema
across the board with 'high', and 'American' film with 'low' culture.
But even in France, domestic origin does not guarantee high artistic
standards, while foreign provenance does not necessarily imply low
cultural quality.

At a second look, there are additional considerations that work
against the restriction of foreign cultural imports. First, limiting the
access to foreign-language-bound products may work to increase
their scarcity value and their prestige, their snob appeal and curiosity
value, and thus, perversely, increase demand. This, of course, is what
happened with American culture under the Nazi regime and with
Western culture in the former Soviet Union, and it may have fed the
immense popularity of Disney and Hollywood in France.

Second, the policy of protecting 'couleur locale' and 'indigenous
values' cuts both ways: local authors and performers may come to
rely too much on familiar notions and facile imitations and end up
being considered 'homely' and boring.

Finally, authors and performers may pressure the government into
granting subsidies for domestic products, to improve their competitive position vis-à-vis foreign imports. This is standard practice in the
European film industry, and less visibly so in the production of TV
drama and documentaries. Domestic literature and the arts are also
routinely subsidized. As mentioned already, in classical trade theory,
government subsidies of products in their country of origin are an
accepted argument for protective barriers by importing countries.
However, for the large language area, such counter-measures are
scarcely relevant: European books, songs and films that have been
subsidized at home hardly represent much of a threat to domestic
producers in the US.

The situation is entirely different for the former French and British colonies, especially in Africa, where the erstwhile colonial language remains the most central (but usually not the most prevalent), and the predominance of texts in the ex-colonial language actually hinders the emergence of cultural and scientific production in the domestic language. On the other hand, in many countries the former colonial language remains the only medium of nationwide communication and therefore greatly facilitates exchange on a translocal level. This theme will recur throughout the following chapters of this book.

At this point, a second concept from classical foreign trade theory is pertinent. Many cultural products can obviously be considered 'merit goods', that is, products that when consumed by some individuals generate favourable consequences for others, even if they do not themselves purchase or use them: 'positive external effects'. For example, a small audience for indigenous poets may keep poetry in the domestic language alive, stimulate poets to go on writing in that language, and maintain and reinforce interest in the poetic heritage. This may be sufficient reason to subsidize poets and poetry books, even for people who do not themselves read poetry but want to be part of a culture in which poetry survives.

Accordingly, merit goods can be defined as commodities that one agrees *others* should be using. The prestige of high art and high tradition may radiate out to people who themselves have no part in them. This also applies to international exchange: people who travel and work abroad have a collective interest in the international prestige of their culture, even if they themselves are not consumers of it. Thus, even the collective cultural capital of small nations may contain elements that are known and appreciated abroad. A Netherlander's standing in the world is somewhat increased by his or her association with Rembrandt, Van Gogh and Appel, or the Concertgebouw Orchestra (none of them tied to the language), or in some circles even by the reputation of Huizinga, Multatuli and Mulisch (in translation).

The 'merit goods' argument is of course the mainstay of the case in favour of cultural subsidies. Another argument is heard less frequently: cultural producers must make a relatively large, high-risk, personal investment that pays off only in the long run, if ever. During their formative years, artists, writers and even scholars often find themselves living in poverty and anonymity, with only a small chance of ever becoming successful. Under such risky conditions, producer subsidies seem justified (although this implies a complementary case for taxing 'windfall profits' reaped at a later stage and age of recognition).

In the preceding section, arguments have been borrowed from the theory of international trade, the theory of (hyper)collective goods, the theory of merit goods, and the theory of collective cultural capital. Together they can support the case for a free trade policy with regard to cultural exchange – no tariffs, no quota – and for a policy of domestic subsidies to producers of high or innovative culture. These grants should support especially risky – that is, advanced, initially contested – forms of expression, on the basis of the estimated probability that at some time in the future they will turn out to have 'merit' as cultural goods. Both free trade and producer subsidies stimulate the accumulation of domestic collective cultural capital; free trade by facilitating the contributions of foreign authors, subsidies by stimulating domestic producers.

But what about 'mass culture'? Do the writers of soap series, thrillers and pop songs also deserve producer subsidies? This question is even harder to answer for sociologists than for other people, since most of them define 'high culture' as the products and practices that appeal to the tastes of the highly educated, and conversely 'low culture' as appealing to the less educated.[19] Most sociologists refuse to discuss the 'intrinsic merits' of cultural goods at all. But an argument for subsidizing the producers of 'high culture' can be based on the authors' and artists' risky and long-term investment in an oeuvre that may pay off only twenty or thirty years later. 'Mass culture' aiming to please a large public immediately is less *risqué* and less risky. Second, unlike 'high culture', 'low culture' is not thought to generate positive external effects, or contribute to the cultural collective good. It is therefore not a 'merit good' and thus not deserving of producer subsidies.[20]

Surprisingly, precisely the same argument applies to the 'high' and 'low' versions of a language. Sociolinguists and sociologists will not attribute any intrinsic superiority to the high register; they are wary of even considering the matter in terms of better and worse; the 'high' version is the sociolect of the highly educated, and there is no more to it. And yet the entire educational system is geared to teaching children the high, that is the 'standard', that is the 'king's' or 'queen's', that is the 'general civilized' version.[21] The students, for reasons of 'their own', often continue to use their home sociolects and usually agree that the 'high' version is better.

In the meantime, competence in the high version of the language represents 'linguistic capital' (Bourdieu). Competence in one of the lower versions provides no such advantage in wider society, but functions as an identity marker that strengthens the bonds with one's peers.[22]

The unequal relations of power and prestige that prevail between different languages in a given constellation, say between the higher, supercentral language and the peripheral or central languages that must compete with it, also exist between the different versions of a single language, say between the standard version and the dialects of the domestic periphery (the 'provinces', the 'countryside' or the 'back-woods'). And, sometimes, 'regional' authors who write the 'dialect', or singers and comedians who speak it, occupy a separate niche, sheltered by the relative unintelligibility of their language variety, and by its low prestige elsewhere.

The next section will again take up the subject of the collective aspects of language, and of culture in general. But first, we need to characterize briefly the position of the third and the fourth party in unequal cultural exchanges: the producers and the consumers of language-bound cultural goods in the widespread language. The treatment can be short, since their position is fairly straightforward and most privileged.

By definition, the users of a language with high Q-value profit from the position their language occupies in the encompassing constellation of languages. Their advantage is a clear case of what economists would call 'location rent'.[23] Whenever someone learns their mother tongue as a foreign language, they profit, as the 'communication value' of their language increases without any effort on their part. The tremendous advantages of this position may be seen when looking at the exports of language-bound cultural goods from the US and Britain. This privilege is not won by birthright alone, through the gift of the native tongue. It can be acquired: quite a few writers, many singers and actors, legions of scientists and scholars have made the effort to acquire fluency in English and reaped the rewards that go with it. Nor does it come solely from a location in Babylon, the anglophone heartland of the US and UK. An astonishing number of writers from peripheral societies where English prevails in some form or function have gained a worldwide stature through their mastery of English prose: for example, Naipaul, Rushdie, Soyinka and Coetzee. Success with the native English-speaking public often brings with it recognition by a globally dispersed audience that learned English as a foreign language. Next comes translation into the many languages that are linked to English by interpreters and translators. Not only the rents from linguistic capital enter the equation, but also the rents from the social capital based on a strategic position in the network of international cultural exchange.

The authors in the large languages have little to fear from foreign imports: translation costs operate as a small but protective impediment, equal to the translation costs in the other direction (as symmetric as transportation costs for that matter).[24] The effort demanded from foreign authors who wish to acquire the required fluency to produce English-language texts serves as another, rather formidable, protective barrier. Moreover, even though foreign-born authors enter the English-language market either directly or through translation, the increase in foreign consumers who have mastered the language proceeds even faster, making any measure of domestic producer protection rather superfluous.[25] It goes without saying that under these conditions, the USA is well advised to support free cultural exchange across the globe, even if it has to do so unilaterally.[26]

The authors of English texts also profit from the generalized prestige of English-language culture abroad, and this again facilitates export of their writings. This prestige is a function not only of the worldwide distribution of English, but also of the global military, political and economic hegemony of America – and what is left of the glory of Britain.[27]

The position of cultural consumers who learned the (super)central language as their mother tongue is as privileged as that of the producers, if not more so. Competition from abroad brings consumers only more variety in supply, while they need not fear at all for the survival of their own language and culture. On the contrary, each day, all over the world, tens of millions of students are busy learning English, in the process improving their own position in the world language constellation and, unwittingly, improving the value position of all other English speakers. All the while, the native English speakers do not even realize what an enviable blessing is bestowed upon them by the sheer accident of their mother tongue and the learning efforts of a myriad of unknown foreign students.

These benefits are almost entirely undeserved and unjustified, but so are most advantages and detriments that befall nations as accidents of geography and history: location, climate, the access to natural resources and trade routes and so forth. Recently, a movement to right the wrongs of language hegemony has spread across the Western world, advocating the right of all people to speak the language of their choice, to fight 'language imperialism' abroad and 'linguicism' at home, to strengthen 'language rights' in international law. Alas, what decides is not the right of human beings to speak whatever language they wish, but the freedom of everyone else to ignore what they say in the language of their choice.[28] If, on the other hand, people want to communicate beyond the narrow circle of their linguistic peers, they will have to learn the (super)central language that links them to wider circles of communication.

3.3   Monoglossia, polyglossia and heteroglossia

The users of a language share it as a hypercollective good. But having
constituted a language community over a long period of time, centuries, maybe millennia, they have gradually accumulated a collection of
texts recorded or memorized[29] in their language. Just as every added
speaker profits all others, every new text increases the collective
cultural capital.

In principle, a language community should be willing to subsidize
new speakers to join its ranks, since they increase the Q-value of its
language for all members. Language courses for recent immigrants are
indeed routinely subsidized in Israel and in European Union countries
such as the Netherlands. For the same reasons, it would be rational
for the British or the American, or for that matter the French or
German, governments to sponsor courses abroad in their respective
languages. But actually many students there are willing to pay for
textbooks and tuition anyway, since they want to improve the Q-
value of their repertoire by adding a widespread language. Governments in wealthy countries, on their part, do subsidize language
instruction at home indirectly by paying for secondary education.
This, too, is rational both for the individual, who acquires a repertoire
with higher Q-value, and for the collectivity, since the domestic
language grows in value as its centrality increases with a gain in
multilinguals in its ranks, that is, students who have mastered a
foreign language. In other words, speakers of a language profit from
the language-learning efforts of some among them without any effort
on their own part; they gain opportunities to find interpreters between
that foreign language and their own, and this is reflected in the
increase of centrality, a factor in the Q-value. The same applies to
speakers of the foreign language, again without any activity on their
part, since its Q-value also grows with the increase of its multilingual
speakers. Where hypercollectivity prevails, language learning is a
win–win game, with benefits for every one. The gain comes at a
cost, however: the expense and effort of language learning itself.[30]

Polyglossia,[31] the coexistence of several languages in one society in
distinct social domains, need not damage anyone. But under certain
conditions it drives people to abandon the language with the lesser Q-
value, usually an indigenous language, often their mother tongue. In
one domain after another a growing number of speakers chooses to
use the more central language. Gradually at first, then at an increasing
rate, the original language is deserted. The language community in its

entirety begins to tilt towards the new language like a ship making water and leaning over ever further until it capsizes. A slow stampede out of the domestic language and towards the imported tongue is under way. This is what sociolinguists call 'language death' or 'language extinction'. It is difficult not to depict the process as a tragic loss. The metaphor of death or extinction conjures up the image of a lost species. A biological species, however, may be saved by safe-guarding the environment where it finds its niche. For a language to survive, a considerable number of people must maintain their speech and maybe their ways of life against the inroads of a changing social and linguistic environment – a rather more formid-able task.

As an increasing proportion of the speakers in the original language community becomes bilingual, the added Q-value of being fluent not only in the exogenous but also in the indigenous language begins to diminish, since more and more people who speak the domestic language can also be reached in the foreign one, until no one is left who speaks the domestic language only and competence in it no longer adds to one's Q-value.[32] Children may now learn the new language at an ever earlier age, with increasing facility, and they may even pass it on to their children as their other tongue instead of the original language. This is by no means unusual. On the contrary, it is the 'normal' course of affairs in processes of nation-formation and colon-ization. A powerful centre extends its political, economic and cultural control over the periphery, adjacent or overseas, and its language spreads across the new territories. This occurred in the French 'prov-inces' with Breton, Flemish and Occitan, and throughout the 'Celtic fringe' of the British Isles with Welsh, Scots and Irish; it happened all over Latin America under the impact of Spanish; while the small languages of memory in India and Indonesia, in South Africa and Senegal, Nigeria and Congo (Zaire), are undergoing the triple impact of the supercentral, former colonial languages, the (super)central domestic languages and the popular, vehicular 'pidgins'.

From an individual perspective it is entirely rational for people to opt for the language with the larger Q-value. Only the costs of language learning and the emotional costs of abandoning one's mother tongue will impede the transition to the dominant language. Once the great majority of the original language community has become bilingual, and diglossia is well-nigh complete, another stage sets in, one that may be called 'heteroglossia'. Here the original language no longer adds much to the Q-value of individual reper-toires (that is, less than its 'maintenance' costs) and it is increasingly being abandoned, as the dominant language takes over.

However, at this point other considerations may become predominant: with the surrender of the indigenous language the collective
cultural capital becomes increasingly inaccessible. Either the texts
must be translated into the dominant language, or the collective
cultural stock is lost. In that case, the individual cultural capital,
predicated as it is on the collective capital, must be written off. (Of
course, the new speakers of the hegemonic language in the process
acquire access to the collective cultural stock of that language community and they may well consider it adequate compensation for their
loss.) Since it usually does not pay for individuals on their own to
translate endogenous texts into the hegemonic language, a collective
effort must be made by the members of the language community in
dissolution. But those who speak and act for this disbanding language
community will most probably prefer to salvage it not by translation
of its heritage, but by preventing the desertion of its members in the
first place: they will insist that a collective effort be made to maintain
the idiom, even if only as a second language. There will be pressure
upon adults to continue to use it, and upon children to go on learning
it as their parents did.[33] Clearly, a community with an effective
coordinating agency, such as a political authority of its own, is in a
much better position to impose its policies than a collectivity that
must rely on voluntary compliance.[34]

Authors, as producers of texts, have a larger stake in the original
language and in the conservation of its cultural stock than others,
because of their costly investment in language skills and in knowledge
of the accumulated texts. Moreover, for them the switch to the
dominant language as a full means of expression requires a much
larger effort than for those who only speak, hear and read it. And,
finally, if and when the domestic language is maintained by a sufficiently large audience, this provides the indigenous authors with a
protected market for their texts, and gives them an added interest in
maintaining the original language.

Thus, unless they make up their mind to become cosmopolitans,
venturing into the high-Q language community, authors will feel
compelled to defend the domestic language. Translators and interpreters, too, have a vested interest in slowing down the spread of the
dominant language and in preventing the desertion from the original
language, so as to maintain a clientele for their services.

It should therefore come as no surprise that specialized producers
and translators of texts are among the first to defend the domestic
language, together with politicians who wish to preserve their local
support base and community leaders or clergy who do not want to see
their congregation disband as its unifying language evaporates.

The 'tipping point' in the transition from diglossia to heteroglossia comes when those who speak both the indigenous and the exogenous language find that the costs of maintaining the local language begin to outweigh the latter's dwindling additional Q-value.[35] That occurs when a considerable majority of the community has already become bilingual. Once desertion sets in, parents no longer teach the language to their children and no longer make an effort to speak it 'correctly' themselves. If the language is to survive at all, individual language maintenance is no longer enough. Young adults must be pressured into the much larger effort of learning what has by then become the language of their elders.

In general, the gains that speakers may reap from the addition of new users of their language find their counterpart under obverse conditions in the increasing losses that the remaining speakers suffer once others begin to desert their language. Since language is a hyper-collective good, and cultural stock constitutes a collective good for the language community, language maintenance raises problems of collective action and confronts individual language users with con-comitant dilemmas: it would indeed make sense for everyone separately to maintain the original language if many others could be counted on to act likewise. However, since one cannot be sure the others will do so, in each individual case maintenance of the original language appears not worth the effort. In such situations people often publicly profess their allegiance to the collective heritage, while privately they neglect their inherited language and their cultural inheritance, and improve the career prospects of their children by making sure they will become proficient in the dominant language.[36]

On the whole, when the language community also constitutes a state, its government can avert a stampede out of the national language, even when a high degree of diglossia prevails. It can do so by safeguarding the domains of domestic politics, national culture, education, law and so forth as the preserve of the indigenous language and by preventing the exogenous language from usurping all prestigious functions. In short, it is the state that can keep its official language 'robust'. Thus, some European countries, like the Netherlands, Luxembourg and Denmark, are rapidly approaching a state of universal multilingualism and pervasive diglossia: up to 80 per cent of the population is more or less competent in English. But, at present, there are no signs of abandonment or neglect of the national languages. The domestic language continues to function in a series of distinct social domains while English dominates in other domains. Even if switching between the two is frequent, the one hardly encroaches upon the other.[37] If there is no reason for alarm, there is sufficient cause to remain alert: English may make inroads into new speech domains and the national languages may continue to lose prestigious functions. But most probably European languages will prove vital enough to maintain their specific domains under the pressure of English.

3.4 Discussion

Although linguists, and especially sociolinguists, have produced a most respectable number of informative studies on the social determinants and functions of language, and macro-sociolinguists have even made language policy and planning their speciality, the rivalry and accommodation between language groups have so far received only scant theoretical attention.

Economists, on their part, have rarely studied language per se. As a result, some of the most remarkable characteristics of language have gone largely unnoticed. Sociolinguists, on the other hand, have looked into the costs and benefits of multilingualism, translation and simultaneous interpretation, but have never gone much beyond cost accounting, neglecting the concepts economic theory has to offer.

In the first chapters of this book, languages, or rather language groups, were studied from a general social science perspective, and it is in this vein that ideas taken from economics have been applied: as part and parcel of a general science of society. In this sense, the political economy and the political sociology of language are part of one and the same approach.

The argument took off from a synoptic position: the concept of a global language system that has emerged in the course of the evolution of the human species. In the next stage the focus was on an intermediate level: the particular, hypercollective character of language that makes for the dynamics between specific language groups, as individuals adopt one language and – after a delay – abandon another: often in a self-fulfilling and self-accelerating mode. In the third stage, the analysis shifted to an individualistic perspective: the Q-value as an indication of the communication opportunities that a language affords its users. This communication value determines individual preferences among languages, but it is itself determined by the position of these languages – their connectedness within the overall constellation. Thus, the analysis proceeds on all three levels, that of the global constellation, of the language groups and of the individual speakers, focusing on the dialectics of the interaction between these levels.

The subject of the present chapter was the unequal exchange of texts between different language groups in the global constellation. The theoretical concepts presented earlier could now be applied to the strategic options of producers and consumers, that is authors and readers, of the texts that circulate through the system. The notions of free trade and protection, again borrowed from economics, helped to clarify the dilemmas that confront authors and readers, both in small and in large language groups.

Clearly, the exchange of cultural goods and practices that are embedded in language, 'language-bound', is much more determined by linguistic barriers than that of non-verbal products and practices, such as music, dance and painting, that cross these bounds more freely.

Language-bound cultural goods percolate through the system as texts, transcending language barriers directly for multilingual users, or indirectly through the mediation of translators. Producers of texts may opt for the domestic market – the 'local' strategy – or try their chances in a more prevalent and central ('high-Q') language for a larger market – the 'cosmopolitan' strategy. Authors in the indigenous language may seek production subsidies. They may also demand protective measures against foreign imports, just as 'infant industries' and the providers of 'merit goods' are wont to do.

At the core of the present analysis is the notion of the effects of individual language choices upon other language users: the concept of hypercollectivity. Initially, the expansion of a language community seems to benefit everyone, but there may come a point where multilingualism spreads so widely through the smaller, more peripheral language community that the domestic language is in danger of mass abandonment. It is at this point that state protection may help to safeguard the national language, robust as it is. But languages that must function without such shelter may indeed be threatened by a stampede of deserters.

Communication in any language leaves a sediment of 'texts' – all utterances that are recorded or remembered in that language. These texts accumulate as a collective cultural capital, available to the members of the particular language group. If, however, the language is abandoned by its speakers, the texts become inaccessible (although they may be salvaged by translation). That is why the users of a language have a collective interest in its survival. The collective character of this capital again creates the familiar dilemmas of collective action in the preservation or the neglect of the language concerned.

This concept of collective cultural capital opens up an entirely new avenue to the analysis of 'ethnic identity' or of 'cultural heritage'. These themes, which are usually discussed in discursive historical, psychological and normative terms, have now become amenable to treatment in terms of a more general theory, immediately connected to the core concepts of social science. This analysis cannot replace the prevalent approach, but allows us to situate it in the wider theoretical context that frames the present study: the perspective of the 'social life sciences'.[38] In this science of human societies, a very long-term, large-scale view of the human species in evolution provides the conceptual background for an analysis of competing (and therefore also collaborating) groups, composed of individuals who in the short run are alert and scheming in protecting their resources and realizing some of their opportunities, with and against one another.[39]

India: the rivalry between Hindi and English

The great human variety which makes up both India's wealth and its burden is also reflected in its multitude of languages. And just as other social differences at times have turned into political cleavages, so have differing languages become a persistent issue of public controversy in contemporary India.

And yet it is a thoroughly modern idea that the choice of a language should be more than a matter of private preference, practical convenience and, maybe, social standing. Under the *ancien régime*, in many lands of Europe, monarchs and their nobles happily spoke French, Italian or German, regardless of the speech among the common people, and this was one issue that was never raised in petitions or protests. Scholars and clerics continued to speak Latin with their peers across the entire subcontinent. Equally, at the Indian courts of the conqueror dynasties the language was Persian, while learned and pious men used Sanskrit, and the commoners spoke their local version of the vernacular languages, the 'prakrits', without the matter ever causing much controversy.

In the contemporary world, issues of language seem to be a cause of persistent and often vehement political conflict. In India, also, the language question has shown itself to be especially intractable. It is not the variety of languages per se that causes friction, and even the spread of one among them at the cost of others need not always provoke animosity. Strife erupts when the authorities select one language among many as the medium of administration, of instruction in the schools, or even of entertainment in the media, and exclude all others from such institutional use. But rulers, even if they wanted to, cannot escape such choices. For more than two centuries India's rulers have had to confront the choice between adopting either Hindi or English as the language of governance, and coping with a multiplicity of regional languages. Even today, this dilemma continues to haunt the Indians. The question to be answered is why a nation of one billion souls, home to not one but several of the great traditions of world culture, has not divested itself of the language of its former conquerors, even though the vast majority would prefer there to be only one language for the entire nation, an indigenous one at that.[1]

4.1   Characterization of the Indian constellation

The Indian language constellation comprises more than India alone; it also covers Pakistan, Bangladesh, Nepal, Bhutan and Sri Lanka, and other countries. All in all, across the subcontinent, more than a billion people constitute a constellation grouped around two major world languages: English, and Hindi in its many varieties.

Nevertheless, in this chapter the Indian Union will be the unit of analysis for three reasons: language policy is made by governments, usually without much regard for neighbouring countries, and the government of India certainly went its own way in managing the language issue. Moreover, the Indian census provides data that are far superior to those of any of the neighbouring countries. And finally, there is a copious literature on language issues in India.

Some eight hundred languages are spoken in India, and the most recent census lists more than 1600 names for them. However, only eighteen[2] are listed in the Eighth Schedule attached to the Constitution. With some exceptions, each one of these is the official language in one or more of the constituent states of the Union. According to the 1991 census, more than 96 per cent of all Indians speak one of these scheduled languages as their mother tongue.[3] Six languages, Bengali, Hindi, Marathi, Tamil, Telugu and Urdu, together are spoken by three-quarters of the population as their mother tongue. Hindi is by far the largest, spoken by 337 million people, or 40 per cent of the population, in one variety or another.[4] Bengali, with more than 8 per cent, comes second. Telugu, a Dravidian language, takes third place with almost 8 per cent. In a linguistic perspective, the main division is between the Indo-European, 'Indo-Aryan' language family of the north and the Dravidian languages[5] of the southern part of the subcontinent. And it is this distinction that also marks a sharp divide of mutual unintelligibility.

Hindi is the first language in six states. It represents the third-largest linguistic group in the world, after Mandarin Chinese and English. Six other Indian languages are among the twenty largest on earth: Bengali (the eighth-largest, if the Bengali speakers of Bangladesh, the vast majority, are added), Telugu, Tamil, Punjabi, Marathi, Urdu etc.[6] By sheer force of numbers they should all count as viable means of communication in every field of contemporary society. Each of these languages, moreover, has a significant literary tradition of its own and functions at present as a means of instruction in a vast and expanding system of elementary and extended education, while deliberately being developed into a standardized canon.[7] As each is supported by its respective state apparatus, it acquires a corresponding 'robustness',[8] and this to a much higher degree than the regional languages which in Europe were slowly being superseded by the languages of the respective central states from the seventeenth century on.

On the other hand, on the Indian subcontinent, the prevalence in some domains of both Hindi and English pre-empts many functions of these regional languages in modern communication: they hardly play a role in higher education and science, whereas for Hindi at least an attempt is being made in these fields.[9] Popular songs, TV drama and films are dominated by Hindi; all-India politics, administration, law, commerce, industry, transport and communications are again carried on in Hindi or in English.[10]

Another fact, rarely mentioned when assessing the strength of the various languages current on the subcontinent, is the illiteracy rate, which has been steadily declining but still hovers around 50 per cent, depending on the particular state: higher in the north than in the south.[11] This implies that language use for a majority of Indians is still very much 'tied to the soil'. Nevertheless, the penetration of electronic (that is, one-way) oral communication through radio and television in some respects compensates for the inaccessibility of printed media. But illiteracy does limit the rural population very much to a 'restricted code', one that is context-bound, as opposed to the 'elaborated codes' of the literate elite, which are more independent of the immediate setting.[12] Hence, for them English and Hindi lack one important characteristic of hypercollectivity: these languages are not freely accessible to all those who are effectively excluded from elementary education as the necessary avenue to literacy and the acquisition of Hindi or English in the 'high' or written version. But even ordinary villagers are commonly competent not only in their village dialect, but also in the dialect of the regional market town, and quite often in the official language of the state. Nevertheless, for many purposes, the 'players in the language game' do not include these vast masses of illiterates, who are not considered as potential language learners to be converted to one or another strategic choice.

For all these reasons, the 'scheduled languages' of India, although 'state languages' in a real sense, are more robust than the regional languages used to be in Europe, but not nearly as robust as the national state languages in contemporary Europe. They are more fluid, more varying over time, more differentiated according to social status (there are marked caste differences, but also occupational and class variations), more penetrable by other, 'higher' languages (such as Hindi and English). They tend to shade imperceptibly from one region to the next, from one version into another, so that, say, a Hindi dialect in the northwestern zone of the Hindi area may be completely unintelligible to a speaker in the southeastern part, and yet the two are connected by a chain of adjoining, mutually intelligible dialects.[13]

The resulting state of affairs is a high prevalence of multilingualism, but mostly among the educated classes. This means in the first place that the overwhelming majority of Indians speaks one language only (although quite probably in several dialects and registers) and a very large majority does not read any. Although India is an extremely multilingual society, Indians are an extremely unilingual people, for the simple reason that the educated classes constitute only a small minority.[14]

4.2   State formation, nation-building and language unification

The nationalism that sprang up in resistance to European colonialism adopted and adapted many Western ideas of nation, state and language. In many respects, the French unitary nation-state that had so successfully conveyed the notion of a monolingual society has served as the paradigm for a succession of liberation movements, in Latin America in the nineteenth century, in Europe after World War I, and in Asia and Africa after World War II.

Time and again, activists aspiring to an autonomous status for their particular group have presented its common language as the unifying element and defining characteristic of their nation-to-be. Such 'linguistic nationalism' required them to single out one particular version among many as their very own standard language and relegate all other spoken idioms to the status of dialect.[15] The symbolic (and often mythological) potential of language as the paramount source of integration has gained saliency only in modern politics, often reinforcing or replacing religion, dynasty, common descent or geographic proximity as constitutive elements of the movement.

The new states that emerged in the twentieth century all attempted to legislate on language practices and strove to adopt a single medium for official use.[16] The postcolonial states that were established on independence during the quarter of a century after World War II equally cherished the ideal of a sole language, an indigenous one at that. But each one of them had to cope with the stubborn legacy of the ex-colonial language.

Symbolic reasons, such as the celebration of common historical origin and present political unity, to the exclusion of some (who in the same act were constituted as minorities), apparently prevailed in the desire for a national language. Thus, it is as a means of expression (of a common soul, a shared identity) that language serves to define a nationality, but it is as a means of communication that it is adopted for a polity and an economy.[17] In the first mode, the discourse is mostly evocative and symbolic, the domain of poets, philologists and historians; in the second, the argument is largely functional and pragmatic, and refers to the requirements of tax-collectors, recruiters, inspectors, merchants and employers, all of them oriented towards the centre and seeking direct access to the population at large. Thus, the entire matter may also be presented as one of practicality, as a necessary choice for a unitary standard of national communication and against the archaic chaos of ancient tongues under the fragmented and divided old regime. Past, present and progress, then, all seem to dictate the adoption of a single, exclusive, domestic, national language. More often than not, both the colonial rulers and their nationalist successors agreed on this issue. The one overriding question was which language was to be selected.

But postcolonial regimes rarely succeeded in imposing a single unitary language across the entire territory. It seemed that the nation-states of Western Europe had indeed accomplished this feat, and the appearance may never have been more convincing than at mid-twentieth century, when regional languages had been effectively discarded from official and public use in these countries. In Asia and Africa many new states achieved independence precisely at the moment that monolingualism in Europe and the US reached its zenith. Since then, Spain has accepted Catalan as the official language of

Catalonia, France has rediscovered itself as a 'pays multilingue',[18] the United Kingdom has granted language rights to its 'Celtic fringe' within the context of administrative and political 'devolution', and the United States must confront large minorities of Spanish-speaking immigrants and their descendants.

Most nationalists took the idea of a unitary national language for granted. Moreover, the underlying notion of language, any language, as a more or less permanent, clearly distinct entity covering a contiguous, well-demarcated territory was also accepted unthinkingly. The emergence of vernacular languages was the result of a 'cultural act', not a 'natural fact', as Sheldon Pollock has argued: 'literary vernacularization is a choice, made at particular moments in history'.[19] This slow transition from the translocal, liturgical and scholarly vehicular language – Latin, Sanskrit, Mandarin – to a series of distinct, territorialized, vernacular (and literary) languages occurred roughly during the same epoch on the Eurasian continent, at its western, European, fringe, on its southern, Indian, tip and in the southeastern, Chinese swath:

> Whereas in 'real life' there may be not languages but only language-continua, a language spectrum and not segments – where 'Kannada' imperceptibly merged into 'Telugu', like 'French' into 'Italian', so that in fact Kannada and Telugu (and French and Italian) should not even be regarded as pre-given points on a spectrum – an important effect of literary vernacularization is to divide that continuum. The language boundedness that results has a logic akin to the logic of spatial boundedness, though each has specific instrumentalities. The former...deploys grammars, dictionaries, and literary texts, to discipline and purify, but above all, to de-fine.[20]

In India, this transition produced the 'prakrit' languages, based on Sanskrit, and the literary languages that emerged in the Dravidian language family. It took the nation-states of Western Europe all of the nineteenth century to drive out the regional languages and introduce the language of the court and the capital as the sole means of national communication. In the process, what initially emerged was a 'planetary' constellation with a series of regional languages hardly connected among one another but all strongly connected to the central language, like satellites circling around a planet.[21] In a later stage, these regional languages gradually lost their functions until they barely survived on the local level, among relatives and neighbours, while one domain after another was usurped by the central language that finally seemed to be the only language left in the realm.

The initial 'planetary' constellations of Western Europe are not unlike the configuration that prevailed under the Mughal rulers in northern India, where the Khari Boli version of Hindi that was current in Delhi functioned as a central language for an array of peripheral Indo-European, Indo-Aryan languages. At the same time, Persian and Sanskrit both survived as courtly and scholarly languages, rather like French and Latin in Europe.

But in the southern part of India, the languages of the Dravidian family prevail to this day and Hindi is still far less current, as either a first or a second language. At independence, the postcolonial Indian state inherited from the British a territory that encompassed much more than the 'great Hindi belt' and where the speakers of Bengali or Telugu, of Tamil or Kashmiri, would not easily accept the dominance of Hindi, no matter how numerous its speakers or how central its position (or even precisely because of its large numbers and core location).

In terms of our galactic model, the language situation that took shape on the Indian subcontinent resembles a *double stellar constellation*: a supercentral language, or rather two of them, connected to an arc of central languages each in turn linked to a ring of peripheral languages. As in European history, in the Indian past also, military conquest and political domination from a central power base explain this core–periphery pattern: what Paris was and is for France, London for Britain, Madrid for Spain, Berlin for the German lands, Moscow for the Russian empire, the Delhi area was and still is for the Indian subcontinent. In India, the Hindi–Urdu–Punjabi group of languages in many variations of widely differing mutual intelligibility acquired the largest number of speakers and Khari Boli, the speech of Delhi, the political centre, prevailed as a standard for inter-regional communication.[22]

However, by the seventeenth century, the typical nation-states of Europe had all achieved some kind of territorial equilibrium and were never after exposed to foreign occupation for long periods of time. The long and grinding process of nation-building proceeded with much less external disturbance. In the course of three centuries an ever expanding administration and an extending school system inexorably imposed the central language of the realm with all the resources the state apparatus could muster.

In India, on the contrary, this was the period of colonization by a foreign power which employed all its advanced resources to impose its rule, first on the existing courts and next increasingly upon the population at large. In the process, the British succeeded in achieving a greater degree of coherence and interdependence on the subcontinent than had ever existed before. Conquest and political hegemony went together with linguistic domination. Among the native elites that were recruited into these pursuits, English spread as the language of colonial administration, commerce and industry, of science and the printed media. Where Hindi and the related languages encompassed a plurality of the population on the subcontinent but left out a large majority, especially in the south, English became the language for all-India communication. By the same dialectics of unification and liberation, the colonial language was also adopted as the link language among the anti-colonial opposition.

This situation is by no means unique; on the contrary, it is quite common in relatively heterogeneous areas which reached a higher level of political integration under the ruling machinery of a colonial power, such as Malaysia, Indonesia, Nigeria, Zaire, South Africa and so on. Since the single common denominator in each of these heterogeneous entities was colonial rule, the anti-colonial opposition had to adopt this definition of the political boundaries for the sake of unity in liberation.

During the colonial epoch, the colonizers were in the position of a central, 'metropolitan' elite, most of them speaking only their mother tongue, which gradually became a supercentral language of the territory. Domestic, regional elites functioned as bilingual mediators between the colonial language and the language of their region. The monolingual colonizers in their central position should be expected to support the spread of their language so as to gain immediate access to the population in the regions. The bilingual regional elites, according to the model, should equally welcome the spread of the central language in regions other than their own, since it would increase the Q-value of their bilingual repertoire, but they should not encourage it in their own region, as that would yield no gain in Q-value and might well erode their collective mediation monopoly.[23]

In many cases, nationalist rejection of the colonial language meant abandoning a nationwide means of communication and, also, undermining the position of bilingual elites, fluent in English, and with an ethnic or regional power base.[24]

However, once the colonies became independent, the monolingual metropolitans, that is, the colonists, disappeared and a coalition of bilingual regional elites usually took power. Group jealousy often kept each regional language group from supporting the language of another as the official medium. At the same time, at least according to the galactic model, bilingual elites did not stand to gain from the spread of the former colonial language in their own region, and feared for their monopoly in mediating between this central language and the language of the region. They preferred to maintain the former colonial language as the central and official language, but not promulgate it as a language of mass instruction in their own region. The peripheral languages remained in place, each as the vernacular in its own region.[25] Nor did they encourage the adoption of an alternative, domestic, lingua franca, since that would also have threatened their monopolistic mediation functions, which mastery of the (formerly colonial) central language conveys upon the bilingual elites.[26]

Mutual jealousy between language groups and reluctance among the bilingual elites to abandon their mediation monopoly may explain at once the persistence of the colonial language in many newly independent countries and the slow spread of this central language among the population at large. As a consequence, French and English hardly lost ground after decolonization, and both became the official language of many newly independent states in Africa and Asia. At the same time, competence in these languages has remained restricted to an educated minority. Within each country, individual speakers of one of the peripheral languages have every interest in learning the central language and sharing in the advantages of bilingualism, all the more so when this language is also central, or even supercentral, in other parts of the continent, and above all when it is the hypercentral language, current across the entire globe: English. In sheer power of numbers, English is second only to Chinese, and when it comes to its connections with other language groups, the unique position of English makes it the most attractive option for second-language learners with an international orientation. This is a self-reinforcing process: people choosing to learn English in one part of the world make the language more attractive in doing so to others in another corner of the globe.[27] This, of course, testifies to the hypercollective character of languages.

As a consequence, India, but also the Philippines, Nigeria, Zaire or Senegal and many more countries, at liberation found themselves confronted with a linguistic dilemma: adopt the former colonial language, for example English or French, as the lingua franca of national politics, administration, big business, higher education and the media, or choose a vernacular language of the territory.

Two political considerations greatly complicated the issue, in India and elsewhere: the nationalist struggle had not been fought to restore the colonial language to a position of hegemony, with all the attendant cultural and political implications. And, on the other hand, the adoption of one from the Hindi group of languages (and which one: Khari Boli, Hindustani?) would greatly favour one category within the Indian nation, exempted from the task of learning an additional language as the remaining vast majority of the population would have to.

4.3   The vicissitudes of language policy in India

Until the advent of the British, language was hardly a political issue in India. It was the introduction of English that posed a problem, both for the colonial rulers and for the native scholars and scribes. The early British administrators and their advisors were very well aware that in India they confronted a culture of great tradition.[28] They knew something about the language of learning, Sanskrit, and the courtly language, Persian. Not wanting to alienate the Indian elites further, they were reluctant to impose English and preferred to adopt the classical Indian languages, which they held in high esteem.

The initiative in introducing English as the vehicular language for India came from the next levy of British progressives: the evangelical Christians, who abhorred the squalor and resignation they found everywhere in Indian society. The Hindu religion was to be replaced by a new Christianity and English was to be the vehicle of this mass conversion. More or less at the same time, the English utilitarians took issue with what they thought was the inefficient, impassive Indian way of life. Their new utilitarian philosophy was to improve the native mentality, and again this campaign was to be carried out in English.

The Indians themselves were rather divided and ambivalent about the issue. Many saw English as a way to personal promotion into the ranks of the civil administration, others realized how far British technology and science had advanced and longed to reap the gains of this progress for their country also. It all required, at the very least, mastery of English.

The anglicists carried the day within the Indian administration and English became the language of British rule on the subcontinent. But as opposition to colonial domination grew, and resistance became organized, the language issue arose once again, this time within the ranks of the Indian National Congress (established in 1885). The colonial administration admitted the use of regional languages in the lower echelons and favoured Urdu for the middle ranks of the civil service. With English and Urdu thus privileged, educated Hindi speakers felt doubly discriminated against. In 1893 students founded a society for the promotion of Hindi, and in 1910 the Hindi Sahitya Sammelan was established.[29] But these were movements for the defence of Hindi; they did not as yet confront the question of which language to adopt for all-India communication.

In the early decades of the twentieth century, Hindi increasingly became the symbol of Indian nationalism. But Hindi leaders promoted a purified version, purged of its Perso-Arabic vocabulary, enriched with new expressions taken from Sanskrit, and written not in the Persian (Arabic) but in the Devanagari script.[30]

Very much in this line, Mahatma Gandhi's rejection of English is first to be understood in symbolic terms, as constituting the Indian nation in the act of liberation from the British.[31] But in the matter of Hindi, Gandhi proceeded with caution. He preferred the adoption of Hindustani as the new national language. His choice was pregnant with symbolism. Hindustani was a vehicular, popular language, a 'bazaar' language for traders and travellers, a dialect shared by Hindi and Urdu speakers, and therefore by both Hindus and Muslims. It was, moreover, considered to be a 'low', non-literary variety, with all the corresponding populist connotations. Purist derivations from either Sanskrit or Persian were to be eschewed. On the contrary, Gandhi welcomed borrowings from a wide variety of languages. What mattered was not the historical origin of expressions but their actual currency.[32]

With hindsight, it can be acknowledged that Gandhi hit on the right recipe for gaining broad acceptance of an indigenous language. Events in Indonesia and Tanzania have demonstrated that it could have worked. But all too often, purist, ethnic cooks spoiled the broth and made anyone else's indigenous language unpalatable for their own group. Gandhi had no remedy against that.

But of course, Gandhi and Congress insisted on the introduction of a single language for eminently practical reasons also. After all, India was to become a federal union and a single market in which administrators and citizens, voters and politicians, recruits and officers, producers and consumers, employers and workers should be able to make themselves understood by one another.

Accordingly, in 1925, the Indian National Congress adopted Hindustani as its primary language. Initially the defenders of Hindi supported the move to Hindustani; Gandhi was even made president of the Hindi Sahitya Sammelan. But when, in 1942, the purist, Sanskritist faction gained the upper hand, he resigned.[33]

During the drafting of the Constitution, in 1948, the partisans of Hindi successfully blocked the adoption of Hindustani. After the secession of Pakistan as a separate Muslim state, Hindustani steadily lost support in India because of being closely associated with Urdu (the Muslim and Persianized version of Khari Boli, written in the Persian script). As a result, Hindi gained adherents and finally carried the vote.[34] But the proponents of Hindi demanded in vain the immediate abolition of English in favour of Hindi: there was to be a fifteen-year grace period. Nevertheless a purified Hindi, with Sanskrit derivations only, was henceforward to be the official language of India.

This partisan insistence on a re-Sanskritized version of Hindi did much to identify the language with native Hindi speakers, with Hinduism and with the north. As a result it alienated the other groups in the Assembly and in the country at large. Where Hindustani could have worked as an integrating force, Hindi now had a divisive effect.

In a separate attachment to the Constitution, the Eighth Schedule, the major languages of India (including Sanskrit) were listed as the so-called 'constitutional' or 'scheduled' languages, which at the time were spoken by well over 90 per cent of the Indian population. Most of the languages on the list were official languages of one or more of the constituent states of the Union.

Initially, the drafters of the Constitution took a strong stance on the political and linguistic unity and integrity of the Union. The Commission that reported on the language question in December 1948 'came out against the principle of linguistic provinces as it was found by the criterion of promoting nationalism "not in the larger interest of the Indian nation and (hence) should not be taken in hand"'. Only after intense agitation erupted in Andhra did the Congress shift its position.[35]

Since then, time and again, language has functioned as a powerful rallying point for regional groups attempting to create a common identity and to distinguish themselves from their neighbours.[36] Bengali served this function in the secessionist struggle that resulted in the creation of Bangladesh; Punjabi functioned in this manner for the Sikh movement towards greater autonomy; and in the mobilization of the Tamil people its language was revered as the divine essence of 'Tamilhood'.[37]

These movements have all been quite violent at times, but it is debatable whether the language issue itself contributed to the violence. David Laitin has argued that in general it does not, since language issues are not monolithic in nature and lend themselves to compromise and accommodation. Moreover, it is not easy to prevent individual speakers from defection, and that alone forces leaders to take a moderate stand. However, the separation of the language issue from 'ethnic', 'cultural' or 'religious' matters seems contrived.

Language matters may not be explosive on their own, but as they are so often part of a separatist, nationalist programme, they have often figured in violent conflict.

The accounts of these struggles are often strongly coloured by partisan opinion, but even the more detached authors tend to relate their story entirely in terms of national, ethnic and religious sentiment. The choice of languages is considered a most momentous matter indeed, but mostly for its tremendous symbolic value. More mundane interests are usually glossed over, and yet certain language groups stand to reap or forgo great practical advantages from such changes. This applies to the process of language unification in the European nation-states of the modern era as well as to language regulation in the postcolonial states of the second half of the twentieth century.

Indian politicians pursued the language issue with much caution. Fifteen years after the adoption of the Constitution, on 26 January 1965, Hindi was to replace English throughout India. However, a commission was appointed to advise on the matter, and after much and heated deliberation within its ranks and throughout the Indian body politic, the all-Indian Parliament accepted an Official Language Act, providing that 'the English language may continue to be used...in addition to Hindi, for all the official purposes of the Union' (wherever it was already in use at the time).[38] In practice, this meant that Hindi, English and the other domestic languages continued to coexist in their precarious balance.[39]

At the same time, the potential for linguistic (and ethnic) strife was much reduced by very different means. The borders of the constitutent states and territories of the Union were redrawn so as to create more homogeneous entities as far as language was concerned. The central government, worried about separatist tendencies, had initially resisted the formation of such cohesive political units. But it consented after acute political agitation erupted.[40] In 1956 and again in 1966 a number of states were indeed repartitioned. As a result, the number of Indians living as minorities in their state of residence was drastically diminished to 16.5 per cent for all of India in 1971, down from an estimated 32 per cent in 1921 and 30 per cent in 1950.[41] Joseph Schwartzberg, who carried out a careful quantitative analysis of the changing language distribution in the reorganized states, concludes: 'In creating a system of essentially linguistic states, India has provided a local political milieu that is conducive to the flowering of many linguistically-rooted cultures.'[42] Accordingly, at the regional level, within each separate state, the sting was taken out of language conflict by the creation of political units that were more homogeneous with respect to language. But the central government was much more reluctant to reorganize states along religious and ethnic lines, and never conceded separatist or secessionist claims.

In the meantime, at the Union level, English and Hindi continued their competition as official and co-official languages of India. The 1991 census in India[43] contained a number of questions on language skills, including second- and third-language skills under the heading: 'Two other languages known' (see table 4.1).[44] As might be expected, Hindi, with the largest number of native speakers by far (339 million), also obtains the highest Q-value (0.37). The second-highest communication value belongs to English (0.07), with only some 180,000 mother-tongue speakers (too few to be mentioned in table 4.1). It is, however, the second language of 92 million Indian citizens, in this respect even outdoing Hindi, which 68 million Indians have acquired as a second language. No other Indian language by itself obtains a significant Q-value, except Telugu (0.01). The only repertoires of some importance are those which contain Hindi or English, or, of course, both, with or without some third language. All other language groups add most to the Q-value of their repertoire by adopting Hindi; English is the next-best option.

The persistence of English, therefore, can only be explained by the facts that it has of old been the language of the Indian administrative and cultural elite, that it is a quickly expanding world language, and that it is still a requirement for the more attractive positions in the labour market. The use of English also excludes the vast majority of Indians, who, being illiterate, have no access to the written version.[45] Moreover, in the southern states English also serves to 'neutralize' Hindi in its otherwise inexorable rise, and that is one reason why it is widely taught there.

4.4 Discussion

The Indian language constellation is considerably more complex than the standard 'planetary' model of the typical European nation-state. This planetary model has two levels: first, the central language of the court and the capital, spoken by the metropolitan elites, often as their only language; second, the regional or peripheral languages. The peripheral languages surround the central language like moons circling a planet: they are connected to the central language through the mediation of bilingual regional elites, each competent in the central

Table 4.1 India c.1991 (speakers in millions)

Native language	Sole or second language															Third language	Total
	HI	EN	AS	BG	GU	KA	ML	MR	OR	PU	TA	TE	UR	AR	SA	LANG +HI&EN	
HI	301	30	0	0	0	0	2	0	0	0	1	0	1	0	2	–	337
AS	1	0	9	1	0	0	0	0	0	0	0	0	0	0	0	3	14
BG	2	4	1	60	0	0	0	0	0	0	0	0	0	0	0	4	71
GU	6	0	0	0	31	0	0	0	0	0	0	0	0	0	0	2	39
KA	1	2	0	0	0	25	0	0	0	0	1	2	0	0	0	6	37
ML	0	2	0	0	0	0	22	0	0	0	0	0	0	0	0	7	31
MR	9	0	0	0	0	0	0	46	0	0	0	0	0	0	0	3	57
OR	1	1	0	0	0	0	0	0	24	0	0	0	0	0	0	5	31
PU	3	0	0	0	0	0	0	0	0	14	0	0	0	0	0	1	18
TA	0	7	0	0	0	1	0	0	0	0	43	1	0	0	0	4	57
TE	1	3	0	0	0	3	0	0	0	0	3	52	0	0	0	2	64
UR	7	2	0	0	0	2	0	1	0	0	1	2	25	2	0	2	43
																	798
Q_i:																	
HI	0.367	0.463	0.384	0.451	0.395	0.437	0.396	0.414	0.394	0.380	0.474	0.478	0.437	0.376	0.367	–	
AS	0.384	0.081	0.001	0.010	0.007	0.008	0.006	0.014	0.004	0.004	0.013	0.016	0.013	0.001	0.001	0.482	
BG	0.451	0.123	0.010	0.007	0.020	0.022	0.018	0.032	0.014	0.015	0.030	0.035	0.031	0.008	0.008	0.538	
GU	0.395	0.104	0.007	0.020	0.003	0.015	0.012	0.024	0.009	0.010	0.022	0.026	0.022	0.004	0.004	0.496	

KA	0.437	0.105	0.008	0.022	0.015	0.004	0.014	0.026	0.010	0.011	0.022	0.024	0.021	0.005	0.005	0.530
ML	0.396	0.089	0.006	0.018	0.012	0.014	0.003	0.022	0.008	0.008	0.020	0.024	0.020	0.003	0.003	0.487
MR	0.414	0.124	0.014	0.032	0.024	0.026	0.022	0.009	0.017	0.018	0.034	0.040	0.033	0.011	0.011	0.518
OR	0.394	0.089	0.004	0.014	0.009	0.010	0.008	0.017	0.001	0.006	0.016	0.019	0.016	0.002	0.002	0.489
PU	0.380	0.085	0.004	0.015	0.010	0.011	0.008	0.018	0.006	0.001	0.017	0.020	0.016	0.002	0.002	0.478
TA	0.474	0.118	0.013	0.030	0.022	0.022	0.020	0.034	0.016	0.017	0.008	0.032	0.031	0.009	0.009	0.545
TE	0.478	0.132	0.016	0.035	0.026	0.024	0.024	0.040	0.019	0.020	0.032	0.011	0.035	0.012	0.012	0.572
UR	0.437	0.118	0.013	0.031	0.022	0.021	0.020	0.033	0.016	0.016	0.031	0.035	0.008	0.009	0.009	0.530

Greenberg's A   0.697

HI = Hindi; EN = English; AS = Assamese; BG = Bengali; GU = Gujarati; KA = Kannada; ML = Malayalam; MR = Marathi; OR = Oriya; PU = Punjabi; TA = Tamil; TE = Telugu; UR = Urdu; AR = Arabic; SA = Sanskrit (the last two have few or no mother-tongue speakers).

A dash − = not applicable.

The rows show the native speakers of a language: speakers of that language only, and those who also speak a second (and third) language, as indicated by the column heading. The total number of speakers of a language may be found by adding to the row total of native speakers the entries in the corresponding column for foreign speakers of that language (avoiding counting monolingual speakers twice).

The prevalence p_i of a repertoire p_i is found by adding the entries in the columns and rows for the language(s) in p_i (while avoiding double counts) and dividing by N^s, the number of all speakers. The centrality c_i of a repertoire p_i is calculated by adding the entries for all *multilingual* repertoires that have a language in common with p_i and dividing by the total of multilingual speakers M^s.

In this procedure, the matrix for Q has been folded along the diagonal: in calculating p_i, c_i and Q_i, the numbers for, say, Hindi speakers who have learned Telugu have been added to the number of Telugu speakers who acquired Hindi, and vice versa. As a result, the entries in the lower left half of the matrix for Q are identical to the corresponding entries in the upper right half.

Figures have been rounded to the nearest million. Entries may therefore not always add up to the corresponding total.

language and one of the regional languages. Each of the regional clienteles is monolingual in its own peripheral language. In the past, they were predominantly illiterate, and for the greater part they still are.

The Indian constellation has three rather than two levels, and at the core there are two 'supercentral' languages, instead of one. This 'bistellar model' has three tiers. First, there are the two supercentral languages, Hindi and English. They constitute the pivot of the system, a double star surrounded by a number of 'planets': the regional language of the system.

Most of the 'scheduled' languages are the official language of one or more constitutent states of the union and are predominant in the corresponding region. Bi- or trilingual elites connect each regional language to one supercentral language or to both. Although in a peripheral position with respect to Hindi and English, the supercentral or stellar languages, each regional language is in its turn central with respect to a number of local languages.

The local languages may be 'tribal' languages, local dialects, immigrants' or minority languages. Multilingual elites connect these languages to the central language of the state or the region.

The mediating elites at both the local and the regional level often speak two, three or even four languages: their local language, the language of their state (which may well be Hindi), the language of the Union (Hindi) and frequently also English. Such a 3±1 formula has been advocated not only as the multilingual solution to India's language problems, but as a general panacea for navigating local, regional, national and global levels of communication.[46]

The dynamics of the model favour the central language, not only because the monolingual metropolitan elites profit from others learning their language, but also because the bilingual regional elites stand to gain if the population of *other* regions learns the central language (they do not profit if their own clientele learns the central language). The peripheral monolingual clientele stand to gain greatly from learning the central language, if they can afford the tuition – this calculation very much depends on the social position they have already achieved.[47] Illiterates lack the opportunity to learn the 'correct' version of the central language.

The dynamics of the bi-stellar model for the Indian constellation are more complicated, especially at the all-India level, since there are two supercentral languages to choose between. At the level of the constituent states, the dynamics of the constellation favour the spread of the central (that is, the state) language. The political and entrepreneurial elites at the state level again stand to gain if peripheral populations learn the central state language. The bilingual mediating elites at the local level equally profit from central language acquisition by other clienteles and do not gain or lose in Q-value if their own clientele learns the state language. In the school system, children may initially be taught in their local mother tongue, but in each case, immediately or later on, they will learn the state language, which is the central language at the core of the subsystem.

The reorganization of Indian states to coincide more closely with linguistic areas did much to strengthen the position of the central languages at the state level and has contributed to the spread of each one across the territory of the corresponding state.

In an essay on language contact in India, Grant McConnell has proposed a scheme that nicely fits the present argument. It shows a 'unipolar' language constellation, in the state of Uttar Pradesh: Hindi apears in the middle of the diagram as the central language of the state, connected by bilinguals to an arc of minority languages. Many of these minorities speak a language that is in the majority in some other state, as its official language.[48]

At the all-India level, we can identify several elites with their quite divergent interests. First of all, there are the political, entrepreneurial and civil service elites, who use only English for communication at the Union level. Next, there are the elites who speak Hindi, both in their home states and for communication at the Union level. Finally, there are the elites who use both Hindi and English at the level of the Union. Again, they may be active in business, civil service, mass media or politics. Often Hindi is their mother tongue, but increasingly they come from non-Hindi states, and have acquired Hindi as well as English.

The various interests of these elites can be identified on the basis of their position in the language constellation. The elites that use only English have a vested interest in its dissemination throughout the Union, since it enhances the Q-value of their repertoire. The most vociferous among them come from the southern states where Dravidian languages are current – they have used the 'English card' to thwart the spread of Hindi at the expense of the other language groups. After independence, the Indian civil service strongly defended the exclusive use of English in the administration to protect its privileged claim to government jobs. David Laitin has developed the argument that the IAS, the all-India civil service, strongly preferred English on the grounds of education and *esprit de corps*, but that it would have complied with explicit and enforced orders from the political sphere *if* Hindi had been imposed.[49]

The elites that make use of only Hindi stand to gain from the spread of Hindi across India for analogous reasons. The supporters of the swift abolition of English were to be found in their ranks, and they are most staunchly in favour of civil service examinations in Hindi (alongside English) and of Hindi as the compulsory second language language in secondary schools in all regions where it is not the mother tongue. Elites in Hindi-speaking states of course use Hindi in communicating at the all-India level and consequently support Hindi against English.

The elites that speak both English and Hindi are basically indifferent between the two: whether students learn the one or the other, their chances for direct communication increase anyway, and the centrality of their repertoire already approaches $1.$[50] Since secondary school students in non-Hindi-speaking states routinely learn English and quite frequently also Hindi, while students in Hindi-speaking areas usually learn English (plus another Indian language, which tends to be one closely related to Hindi, such as Sanskrit), a fast-growing number of educated Indians speak both supercentral languages.

Under these conditions, it follows that the coexistence of English and Hindi at the Union level may well be inefficient (a single national language would save expenditure and learning effort), but it is nevertheless an equilibrium solution in the sense that no effective majority can be found for the alternatives of either English only or Hindi only. Apparently, for individual students it 'pays' to learn English or Hindi, or both, because the two languages so much increase communication opportunities.

When independence came, English was spoken by a very small, albeit also very influential minority (the Congress party, the civil service, big business). If the non-Hindi-speaking groups had not been alienated by the attempt to impose a 'pure' version of Hindi, and if instead the more 'neutral' Hindustani had been introduced – as Gandhi had always advocated – the national language of India today might well have been indigenous, even 'hindigenous'. Having overplayed its hand, the Hindi party had to accept that English would remain the co-official language indefinitely. Moreover, it has now become the most widely used language after Hindi: in a recent poll 71 per cent of respondents said they 'understood' Hindi, and 31 per cent answered the same for English.[51] Since approximately 40 per cent of all Indians are Hindi mother-tongue speakers, this means that another 31 per cent of Indians must have learned the language later, exactly the same percentage as that of Indians who acquired English. Clearly, as second languages, Hindi and English are now on a par.

The Q-value of English in the Indian constellation is about half that of Hindi. This is considerably more than it would have been in the first years after independence. Moreover, allowance must be made for the Q-value of English in the global constellation, an added reason for both Hindi- and non-Hindi-speaking students to add that language to their repertoire.

Learning English is certainly the best choice a native Hindi speaker can make. And in fact, that is what most students from Hindi-speaking areas do. (They very rarely learn other Indian languages. The others learn Hindi. Here too, language learning proceeds 'upward'.) The fact that so many Hindi-speaking students learn English greatly contributes to its Q-value, and thus makes the language more attractive also for students from non-Hindi-speaking areas who are faced with the choice between English and Hindi.

For the speakers of other Indian languages, according to our calculations, learning Hindi adds more to the Q-value of their repertoire than learning English (although we must allow for global motivations in picking English). English is usually learned in school, and its place in the curriculum is determined by decisions at the state level (on the recommendation of the Union government). The governments of non-Hindi-speaking states pursue such collective objectives as the containment of the expansion of Hindi. At the same time, for individual students it may be more rewarding in terms of Q-value to learn Hindi rather than English. There are indications that in non-Hindi states students at the intermediary level 'voluntarily' opt for Hindi as a subject of instruction. Many also pick up Hindi in informal situations and from the mass media. If their perspective (their 'definition of the game') is Indian society, in terms of the model they are perfectly rational in choosing Hindi, since it increases their opportunities for direct communication in Indian society more than any other language. Only if they define the whole earth as their world, that is, if they aspire to an international career in business or science, would English be the better choice – but they can always add English to their repertoire if and when they make it to college level, that is, when their global aspirations become more realistic.

After half a century of nationalist agitation and another half-century of independence, the original prospect of one domestic language, Hindi, for all of India has disappeared. Apparently, there is not much support left for Hindi as the sole official language of the Union, while the great national Gandhian Congress tradition withers away in the course of time. 'Perhaps it could be said that Hindi has lost its battle.'[52] Indeed, the policy at the central level is ambiguous at best and makes for great insecurity among those who must decide what second language they, or their children, should learn. The non-Hindi states successfully play off the option of English plus their particular state language against the promulgation of Hindi. But betting on the slow disappearance of Hindi from the all-India scene would ignore the strength that lies in sheer numbers and in the very dominant position of Hindi in modern mass culture.

The triumph of *bahasa Indonesia*

The language constellation of Indonesia is a small miracle. In a world where Western languages have continued to function as the medium of wider communication in almost all formerly colonial countries, the Indonesians successfully adopted one of their domestic languages for the purpose: *bahasa Indonesia*, the language of Indonesia. But the true enigma, at least to an outsider, is that they bypassed yet another language of the land as their national medium, the mother tongue of about half the nation's citizens, the language of its political centre of gravity and its economic core, a language of millennial courtly, religious and literary tradition: Javanese. Indonesians, and most experts on Austronesian languages with them, offer very good reasons why Javanese was spurned and a modernized version of Malay adopted as the national language. There is only one minor problem with these arguments: by implication, they also explain why India adopted Hindustani, Kenya Swahili, and the Philippines Pilipino[1] as their single national language. But, in fact, none of these countries did, although their nationalist movements agitated for it all along.

5.1 Gandhi's dream

In many respects, the position of Javanese in Indonesia is similar to that of Hindi in India. Moreover, the role of Malay during the colonial era might be compared to that of Hindustani, although Malay differs much more from Javanese than Hindustani does from Hindi. As in India, so in Indonesia there are a number of other major languages, but none of them with the numbers and the pedigree of the principal 'scheduled' languages of India. Initially, the itineraries of the two languages were quite similar. The All-India Congress adopted popular Hindustani as the all-India linking language in 1925. In 1928, the Indonesian nationalist youth congress opted for Malaysian (not Javanese) as the language of the movement. But in India, the Hindu nationalist movement pressed for a purist version of Hindi which all other parties found hard to accept. The Dravidian language groups, for their part, played off English against Hindi to block its spread. In Indonesia, on the contrary, the Javanese accepted Malay without a murmur, while the Dutch option was hardly considered. Briefly, what happened in Indonesia with *bahasa Indonesia* was Gandhi's dream for India: it was in fact what all postcolonial nationalist leaders professed as their ideal for the independent country. But only one or two of them came even close to realizing it.

The selection of Indonesian and its successful spread across the archipelago are a unique case in the records of comparative macro-sociolinguistics.[2] But to those who are familiar with the languages of the archipelago, the Indonesians themselves in the first place, it appears just natural. Only outsiders will sometimes marvel at the surrender of Javanese for the sake of Indonesian.

'Ah, but you don't know Javanese', an Indonesian would sigh at this point. And a knowledgeable Indonesian would go on to point out that it is an impossible language, wholly unsuited to the demands of modern life. It has a high and a low version, *krama* and *ngoko*. Unless they are quite intimate, respectable persons among themselves speak *krama* with its elaborate vocabulary, replete with ancient terms of Sanskrit origin. Superiors use *ngoko* to address their inferiors, and these servants are expected to answer in a simplified version of *krama*.[3] What is worse, there are dozens of forms of address, each appropriate to a specific relation of deference and unsuited for any situation that is not carefully defined in the terms of traditional etiquette.

Malay, by contrast, has been the language of commerce and traffic for maybe a thousand years, spoken by traders and voyagers all over the archipelago. It is the language that carried the message of Islam, and the language in which Portuguese priests and later Dutch ministers converted the local people to Christianity. Although Malay is the native language of the eastern part of Sumatra and the coastal areas of Kalimantan, Indonesians do not associate it with any region or ethnic group in particular, whereas Javanese to them is inseparably connected to the hegemony of Java.

5.2   The rise of Malay

The nationalist movement accordingly decided to adopt Malay in the version called *bahasa Indonesia*, and the Javanese representatives concurred: 'different ethnic groups are willing to sacrifice their ethno-linguistic pride for the sake of the urgent needs for national unity'.[4] This applies to the Javanese in the first place. In fact, in the 1920s, the first cohort of Javanese students in the Netherlands initially experimented with notions of a Javanese renaissance, but soon joined their fellow students from 'East India' in an all-Indonesia nationalism.[5] Javanese nationalists seem to have welcomed *bahasa* as enthusiastically as did the nationalist pioneers from the other islands.[6] If there was any afterthought of collective self-interest on the part of the Javanese at all, their generosity may be interpreted as the sacrifice of a queen to win an endgame, the surrender of a language to gain an empire. After all, the Javanese did succeed in maintaining and consolidating their hold over the Indonesian archipelago.

   After the Dutch efforts to foment separatism in the late 1940s, there were very few attempts to secede, until the collapse of the Suharto regime some fifty years later. The case of East Timor stands apart: that island never belonged to the Dutch empire, the political predecessor of the Indonesian state, and was annexed by the Republic when the Portuguese left in 1975. New Guinea, which indeed had been part of the Dutch Colonial empire, briefly and unsuccessfully resisted incorporation by Indonesia after the Dutch abandoned it in 1965. Recently, separatism has surged on several islands and the regime seeks at once to pacify the rebels and hold the Republic together. At the time, the institution of a national language, itself not identified with Javanese hegemony, may well have contributed to the acceptance of an Indonesian nation in which Java predominated. But if the Javanese leaders could operate with so much foresight and willingness to compromise, why did regional elites in a similar position in other newly independent nations not act with the same generosity and providence?

   And then, there was a third language, used all over the archipelago, but abandoned without much ado, once the country became independent: Dutch. Of course, after the fact, it seems obvious that a language of minor importance in the rest of the world, spoken by only a smattering of the domestic elites, abolished by a stroke of the pen under the Japanese occupation, would disappear without a trace. The common-sense explanation appears wholly adequate, but here again comparative and theoretical considerations reveal anomalies: why had the Dutch language hardly spread after more than three centuries of Dutch presence and more than a century of intensive colonization? Spanish, Portuguese, French and English had gained substantive numbers of speakers in their respective African and Asian colonies.[7] When independence came to each of these countries, the anti-colonial elites had long been accustomed to communicate among themselves in the language of the colonizer, and read their socialist and nationalist authors in that language. Moreover, the same held for the Indonesian nationalists: the leaders had almost without exception learned Dutch and with one another they spoke it with zest[8] (long after the Dutch had left, many continued to do so at home and in the corridors of power). But in public and beyond the inner circles, Dutch lost all its functions in Indonesia.

Clearly, as the grand exception in the pattern of postimperialist language constellations, Indonesia is the test case for any attempt at comparative explanation of the spread of competing languages. That alone is sufficient reason to discuss the language constellation of Indonesia at some length. Moreover, the story is fascinating in its own right.

The Indonesian archipelago stretches from the Malaysian peninsula in the west and the islands of the Philippines in the north, in an arc of some 5100 kilometres, up to the Australian subcontinent in the east: 'the belt of emerald' is made up of some 13,000 islands (of which 6000 are inhabited), together covering almost two million square kilometres.[9] The sole common denominator of the peoples that inhabited these isles was their shared history under the Dutch colonial regime, and it was this past that distinguished them from adjacent societies. From early on, Java, with some 60 per cent of the population of the archipelago, formed the political and economic core of the Dutch East Indies. In an arc around this centre live a vast variety of peoples, speaking a multitude of languages, possibly more than five hundred: roughly one-tenth of all the known languages in the world. Some three hundred, including all languages with more than a hundred thousand speakers, belong to the Austronesian family. Another two hundred languages found in the archipelago, half of them numbering less than a thousand speakers, have been classified under seven other language families.[10] At the other extreme, there are fourteen languages with more than a million native speakers.[11]

According to the 1990 census, the population of Indonesia numbered 180 million people. (By the end of the millennium it had increased to some 225 million.) Almost 40 per cent of Indonesians over 4 years of age speak Javanese as their 'first' language and almost all of those live on the eastern two-thirds of Java (and the southern tip of Sumatra).[12] Sundanese, spoken on the western third of Java, comes second, with twenty-five million speakers. About the same number of people mentioned *bahasa Indonesia* as their native tongue. Most of them live in the areas where the language has been indigenous for centuries: the eastern half of Sumatra with the adjacent islands, and the coastal zones of Kalimantan (Borneo), plus one most significant enclave: Jakarta, where a Malay vernacular has been current for centuries and has now made its way into films as a fast and snappy version of Indonesian.[13] Madurese, the language of the nearby island of Madura, has almost seven million speakers. Five other languages, Batak, Minangkabau, Balinese, Buginese and Banjarese, are each spoken by roughly three million speakers.

When respondents were asked whether they knew Indonesian (as either a first or second language), more than 130 million people said they did: 83 per cent of all Indonesians more than 4 years old.[14] Steinhauer provides a healthy caveat: 'there may be a tendency to answer "yes" as a sign of one's good citizenship, where "a bit" or perhaps "no" would have been more in accordance with linguistic facts'.[15]

A closer inspection of census figures reveals some consistent and significant trends. First of all, the percentage of respondents who said they could speak Indonesian has been growing at a spectacular pace in every region of the Republic. On the eve of World War II an estimated 15 per cent of Indonesians spoke some version of Malay, either as their mother tongue or as a second language. It is quite likely that the population movements caused by the Japanese occupation, by the subsequent war of liberation against the Dutch, and by economic migration since then contributed much to the spread of Indonesian as a popular vehicular language. But once the Republic was established and began to build up its institutions throughout the realm, a different dynamics took off: mass elementary education. According to the 1971 census, 62 per cent of boys and 58 per cent of girls between 7 and 12 years of age attended school. By 1990, more than 91 per cent did (and even slightly more girls than boys).[16] During the first three years of elementary school, children are taught in the major language of the region, or in Indonesian, if several minor languages are locally current. From the fourth year on and throughout the educational system, the language of instruction is Indonesian.[17] This explains the spectacular spread of Indonesian as a second language across the archipelago after independence. Knowledge of Indonesian is found more in urban than in rural areas, somewhat more frequently among males than females, and considerably more among adolescents (above twelve years) than among the older generations.

For a quickly increasing number of children, Indonesian is also the first language they pick up, as parents with different native languages adopt the vehicular at home, or when parents hope to provide their offspring with a head start by using Indonesian with their children even though they themselves share another mother tongue.[18] In fact, the number of native speakers of Indonesian went up from less than fifteen million in 1980 to more than twenty-four million in 1990, an increase of over 60 per cent in ten years; discounting the overall growth of the population (about 22 per cent), this still implies a rise of more than a quarter in a single decade.[19] Yet, even today, the number of native speakers of Indonesian does not come near the figures for mother-tongue speakers of Javanese, and just barely matches those of Sundanese.

From the outset, the nationalist movement rejected Dutch and Javanese in favour of Indonesian as the national language that is now spoken by almost all citizens of the archipelago, if not as their mother tongue, then as the language they learned in school. Moreover, Malay is also the national language of Malaysia (and Brunei), co-official with English. Since independence, it has steadily increased in importance there, as it is the language of instruction throughout the educational system, with English as a compulsory subject. At present, Malay holds its own against English in most domains of domestic use.[20] The most important language of the Philippines, Tagalog, and the reconstructed national language, Pilipino, are also closely related to Malay.[21] Hence, as a variety of Malay, *bahasa Indonesia* serves to connect with other constellations in the South East Asian region. This certainly adds to its communication value.

5.3 The demise of Dutch

This rather unusual situation raises a number of questions. Why did Dutch, the language of the colonial regime, disappear so swiftly and completely? Why was Javanese, the language of more than half the population and almost all of its elite, spurned as the national medium in favour of a Malay dialect? How could Malay, always the native language of only a fraction of the population, of old widely dispersed as a lowly bazaar language, in less than half a century be transformed into *bahasa Indonesia*, the official language of the Republic and the second language of the vast majority of its citizens?

Let us begin with the riddle of disappearing Dutch. And a riddle it is. After all, in most 'postimperial' countries the language introduced by the colonizers continues to function as the language of politics, of parliament, of the courts and the administration, of education, especially its higher echelons, of the media, certainly its more 'serious' section, of technology and, above all, of the higher segments of the labour market. Why did not Dutch linger on in Indonesia as French did in so many western and central African countries, or, of course, English in India?

Again, there is a current answer, but this time it does not refer to 'the character of Javanese' but rather to 'the character of the Dutch'. In this view, the Dutch themselves prevented their language from spreading among the population, in stark contrast with other colonizing nations. But why should an occupying power forgo the opportunity to facilitate communication with its subjects by seeing them learn its language?

The history of the Dutch language in the East Indies has been extensively documented.[22] Indeed, it appears that the Dutch were never very keen on having the Indonesians learn their language in large numbers. When finally, in the late 1930s, they came round to promoting Dutch as a language of communication, it was too late: the educated elite had already opted en masse for Indonesian. A few years later, in 1942, the Japanese conquered Indonesia, and quickly prohibited the use of Dutch in public, and even in private. For practical purposes they supported the spread of Indonesian: in the long run they intended to impose Japanese on all the occupied territories. It was not lost on the Indonesian population that the Dutch motherland was overrun in a matter of days by German armies, that the Asian colonies fell to the Japanese invaders without much of a struggle, and that by 1945 it was a British force that took over the Dutch colony. The prestige of the Netherlands as a colonial power and of Dutch as its language of domination was shattered.

When the Dutch tried to reclaim their overseas possessions, they found a country up in arms and torn by civil strife. They now confronted a self-proclaimed independent Indonesian Republic, and after more than four years of tense confrontations and intermittent warfare, the Dutch presence in Asia came to an unhappy end.[23]

Already in 1945, the Indonesian Republic had adopted *bahasa Indonesia* as its official, national language, and, as if to rub salt into

Dutch wounds, English was selected as the official foreign language.[24] It seems hardly surprising that a language spoken by so few, resented by so many, robbed by events of its hegemonic halo and tainted as the enemy's idiom, was finally abandoned.[25] But, once again, quite similar events occurred in the French colonies and nevertheless French continued to be widely used. Even if the British were never so defeated, they too lost some colonial possessions to the Japanese and after having reconquered them had to face bitter struggles with indigenous nationalist forces. Yet English to this very day retains a central position in those former colonies. Why, then, did Dutch disappear so completely from the Indonesian islands?

By the end of the nineteenth century, as the colonial regime extended and intensified its domination in the East Indies, it also provoked a vivid demand for western education among the indigenous elites. And it was Dutch, the language of power and knowledge, that promised to open 'the way to the west' (*Jalan ke Barat*). Initially, among both Dutch educationalists and Javanese intellectuals, voices were heard that proposed to teach Dutch, even teach in Dutch, on a large scale. Only instruction in a Western language could break the stagnation of traditionalism. The colonial authorities, however, were most reluctant to provide education, especially in Dutch. It might all too easily become a 'nidus of mental infection'.[26] Students might encounter 'all sorts of immorality, dis- and misbelief',[27] and would no doubt shed their humility towards their ruler once they had mastered his language and began to consider themselves his equals on account of it. These concerns were entirely justified. By far the better part of the Indonesian students who learned Dutch during the first four decades of the twentieth century also absorbed Western theories of nationalism and converted to some brand of socialism.

As in so many other colonial and multilingual societies, the language of the oppressor became the medium of liberation that united the small circle of nationalist leaders of different origins and connected them with the world outside, with its unsettling ideas, its popular heroes, and its great upheavals.[28] However, had the young rebels remained ignorant of the outside world, they might still have rebelled, but along entirely different lines – they might have taken inspiration from Islam, for example. And, had they not learned Dutch, they would nevertheless have heard of novel ideas and contemporary events by more roundabout means.

Some of the Dutch administrators believed that their indigenous assistants and clients would become less respectful if allowed to address their superiors in their own language. Did not the Javanese address their underlings in *ngoko* and expect to be answered in a very restricted *krama*, while the underlings talk *ngoko* among themselves? These feudal inequalities were to be reproduced in the colonial context, with Dutch in the position of high *krama* and Malay passing for lowly *ngoko*.

But these were all fleeting concerns on the part of the Dutch, often intimately held, no doubt, but very rarely confided to print. Yet for each of these opinions an opposite was also current. Knowledge of Dutch would elevate the *inlanders*;[29] it would help in the recruitment of competent administrators, familiar with Dutch manners, laws and procedures; it would imprint Dutch culture on East Indian society. Foremost in the mind of the colonial government in Jakarta (formerly Batavia) and The Hague was the objective of cutting expenses and avoiding costly outlays on schools for the local population.[30] The Dutch (this much was also made abundantly clear by Kees Groeneboer) never wanted the natives to speak their language.

But in our scheme of things this creates a major problem. Speakers are expected to welcome others learning their language and even be willing to stimulate it, since it will increase the Q-value of their language. Thus, the Dutch should be expected to have favoured the learning of Netherlandish by the natives. But they did not. On the contrary, they restricted attendance in schools with Dutch instruction to children of Europeans and a very limited number of the offspring of the *priyaji*, the native nobility.

This indifference, bordering on cultural self-effacement and even self-contempt, has been a pertinent trait of Dutch cultural policy beyond the borders. Until recently, the Dutch made little effort to promote their language and culture abroad, and in general tend to consider any foreign interest in their language with some suspicion. In the East Indies, they rarely communicated directly with the local population, no matter in what language, and they restricted their interactions mostly to the local *priyaji* and subaltern native administrators. Malay was good enough for those ends. Van Doorn concludes:

> What the administration aimed at at any cost, was maintaining [East] Indies as an exploitation colony, as a source of profit for the Dutch state, managed efficiently by a corps of civil servants; what the administration rejected was the development of [East] Indies – intentionally or spontaneously – into a settlement colony where immigrants from the Netherlands would take root and constitute an established, economically independent and politically active, white settler population.[31]

Thus, until the 1930s the Dutch carried on a minimalist regime and made no attempt to win over the indigenous population. Hence, they were hardly interested in establishing all-Indonesia networks of communication and remained unwilling to expend the considerable effort and make the investment needed to spread their language among the vast and mostly illiterate masses. An increase in the Q-value of their language in Indonesia simply was not worth the necessary expense.

Groeneboer gives a detailed account of the passivity and indifference of succeeding governments in the Netherlands and colonial administrators overseas, whenever the language issue was brought up. And if it was raised, it was by reform-oriented educators who responded to a clear and pressing demand from the local elites. When, finally, in the 1930s, the Dutch began to realize that Malay was spreading quickly throughout the archipelago and decided that they should react by propagating Dutch, it was too little and too late. A few years later the Japanese government with one stroke of the pen outlawed the use of Dutch, and, come the Revolution, the independent Indonesian government abolished the language.

5.4 The rejection of Javanese

With Dutch out of the way as a viable option, the second question presents itself. Why did Malay prevail over Javanese as the national language, *bahasa Indonesia*? The current answer is simple:

> Malay... was chosen mainly because, since it had been used as a lingua franca in the archipelago for centuries, it was already understood by many citizens of the new Republic. The only other language that was seriously considered at the time was Javanese... However, since Javanese with its complex speech levels was considered to have encouraged the existence of a feudalistic social system and further since it is much more difficult to learn than Malay... the Javanese themselves readily agreed to the choice of Malay.[32]

In fact, it is not easy to find a trace of dissent in the sources.[33] Moeliono mentions that Yamin, the secretary of the 1928 Youth Congress, circulated a scrap of paper with his proposal for the wording of the oath among the committee members while a speech was going on to avoid further lengthy debates about Malay as the language of unity. Yamin suspected that Javanese, the language of the majority, could be a possible contender.[34]

Thus the nationalist youth movement held its first conference and solemnly swore the 'Sumpah Pemudah'.[35] From then on *bahasa Indonesia* became the language of Indonesian nationalism. Instead of the *brabbelmaleis* (Malay gibberish) of the colonial administration came a 'preposterous Malay' which became the 'revolutionary Malay' that spread as the nationalist movement gained adherents.[36]

A closely related question has haunted an outsider, a lifelong observer of Indonesian culture, Benedict Anderson: how could Javanese literature with its more than millennial tradition decline so suddenly, so deeply, while at the same time Malay writing gained ascendancy? And Anderson adds: 'I used to think of it as a black hole.'[37] One answer that he proposes stresses the role of the Dutch, who preferred Malay to Javanese for purposes of administration, as their empire extended further and further beyond Java, across the entire archipelago. A second answer focuses on the importance of the nationalist movement to 'national unity' and hence to a unifying language 'that was also not the colonial language': Malay.[38]

Anderson argues quite plausibly that this was not the beginning, but rather the culmination, of a linguistic transformation in which for three decades 'Javanese steadily lost ground to bahasa Melayu in the world of commerce, politics, and literature'. And he concludes: 'it was less nationalism that created a common language than that a common language helped create nationalism'. Even if this is true, it still begs the question of why this common language emerged at all and why it was Malay rather than Javanese. Anderson explains the rejection of Javanese in terms of a double crisis within Javanese society. The Javanese elites were so deeply compromised by more than three centuries of collaboration with the Dutch colonizers that their culture seemed utterly devalued to the generation that came of age at the beginning of the century. But much the same occurred in many colonized countries. Unique to Java were a rarefied court culture, deeply alienated from the rest of the nation and utterly dependent on the Dutch, severed from its endogenous roots, and the concomitant excrescence of *krama* as an increasingly artificial prestige language. Anderson argues that almost everywhere else the nationalist movements could turn to an 'uncontaminated' native language and transform it into an egalitarian vernacular, but that Javanese, in its *krama* version, was already 'native' and did not allow such 'vernacularization'. In a comparative perspective, this explanation is less than convincing. In many colonies the domestic languages were equally 'contaminated': by class and ethnic connotations, and by association with a collaborating indigenous elite. That certainly goes for Hindi in India, where the 'uncontaminated' and 'native' version, Hindustani, was nevertheless spurned.

Anderson's is a most sophisticated presentation of the argument that Javanese by its sociolinguistic features does not lend itself to being turned into a popular vehicular language – and the present summary does not do justice to the richness of his reasons. Yet it does not give a satisfactory explanation of why a version of Malay became the *bahasa Indonesia* and Javanese did not.

One domain of Javanese, the religious vocabulary of Islam, did in fact resist the pressures of 'kramanization', as Anderson himself points out (quoting Uhlenbeck):[39] if the egalitarian pressure of Islam apparently withstood it, then why did the nationalists not succeed in doing away with the excesses of kramanization? And then, of course, there was and is *ngoko*, the 'low' version of the language that could very well have been turned into a national vernacular.[40] As a matter of fact, early Javanese rebels proposed precisely that and, not unexpectedly, encountered massive resistance from the Javanese establishment.[41] Anderson concedes that *ngoko* might have been transformed into a vehicular, if the only alternative would have been Dutch. But there was another option: Malay. With this last turn in the argument we are back to the question: why Malay? Why not Javanese, or its *ngoko* version?

It would have meant nothing less than a revolution to abolish *krama* in Javanese and create from *ngoko* a vernacular suitable for the entire archipelago. It would have required the abolition of the endlessly intricate forms of address, the code switches between high and low; it would have compelled almost half of the population of Indonesia to learn another language for wider communication. But then, precisely such a revolution did occur! That was the transformation of Malay into *bahasa Indonesia* and the spread of that language throughout the population across the entire territory of the Republic in half a century. That revolution, too, required that people adapt to switching codes, not between high and low registers as in Javanese, but between 'far' and 'near', that is between *bahasa* and their local language. It equally demanded the abolition of most forms of address, and the introduction of the single pronoun 'anda', very similar in meaning to the modern English 'you'. Anderson argues that this became unavoidable with the development of the mass media, in which 'messages must be communicated to a mass and abstract audience'.[42] This excludes the use of highly specific and finely differentiated forms of address.[43] The institution of Indonesian as the language of a quickly transforming society required a lexical operation on a vast scale (one which, however, would have been equally necessary had Javanese been adopted). But most important in the revolutionary turn to Indonesian was that now not just some 40 per cent of the population would have to master a new language of wider communication, as they would have had to had Javanese been introduced, but more than twice as many: 85 per cent was to learn Indonesian – everyone who did not start school as a native speaker of Malay.

Could Javanese have been transformed into a language more suitable for modern society? There have been a few such language reforms, in societies of much smaller scale, but with equal impact. In Israel, for example, Hebrew was transformed into a modern vernacular after having been a strictly liturgical language for almost two thousand years.[44] And when it comes to reforming the forms of polite address that so much complicate the encounters among mutually unacquainted Javanese, there is at least one precedent in the replacement of 'Lei' by 'Voi' in Mussolini's Italy.[45]

Could it be that Javanese is much more difficult to learn for schoolchildren and individual adult students? The widely current argument that Malay is easier to learn is dubious: linguists believe that all languages are equally complex, but each in different respects, and that the difficulty of mastering them depends on the distance between the language to be learned and the language already acquired. Moreover, those languages are considered easy to learn that are already current in the environment (and therefore faintly familiar from the start) and that are vernacular (so that mistakes are not considered that much of an embarrassment). The latter consideration does give an edge to 'popular' Malay over 'stratified' Javanese.

5.5   Discussion

It would have required a revolution to adopt a low version of Javanese as the language of Indonesia. A revolution of such impact did in fact occur in Indonesia, but, instead, it made Malay into the *bahasa Indonesia*. The introduction of Indonesian throughout the archipelago occurred so swiftly, so incisively and so completely that the process must have corresponded to profound structural characteristics of Indonesian society. But the explanations that have been proposed do not stand up to comparative scrutiny.

Yet the political economy of language suggests a plausible explanation. At some point, most probably at the Sumpah Pemudah conference, the leaders opted for Malay against Javanese. They must have done so because they felt that the communication values of Malay and

Javanese were roughly equal: Javanese languages were much more prevalent, but Malay was more central. In fact, the Q-values of Malay may be somewhat larger than that of Javanese.[46] The representatives from the outer islands, who spoke neither Malay nor Javanese, were swayed to choose the former. The Javanese were willing to concede on the language issue for nationalist reasons and because it seemed that it might ensure the continued domination of Java in all other areas of society. Moreover, the young nationalists all appreciated the 'democratic' and 'all-Indonesia' character of Malay.

Table 5.1 shows how Dutch is rejected in favour of either Malay or Javanese by all parties on account of its minimal Q-value. It represents the 'dominated' outcome. The representatives speaking regional languages are assumed to prefer Malay to Javanese, given the respective Q-values. The Javanese, however, would vote against Malay. None of the regional languages is an option since their Q-values do not come anywhere near those for Malay or Javanese. Depending on the numerical strength of the delegations, majority voting might have produced either the one or the other outcome: Javanese or Malay. In the end, the Javanese supported the – apparently unanimous – adoption of Malay. Most probably, they did so for reasons extraneous to their language preferences, out of concern for the unity of the nationalist movement and as a strategic gambit to maintain in a future independent Indonesia Java's hegemony in political and economic affairs.

Once the nationalist youths had selected Malay, the dynamics of mutually reinforcing expectations were set in motion: people throughout the archipelago believed that Malay was the language that most others would learn and hence opted for it themselves, thus reinforcing similar expectations in others. This is a direct consequence of the hypercollective nature of languages. Thus, once Malay had a slight edge over Javanese in the perception of the Indonesians, a slow but powerful movement got on its way.

Throughout the 1930s, Malay spread at an increasing pace. In 1938, at the occasion of the First Indonesian Language Congress,

Table 5.1   The language dilemma in Indonesia, *c.1930*

Preference for national language	Speakers of Javanese	Speakers of Malay	Speakers of regional languages
Javanese	1	2	2
Malay/*bahasa Indonesia*	2	1	1
Dutch	3	3	3

the choice of a national language was confirmed once more,[47] again raising confidence in Malay as the medium of communication for the entire archipelago, and prompting people on all islands to invest their learning efforts in that language rather than in its rivals.

The new Republican government, dominated by the nationalist movement, continued its pre-war language policies and made Malay the national language, compulsorily taught in the rapidly expanding elementary school system. With the full momentum of the state behind it, *bahasa Indonesia* could now be introduced as a compulsory subject and as the language of instruction at higher levels throughout the school system that was rapidly being set up all across the territory of the Republic, until the present level of saturation had been achieved.

In retrospect, the outcome of the Youth Congress of 1928 gave Malay a slight edge over Javanese, which was then confirmed by mutually reinforcing expectations, until after independence the nationalist regime imposed the language as *bahasa Indonesia* across the whole archipelago. In India, at about the same time, events took a slightly different turn, when the cause of Hindustani, as advocated by Gandhi, was lost to the Hindu purists. Hence, popular expectations kept alternating between English and Hindi and, after independence, the regime continued to hesitate between favouring the one or the other.

Since the end of the Suharto regime, strong religious, ethnic and regional movements have surfaced in Indonesia, all of them demanding a larger measure of autonomy against the centralist impact of the Republic. No doubt this will also have its consequences for language policy. Indonesians from all islands will claim a greater role for their regional language in public affairs, education and the media. The disintegration of the Soviet Union may serve as an example: it also brought about the rapid collapse of Russian throughout the former empire. But there are some differences. Russian was the language of Russia, the core of Soviet domination. In Indonesia, that place belongs to Javanese. *Bahasa Indonesia* certainly was and is the language of the Republic, but it is also, rightly, perceived as an ancient vernacular and a popular vehicular language. It is, moreover, current in neighbouring countries too, which adds to its attractiveness. If and when the outlying populations become autonomous or secede entirely, they will face a choice between *bahasa Indonesia* and English as their language of wider communication. Unless, of course, the peoples of the archipelago become completely alienated from the Republic in the course of a violent struggle for independence and come to see *bahasa Indonesia* as the language of the enemy, they are quite likely to reserve a major role for Indonesian.

Africa: The persistence of the colonial languages

Nowhere is a greater diversity of languages to be found than south of the Sahara desert. There may be a thousand, or more, or less – once again, the issue of which varieties must be counted as separate languages is controversial, and the controversy has strong political overtones. Colonial authorities may have exaggerated the differences between the speech of adjacent villages in order better to divide and rule.[1] More often than not, the local elders would readily confirm their singularity to bolster their own local authority. But all things considered, the multiplicity of languages in Africa remains awesome.

For more than a thousand years, Arabic has been the great vernacular and liturgical language of North Africa, from Morocco to Egypt. On the southern side of the Sahara desert and on the eastern seacoast of Africa, Arab traders had been active many centuries before the first European explorers arrived. Hence, their language and religion had spread throughout the area. In the first half of the nineteenth century, even before European colonization got under way, Muslim reform movements swept West Africa and, with the faith, spread the language.[2]

There were, of course, still other linking languages which the indigenous merchants brought along with their merchandise, such as Hausa, Igbo, Soninke and Swahili. And there were the languages of warrior kingdoms such as the Wolof, or the Fon, who acquired their weapons from European traders in exchange for the ivory, gold and slaves that they could now exact at gunpoint from their neighbours.

The European exploration of the continent began early in the fifteenth century with Portuguese expeditions to the western coast.[3] For four centuries the European presence was limited to 'factories' on offshore islands, or near river estuaries. Here, in 'distant contact',[4] the first African–European pidgins developed, first in interaction with Portuguese, later also with English and French.

It was not until the end of the nineteenth century that the European scramble for Africa really got on its way, greatly accelerated by the Berlin Conference of 1884–5. The Western powers now began to explore and exploit the interior, making inroads into the savannah and the rain forest from their operating bases on the coast, usually staying close to the rivers on their trek inland.[5] The workers who were recruited from the villages along the colonizers' path developed a pidgin to talk to their bosses and to the labourers from other communities, when they did not share an indigenous language.

In the Sub-Saharan region, many hundreds of local idioms exist, often spoken by no more than a few thousand people, without written texts (except the Lord's Prayer transcribed by the local missionary), without any protection from the authorities, without validity in the courts of law or the corridors of administration, hardly used at all in the schools and almost entirely unknown a day's march away. Like the deity in Maimonides' conception, these languages are always described by what they are *not*. It is very difficult to describe them in their own terms as languages of conversation, narration and memory.[6] We have called them the languages of memory, since people record texts by memorizing them, rather than by entrusting them to paper. Most probably, memory among the peoples without writing is used more intensely and developed to greater capacity than that of people who live with writing and can always 'look up' what has been confided to paper. The structure, the keywords, the melody and the gesticulation that go with stylized narratives help people to memorize and reproduce them.

In terms of the galactic model, this is the first level: that of the peripheral languages. Many go under different names, but may be very similar indeed. On the other hand, in the absence of written texts that standardize usage over time and across distances, speech may change more rapidly from one generation to another and from one village to the next.[7] Johannes Fabian has pointed out that the colonial authorities had an interest in stressing the differences between adjoining languages and exaggerated them accordingly, for example in the Belgian Congo.[8] This was certainly intended to stymie the emergence of a unified nationalist movement.[9] The Africans themselves probably did not mind this distortion too much, as it tickled their narcissistic sense of small differences and allowed them to boast their great fluency in languages that after all may well have been, for the greater part, dialects of one and the same language.[10]

In each area, there was and is at least one language that serves to connect a number of different peripheral language groups, all of which included some multilingual speakers who were competent in this central language. This is the second level of the galactic model: that of the central planets, surrounded by their peripheral moons. There may be a few dozen of these central languages, together covering the entire continent. Usually, a central language gained its position because it was used at the court of a conqueror dynasty that had subjected the neighbouring peoples; for example, the Wolof in Senegal or Fon in Dahomey (presently Benin) and the Igbo, Yoruba and Hausa in eastern, western and northern Nigeria. The rule of these kingdoms came to an end once the colonial powers penetrated the interior and defeated them on their own ground. Yet their languages continued to spread, as indigenous recruits, porters and labourers followed the colonial armies, helped build the new roads and railways, laboured on the plantations and settled in the sprawling capital cities from which the colonies were ruled.

In other parts of Africa, in what is now known as Congo or Zaire, and in the area of present-day Kenya and Tanzania, the colonial regime promoted the spread of indigenous vehicular languages, some of them with a long pedigree, such as Swahili, some of them, like Kikongo and Lingala, pidgins newly formed out of local languages.

And, of course, each colonial regime imposed its own language, in the missionary posts as the language of conversion, as the language of command in the army barracks, then as the language of administration in the outposts of government, somewhat later as the language of education, if not in the village schools then in the elite schools for continued education. Next to Arabic, the colonial language was the written language par excellence; it was also the only printed language, the language of newspapers and books, and still later it became the language of radio and television.

Colonial conquest brought about an increase in the scale of social life; it lengthened the chains of interdependence linking villages or regions that before had been mostly separate and self-sufficient. Hence, a number of languages expanded on a corresponding scale – some indigenous vernaculars, a few newly emerging pidgins and the language of the colonizer – each connecting a series of peripheral languages. The colonial language in its standard version was reserved for those who had gone to school and learned to read and write. But one could pick up a pidgin or a domestic connecting language as one went along, in the streets and from one's peers. This simple act made for a true diglossia (or triglossia and even more complex constellations): the domestic languages, spoken by the great mass of the people, for mundane, everyday functions, and, for the 'high' functions, the colonial language, written and spoken by the colonizers and those who served their regime.

When in the 1960s independence came for most of these African colonies, not surprisingly the language of the European occupiers was already ingrained in these societies as the language of politics and administration, of large enterprises, of the sciences and the national media. And, for similar reasons to those in India, the nationalist movement, uniting factions from different ethnic and geographic origins, found itself compelled to opt for the language of its colonial opponent.

6.1   A two-by-three comparison

Why has the former colonial language maintained its central position so tenaciously in most African countries? It coexists in some countries with a domestic mother tongue shared by almost the entire population, in others with a native language that is spoken by the overwhelming majority as either a first or a second language, and in still other countries it functions side by side with three or four different indigenous, vehicular languages.

In the social sciences, a question like this can only be answered by making comparisons. Here, the comparison will be between three types of language constellation, each time in a francophone country and in a country centred on English.[11] The first type of constellation to be compared between both language zones is one in which the colonial language has remained the official medium, while more than 75 per cent of the population speaks one and the same native tongue. This is the case in Rwanda, where almost everyone, Hutus and Tutsis alike, speaks Kinyarwanda as their mother tongue,[12] yet, until recently, French was the sole 'official' language. Its English-oriented counterpart is Botswana, where 80 per cent of the population are native speakers of the indigenous language, Tswana, while nevertheless English has remained the official language there.

The second language constellation is one in which at least three-quarters of the population speaks the same domestic language, but either as a native or as an acquired language. In the francophone zone, Senegal is the example: Wolof is the language of some 75 per cent of the population, a good part of which speaks it as a second language. French has remained the official language in Senegal. In the English zone, Tanzania is the case in point: Swahili is the domestic language that is known to more than 90 per cent of Tanzanians, while it is a mother tongue for a small but growing minority. But Swahili is, next to English, the official language of the land.

Finally, there are countries of the third type, where several indigenous languages are current, but none of them comes anywhere near a majority position. This is the case in many African countries, but here the focus will be on Nigeria for the sphere of English and on Congo/ Zaire for the francophone world. In either case, the former colonial language remains paramount, strong nationalistic qualms about its use notwithstanding.

The choice of cases for comparison already suggests that the particular configuration of domestic languages in each country may explain at least in part the tenacity of the ex-colonial language. Thus, it should not surprise us too much if in countries with several major domestic languages, mutual rivalry prevents any one of them from becoming the national medium, thus leaving the field to the former colonial language. This occurred in both Congo/Zaire and Nigeria (and in South Africa, which will constitute the subject of chapter 7). What does seem to be an anomaly, on the other hand, is a country where well-nigh everyone understands and speaks the same native tongue and still the colonial language cannot be dislodged from its predominant position: Botswana, Swaziland, Lesotho, Rwanda and Burundi.

The intermediate case is one in which the domestic language is the native tongue of a minority, but also the acquired language of a good part of the population, making it the idiom of at least three-quarters of the population. This is not an exceptional situation, either: it applies to Senegal and Tanzania, but also to Benin (Fon), Togo (Ewe), Central African Republic (Sango) and Mali (Bambara).[13]

The analysis will proceed in terms of the galactic model with its four levels – local, central, supercentral and hypercentral. Wherever the available data allow it, the Q-values for the languages in each constellation will be estimated. Statistics of language skills are almost non-existent for Africa. This lack of reliable data has provoked a heated debate among experts on African languages. Chaudenson, a leading scholar in the field, has rejected all 'demolinguistics' as inadequate since figures are usually based on the number of people that have achieved a certain scholastic level. These statistics are dubious in the first place, since the authorities have good reasons to embellish them, and moreover, the level of schooling means very little in terms of actual linguistic competence. In fact, people may have studied a Western language – according to the record – for many years without being competent in it at all.[14]

Yet such data on school attendance are not entirely worthless as indicators. First of all, time series do convey a sense of the direction in which language skills are headed. Second, for the present purposes, only a very rough impression of the distribution of language skills is required. The present analysis purports to reconstruct the choices that prospective language learners make, and they decide on the basis of quite intuitive impressions. So, for our objectives, the data need not be all that good.

But even more so than in the Asian cases, in Africa we must take into account the high degree of illiteracy which effectively prevents access to the standard version of the colonial language. It is taught in schools or private courses and cannot be picked up informally, like its pidginized versions and the indigenous languages. The result is an actual group monopoly by the educated elites of the official, ex-colonial language. This fact plays a central role in the present argument. The second theme in the explanation is that of 'language jealousy', the refusal of a domestic vehicular language that is closely identified with a large and influential ethnic group. By the spread of its language, this group might gain even greater weight in the country's ethnic balance. In the long run, the gain of an ethnic language vis-à-vis its lesser rivals might provoke a general stampede towards it: for the losing languages this evokes a grisly vision of diminishing prestige, dwindling resources, shrinking domains of usage and increasing neglect, until parents do not even bother any more to pass the language on to their children and it simply disappears. In other words, from a collective point of view, some language jealousy need not be only spiteful or irrational. After all, languages are in competition (although often latently so) and a gain for the one might entail a loss for the others. As the lesser language loses out, the collective cultural capital that it incorporates may well be lost with it. From an individual perspective, advantages may be gained by learning the predominant language and not much may seem to be lost by neglecting one's own language (in favour of one with a higher Q-value). Thus, rational, individual choices may bring about a situation that goes against the collective interests of those concerned. It is this course of affairs that Laitin has characterized as 'private subversion of the public good'.[15] Apparently, in order to maximize individual career opportunities, individual citizens, and parents of schoolchildren especially, privately decide against the domestic language which for nationalist reasons they publicly support as a collective good.

6.2   Three francophone constellations south of the Sahara

The former French possessions overseas, almost without exception, have remained members of the 'Francophonie',[16] the French counterpart of the Commonwealth that encompasses the erstwhile British colonies. As the name suggests, more than anything else the common denominator of this entity is the language, French. Quite apart from other political designs, the foremost objective of the French government is to protect and promote French in all those countries where it was once the colonial language.[17] Although the global position of French has been steadily eroded since World War II, in many of the former colonies it maintains its functions as the official and the international language. This seems to be the result of a sustained campaign by the French government, and the theory of 'linguistic imperialism' naively suggests as much. In fact, it is much more likely that it is the particular language constellation in each of the former colonies which goes far to determine the position of French vis-à-vis the other languages there. While individuals strive to maximize their communication chances, over time their choices combine with each other to reproduce the overall constellation.

6.2.1   Rwanda

The vast majority, over 90 per cent, of the population of Rwanda speak Kinyarwanda,[18] which as 'Kirundi' is also spoken by almost all inhabitants of neighbouring Burundi and widely used in eastern Zaire and Uganda. With some 15 million speakers (in 1990) Kinyarwanda is the Bantu language spoken most widely as a mother tongue (Swahili outnumbers it but is mostly acquired as a second language).[19] Kinyarwanda was proclaimed the 'national language'.[20] Nevertheless, as in Burundi, in Rwanda the official language is French, one of the languages of the Belgians who occupied the two countries from 1918 (when the Germans were made to abandon their African possessions) until independence in 1959. The position of

French is rather peculiar. Since all Rwandans can communicate with all others in their native tongue, another language adds nothing to their communication potential – not in the Rwandese constellation, that is. But beyond the borders, French allows them to communicate with all the member countries of the Francophonie and with French speakers elsewhere; it provides access to journals and reviews, to radio and TV broadcasts, to extended education, to science and technology, medicine, literature and the arts.

If indeed all Rwandans speak Kinyarwanda, the prevalence, p_k, of that language equals 1. Since everyone speaks it, it follows that all multilinguals must have it in their repertoire, therefore also $c_k = 1$, and $Q_k = p_k.c_k = 1$. Within the Rwandese constellation, no added language can increase the Q-value of the repertoire: it does not pay to learn French or any other language for that matter. Hence, either learning French must be aimed at communication beyond the borders of Rwanda, or other considerations must have played a role.

What could be the reason for using French as the language of government and administration inside Rwanda itself? There are a number of arguments for maintaining the language of the former rulers: at independence all laws and regulations, all court verdicts, all archived correspondence, reports and minutes were in French. All higher indigenous civil servants wrote and read French, and in the lower echelons at the very least they understood and spoke it, while they were all fluent in their mother tongue, Kinyarwanda.

But this in itself was insufficient reason to hold on to French as the official language. The laws could have been translated, and the written records of government would have remained easily accessible as long as a large number of civil servants could still read them in French and if need be translate them into Kinyarwanda.

The most plausible explanation of the continuation of French as the official language of Rwanda is that the civil servants wanted it. Jobs in the administration were almost the only white-collar positions in the country and fluency in French was well-nigh indispensable for them. Moreover, under the prevailing circumstances, competence in French, that is standard French, as distinguished from patois, was not available to the large majority of the population, since written French was taught only in secondary schools and private courses. Only a small part of the population went to school at all. Less than 1 per cent of Rwandans continued their education past the elementary level and even fewer went on to learn written French. Very few Rwandans could and can afford continued education. As a result, at independence, the French-speaking administrative elite enjoyed a group monopoly on the use of the colonial language and hence on civil service jobs. The language remained a hypercollective good, but only with respect to those who had completed secondary school. All others found themselves excluded from the written variety. In fact, the educational system has hitherto operated as a most effective mechanism of exclusion.[21]

Since it would require a major collective effort to translate the records into Kinyarwanda, there was and is little danger of individual defection, that is of civil servants individually switching to Kinyarwanda, since they will continue to consult texts in French (except when talking to the public as 'street-level bureaucrats'). On the contrary, it pays for these elite parents to make sure their children get a good education, become fluent in standard French and can join the ranks of the civil service in their turn. Thus the elites have succeeded in appropriating French exclusively for their own ranks, and this puts at their disposal a vehicular language of global scope, a truly super-central language. Since they have in fact collectively monopolized the system of continued and higher education, they have effectively excluded 99 per cent of the Rwandese population and ensured for themselves privileged access to the key positions in government and business. Fluency in French constitutes the password for admission to these positions.

Yime-Yime Katesi has raised the question of why the colonial languages continue to function as official languages, languages of administration, of the law and of education in states such as Rwanda, Burundi and Lesotho where linguistic homogeneity prevails.[22] And he suggests one possible answer: because the foreign language serves to consecrate the power of those who can use it. And Katesi quotes the French linguist Alexandre, who already in 1967 spoke of a social class defined by its monopoly of the use of a universal communication medium such as French or English, the acquisition of which represents a genuine form of capital accumulation.[23]

This exclusionary use of French not only affects institutions, by limiting access to extended education and monopolizing the higher echelons of the labour market. It actually sets limits to the ambitions and the self-esteem of those who find themselves excluded. French being the unattainable language for the vast majority of Rwandans, by its very exclusivity justifies their exclusion, since, necessarily, they are the uninitiated, the ignorant. Thus, perversely, the exclusion produces its own legitimacy.

French not only was the language of the colonial ruler, but continues to be the language of all scientific and technological knowledge, of administrative and legal expertise, of political discourse, of wealth, power and prestige. Even today, it is the only written language, unintelligible and inaccessible to the common people. They may be ignorant of all the codified knowledge; they are not at all ignorant of their ignorance. They have understood very well that they do not understand it, and that is why they agree with their own disqualification.[24]

In this manner, language is perverted from a means of communication into a means of exclusion with the complicity of the excluded themselves, who in this respect display their loyalty to the privileged. Each time that someone has proposed replacing French as the language of instruction by an indigenous language, the parents have been the first to reject the idea: they want for their children the education that provides the best chances on the labour market and therefore, if they can afford it, schooling in the hegemonic language, French in the present case.[25] While this seems justified in each individual case, collectively the parents maintain a system of selection that excludes the vast majority of children. Even the most progressive members of the elite hesitate when it comes to diminishing the career prospects of their children by preventing them from learning the languages in which they themselves were educated to become the progressives they have remained. Ntole Kazadi[26] adds that it is not enough to know French in order to have access to the privileged positions; witness the thousands of young secondary school and college graduates who nevertheless remain without a job. Indeed, French may not be a sufficient condition, but it is certainly a necessary one.

In the background, the dilemma of collective action hovers once again. Already at this point it may safely be concluded that educational reform cannot be brought about solely by private, grass-roots initiatives. It requires collective action of a scope that matches the scale of the problem, in this case at the national level. In fact, that was the promise of the 'kinyarwandization' policy proclaimed in the 1980s, but abandoned since 1989.[27] At present, Kinyarwanda is used as the language of instruction at the elementary level, while the new regime has introduced English-language secondary schools in addition to the French *lycées*.

In Rwanda, and for that matter in Burundi, French was superimposed upon an almost entirely monolingual society, and it seems that the colonial language – possibly for precisely that reason – is less deeply rooted there than in other African countries. Since the forces of the Rwandan Patriotic Front took power in Kigali in 1994, it seems that English, the language of the armed forces during their long exile in Uganda and also the language of friendly foreign powers, is rapidly spreading. It has even been declared a 'co-official' language.[28] Since there were at most a hundred thousand Rwandans who were fluent in

French, one may well envisage that in the wake of these upheavals the former administrative elite will be replaced swiftly by officials who were educated mostly in English. Under identical conditions of collective monopolization, English will turn out to be just as effective a means of exclusion, disqualification and mystification as French proved itself to be before.[29]

6.2.2 Senegal

In Rwanda the vast majority of the inhabitants share a domestic mother tongue. This should be distinguished from a constellation in which a very large majority speak the same domestic language, but where a sizeable proportion acquired it as a second language. This is the case in Tanzania and Indonesia, but also in Senegal.[30]

Within the world of 'Francophonie', Senegal is the exemplary case. French language and culture have played a larger role there than anywhere else in Africa south of the Sahara. The Senegalese have contributed an impressive array of scholars, writers and administrators to the francophone world and to France itself. The poet, scholar and statesman Léopold Senghor, 'membre de l'Académie', was by far the best known among them, but by no means the only one. For more than three centuries, much longer than elsewhere, French spread among the Senegalese elites, who adopted it quite readily.

Relations between the different ethnic groups that make up the population of Senegal seem less tense than in many other countries on the continent.[31] And the fact that the language of the most numerous group, Wolof, is used as a vehicular language by a large share of the other groups suggests a modicum of ethnic harmony. The Wolof people make up about 43 per cent of the population, but almost 50 per cent name Wolof as their mother tongue. Calvet explains the disparity by pointing out that marriages between a Wolof and a partner of different ethnic background are quite frequent and that the children usually learn to speak Wolof at home rather than the other parental language.[32]

Moreover, according to the 1988 census, about 22 per cent of the population have learned Wolof as a second language. All in all, some 71 per cent of respondents reported speaking Wolof.[33] If this figure is less than experts had assumed until then, there is no doubt at all that Wolof is gaining in popularity: it is expanding rapidly, much more in the cities than in the countryside, and more in Dakar than in faraway

Table 6.1 Senegal around 1988 (speakers in hundred thousands)

Native language	Sole or second language								Third language LANG+ WO&FR	Total
	WO	FU	SE	DI	MA	SO	FR	Other		
WO	18	1	0	0	1	0	7	7	–	33
FU	6	4	1	0	0	0	1	2	1	15
SE	3	0	4	0	0	0	1	0	1	9
DI	1	0	0	1	0	0	0	0	0	3
MA	1	0	0	0	1	0	0	0	0	3
SO	0	0	0	0	0	0	0	0	0	1
Other	1	0	0	0	0	0	0	1	0	3
										68
Q_i:										
WO	0.582	0.853	0.702	0.595	0.628	0.582	0.649	0.697	–	
FU	0.853	0.094	0.200	0.114	0.128	0.094	0.244	0.233	0.892	
SE	0.702	0.200	0.026	0.036	0.054	0.026	0.122	0.160	0.738	
DI	0.595	0.114	0.036	0.001	0.010	0.001	0.067	0.072	0.662	
MA	0.628	0.128	0.054	0.010	0.005	0.005	0.090	0.096	0.697	
SO	0.582	0.094	0.026	0.001	0.005	0.000	0.052	0.056	0.649	
Other	0.697	0.233	0.160	0.072	0.096	0.056	0.216	0.056	0.770	
Greenberg's A	0.373									

Source: Data from the 1988 census, after Calvet, 1994.

WO = Wolof; FU = Fulani; SE = Serer; DI = Diola; MA = Mandingo; SO = Soninke; FR = French

A dash – = Not applicable.

The number of first- and second-language speakers of each language is reported by Calvet. The percentage of French speakers is estimated at 18 per cent on the basis of Daff, 1991, and Diouf, 1994; the numbers of second-language speakers of Wolof and French are assumed to be proportional to the number of first-language speakers of each language, except for Wolof: there the proportion is set higher, since the Wolof need not learn another indigenous language. It is assumed that native Wolof speakers have learned other domestic languages in proportion to the number of native speakers of these languages.

towns such as St Louis in the north, or Ziguinchor in the south (Casamance), where its status is ambiguous.[34]

The 1989 census did not count the number of French speakers. But Daff estimates, with all due provisos, that some 12 per cent speak a 'stable' French, and another 30 per cent a 'broken' version.[35]

The communication value (Q-value) of Wolof (0.60) is far superior to those of all other languages spoken in Senegal (table 6.1). Fulani comes second (0.09) and French in third position (0.05), before Serer (0.03). No other language obtains a significant score. As a consequence, all other language groups are best off by learning Wolof. And in fact, this is the most current second language. However, Senegalese can realize a higher communication value by adding Fulani or Serer to their repertoire than by learning French. And yet, after Wolof, French is the second language learned most frequently, and the trilingual repertoire with Wolof and French is rather current among native Fulani and Serer speakers. It is indeed unusual for Senegalese to learn a language other than these two.[36] In the present case, also, the fact that French still continues to function as the official language of Senegal must be explained by its role as the language of the administration, unavailable to those who have not gone to school, and therefore an instrument of elite closure. Even more than Hindi in India, Wolof in Senegal could function as a national language, if language jealousy did not prevent it and the elites were willing to abandon their monopolistic language, French.

Wolof and French, in fact, spread more or less at the same time, during the colonial and postcolonial era: French as a language of the administration, the school system and Christian missionaries, Wolof as the lingua franca of the police, railway workers, dockers, labourers, immigrants to the cities on the seacoast, and also the wandering imams that spread the Muslim faith and helped found the *confréries* that now control much of economic and social life in Senegal.

According to Louis-Jean Calvet, once again, 'as its functions slowly shifted, Wolof became almost synonymous with the language of one kind of power, economic and symbolic power, but not the language of power per se, which is still French'.[37] Wolof is the indispensable language for urban settlers, while French is required for government employees. The two languages are acquired in different ways which reveal their different status: through 'spontaneous' acquisition in the one case, through instruction in school in the other. Yet an informal version of French can also be learned in the streets (one finds French speakers in the informal economy, among the street pedlars who have never been to school).[38] Calvet wonders which language yields the most rewarding linguistic capital, in Bourdieu's terms, and what is the status of those 'ethnic' languages that are dominated by both French and Wolof.

These questions are answered in an entirely different context by Leigh Swigart:[39] 'Asked which languages one should acquire first when settling in Dakar, my interviewees, no matter where they came from, almost unanimously mentioned Wolof. The official language, French, came second.' Clearly, his respondents, expert as they were in the theory of language constellations, picked the languages with scored the highest Q-values.

Although the 1988 census figures suggest that scholars had over-estimated the prevalence of Wolof, it does seem that the language is gradually losing its ethnic markers, according to the reactions that Swigart collected: 'it is no longer an ethnic group, it is just a language', said one Diola (from the south); 'it is a mixture', according to a Fula (from the north). Or as a third, a Serer (from the south (east)), expressed it: 'Wolof has no culture at all.'[40] All these statements come down to one and the same point: Wolof is a neutral medium, and speaking Wolof by no means implies abandoning one's own ethnic identity, whatever it may be. Such ethnic transparency is the highest ace for a language in full expansion as a vehicular. Moreover, the Wolof of the streets and the markets – with a simplified grammar and a vocabulary enhanced by French and even English words – is quite removed from the ancient Wolof that is still spoken in the villages.

Nevertheless, in Senegal French is the only official language,[41] the first language of instruction even in elementary school, the only language of the printed media, the dominant language of television and advertisement, and – an equally important fact – the privileged language in the labour market and in the corridors of power.[42] Pierre Dumont contends:

> There is no doubt that if one day the schools would teach in Wolof, Fulani, Serer or Diola, it would entirely transform Senegalese society. First of all, the privileges that since colonial times were the reward for fluency in the French language would come up for brutal criticism. And one may be assured that the masses that have been taught in African languages will then compete for power with the established elites, which for the time being are French educated, graduates from the 'École française'...as opposed to the traditional schools, especially the schools of the Koran.[43] (Author's translation)

But major efforts in that direction notwithstanding, nothing has come of such education in the national languages, for two reasons. Parents privately prefer what as citizens they publicly reject: French. This is the first fundamental dilemma that confronts the citizens of so many former colonies. But had the parents opted for a domestic language, they would have been at odds over which one to select.[44] This is the second, equally paralysing, dilemma. Finally, had they wanted to avoid the choice, funds would have been needed to finance textbooks and courses in all six domestic languages.

Yet, even though its population has been so deeply immersed in French, there is in Senegal a widespread domestic language that has gradually been divested of most of its ethnic connotations, but not of all by far. The strength of Wolof constitutes its weakness: the dominant position of the Wolof makes the other ethnic groups wary of formally entrusting to their language all the functions of national communication. Hence, given its high Q-value, Wolof is very likely to continue its expansion, but it may well remain restricted to informal, low-prestige functions.[45]

6.2.3   Congo/Zaire

The third case in this first series of comparisons among francophone countries is that of a country with several domestic, widespread, vehicular languages, none of them, however, encompassing a majority of the population: this is the situation in Zaire, renamed Congo (Democratic Republic of Congo) in 1997. The one official language is French, medium of the administration and the courts of law, of the media and – except for the first classes – of the school system. At least three hundred indigenous languages are spoken in the country:

> divided over three subsequent levels: the first comprises the 300 or so local languages that support the essential foundations of tradition and ethnic communication. The second consists of the four languages that are called 'national' but which are in fact vehicular, inter-ethnic media and cover each a specific area – Kiswahili in the east, Lingala and Kikongo in the west and Kiluba in the centre; the third level, finally, is that of French.[46]

This characterization by Nyunda ya Rubango fits the galactic model, with its peripheral, central and supercentral levels. The former colonial language remains the pivot of the constellation, even though it is estimated that no more than 4 per cent speak it with some fluency.[47] The prevalence of the great vehicular languages of Zaire is unknown. They are more current in the cities than in the villages, among the educated than among those who never went to school (they are each in their region the languages of instruction in the first classes of elementary school).

According to estimates, roughly half of all Congolese speak one of the four vehicular languages as a second language, in addition to one out of a multitude of mother tongues. But a growing number now learn one of these linking languages at a young age at home: a 'vernacularization' of the vehicular languages is on its way, albeit mostly in urban settings (very much in the same way as with Wolof).

Mwatha Musanji Ngalasso[48] has studied the prevalence of Kikongo in one river-town, Kikwit, in the southwest: it has become the language of instruction in the schools, the lingua franca of urban youngsters from the surrounding villages, where more than twenty different languages are current, all more or less similar to Kikongo. It is the mother tongue of growing numbers of children born in the city. Kikongo, Ngalasso remarks, is now the language that conveys a sense of identity, even 'complicity', and solidarity. But already another vehicular language is spreading rapidly in the Kikwit region, while Kikongo continues to grow. This rival language is Lingala, the language of the capital city Kinshasa, promoted by the former president Mobutu and his single-party regime. To speak Lingala is to show everybody that one has been in Kinshasa and is no longer just a nobody from Kikwit. Moreover, during the Mobutu period Lingala marked one as an activist in the Mobutu movement, a distinction that became dubious after Kabila took over and civil war broke out. What matters, however, is that even the choice of a vehicular language carries a range of meanings, such as 'big-city slicker', 'educated person', 'reigning party activist', and so on. These identity markers may provide an independent motive in choosing to learn and use a language; they may be highly correlated to its communication value, and even be epiphenomenal, in the sense that people choose on the basis of Q-value and value the identity markers that come with it, *because* it provides the better opportunities for communication.

At roughly the same time, during the mid-1990s, Lingala was reported to be gaining speakers in the eastern region of Congo/Zaire also, in the town of Bukavu, very near the Rwandan border, an area that traditionally used Swahili as its vehicular language, next to French and a local 'hybrid' of Swahili, 'indoubil'.[49] Hence, if Lingala, from the western side of Congo/Zaire, could make converts in this remote area, it was certainly not for lack of alternative means of vehicular communication. Clearly, in Kikwit as in Bukavu, Lingala represents the language of the political centre, Kinshasa. The military and the civil servants all speak it. It is the language of the lower ranks of central government, and hence of radio and television, and therefore of popular music and entertainment. Thus it can make one sound important and 'cool' at the same time. On the basis of his observations of the competition between French, Swahili and Lingala in Bukavu, Goyvaerts even speculates that in the end 'Lingala may well become the exception, an African language that succeeds in conquering its country'.[50]

This might indeed happen, if the language remains free of any association with a strong ethnic group. In fact, Kikongo, Lingala and Swahili seem to be relatively free of ethnic or regional connections. Lingala, moreover, has its base in the capital, another advantage. So far it lacks the support of a strong nationalist movement that might help it conquer the schools, the media, parliament and the courts, as happened with Malay in Indonesia or Swahili in Tanzania.

The observations by Goyvaerts and Ngalasso signal a grass-roots process of national integration, against all the odds of political fragmentation: an increasing orientation of provincial town dwellers towards the national centre of politics and culture, military power and economic clout. This undercurrent may well be reversed by civil war, foreign intervention and separatist strivings, but it did manifest itself unmistakably in the language choices of Zairese in the outer regions.

Lingala, like Kikongo (also known as Kituba or Monokituba in neighbouring Congo Brazzaville) and for that matter Sango (the lingua franca of the Central African Republic),[51] is a rather young language that emerged during colonial times. Whereas Wolof and Mandingo are ancient court languages that spread by conquest and trade, and were described in detail by European travellers more than three centuries ago, these recent Congolese languages have their origin among the Africans who were recruited by the explorers, conquerors and traders who travelled inland along the river Congo and its tributaries during the later part of the nineteenth century. William Samarin has shown that the Belgian colonizers did not speak the indigenous languages and used local translators (usually very young children) in their contacts with the locals.[52] Workers were recruited along the way, and as they made up a very mixed lot they had to make themselves understood in an improvised pidgin. In a fairly short period of some ten years new languages emerged to meet the needs of the workers and later on the traders, soliders, sutlers and missionaries that traversed the newly conquered areas. Before the Europeans came, no vehicular languages existed in this region, and the villagers learned the rather similar languages spoken in adjacent settlements.[53] Swahili, on the other hand, has an old pedigree on the eastern seashore and it also has a long history in eastern Congo/Zaire as the vehicular language of Arab traders and Katangese miners. As Johannes Fabian has shown, Swahili was promoted by the Belgian authorities to stop the progress of both English and Kabanga, a regional language that might carry with it influences from South Africa.[54]

Congo/Zaire thus has four major vehicular languages, all of them quite widespread in their region, three of them, moreover, largely devoid of ethnic ties. That is why they are quite easily adopted throughout the country according to the actual needs for communication and the prevailing lines of ethnic identifications. Acceptance and acquisition are much facilitated since the languages are of African, even Congolese, origin and all belong to the Niger–Congo language family, which comprises the local languages that most Congolese have grown up with. However, as usual, the problem is which one to select among the several available options. It appears that Lingala, as the language of the capital, may hold the trump card. But recent upheavals may yet entirely change the game.

There is of course another language that occupies a central, even a supercentral, position in all of Congo/Zaire: French. It is the only official language (the constitution does not even mention other languages). Hence, it is the language of the law, of national government and administration, of the courts and even of local government. Until 1974 only French was used throughout the school system, but since then, domestic languages have been adopted for teaching in the first years of elementary school, without, however, so much as touching the complete monopoly of French in secondary and higher education. In Congo/Zaire, too, parents have shown themselves quite unwilling to have their children taught in Congolese languages, fearing it may harm their chances of landing prestigious and rewarding jobs, but also because they consider other domestic languages as a threat to the survival of their own group language, and do not expect that any of these vehicular languages will be understood beyond the borders of the region, let alone outside of Congo/Zaire (with the exception of Swahili). French, on the other hand, is a world language that promises attractive careers and is too 'remote' to present much of a threat to local idioms. Once again, in the final years of the Mobutu regime, at most 10–15 per cent of children in the relevant age cohort attended daytime secondary education, and most of those left school without a diploma. It is unlikely that matters have much improved since then. In this case, too, the Congolese, as citizens, denounced French in public, but as parents coveted it in private for their children, who nevertheless rarely learned it well enough to qualify for the better jobs.[55]

An earlier publication presented estimates for the Q-values of the vehicular languages of Congo/Zaire, including French.[56] For lack of reliable data it was necessary to make very rough estimates. In this most fragmented language constellation, all languages obtained rather low scores. The Q-values obtained with these guesstimates for the Congo/Zaire constellation were: Lingala 0.036; French 0.02; Swahili 0.012; Kiluba and Kikongo both 0.006. French scored higher in Congo/Zaire than in Rwanda, and lower than in Senegal, a result that agrees with the ranks for 'corpus' that Chaudenson assigned to French in these countries.[57] The rather feeble position of French in Congo/Zaire as compared to its score in Senegal may well be the result of the difference between Belgian and French colonial policies: Belgium, like Britain and Germany, facilitated above all the acquisition of domestic languages, whereas France always propagated French. The fact that French obtained a higher score in Congo/Zaire than in Rwanda (both formerly Belgian colonies) may be explained by the language constellation in those countries: French might be more prevalent in Congo/Zaire, where the coexistence of four different domestic vernaculars makes the ex-colonial language indispensable, whereas in Rwanda (and Burundi) almost all citizens speak the same domestic language and French is rather superfluous for domestic communication.

One language has entirely disappeared from Congo/Zaire, Rwanda and Burundi: Dutch, which in its Flemish version was nevertheless used in colonial times and was accorded equal status with French in the Colonial Charter of 1908. In Belgium at the time, Flemish was relegated to a position much inferior to French. In the Belgian Congo of those days, Flemish was used only in the mission settlements and in small trade. According to Nyunda ya Rubango: 'Although it was the poor cousin during the colonial epoch, Dutch ever since has borne the negative image of colonization. That the very expression *Flemish*, referring to individuals, the people, the language, is maligned in the popular speech of Zaire until this very day, is not at all coincidental.'[58] And yet the great majority of the Flemish were opposed to the colonial enterprise. Even Nyunda did not succeed in coming up with an explanation for the Congolese contempt for Netherlandish.[59] As a result, it was French alone that usurped all the functions of the official language in Congo/Zaire, while Dutch has completely disappeared from Central Africa after decolonization. It is now spoken in an indigenized version, Afrikaans, in South Africa, where, as the language of Apartheid, it labours under the same contempt from the blacks there.

In all three cases presented here, French continues to function as the language of government and administration, of continued education, of the media, of science and technology, of literature and high culture in general. In brief, it still is the language of high prestige, of individual linguistic capital à la Bourdieu. At the same time, as this 'stable' version of French can only be acquired in written courses, it is also the collective monopoly of the educated classes who have appropriated the civil service, excluding the vast majority of the illiterate and poorly educated. But French in Rwanda, Senegal and Congo/Zaire is not without competition. In terms of its communication value, its linking functions, the Rwandese can do without it, and well they may in the near future, switching to Kinyarwanda for domestic purposes and English for navigating the global system. The Senegalese are caught in the paralysing dilemma that has by now become a familiar feature of former colonial societies. They could indeed switch to Wolof, and for many purposes they already have, but the native speakers of the other languages cannot bring themselves to raise the status of Wolof above that of their own tongues. In Congo/Zaire finally, four domestic languages compete as vehicles of regional and possibly even national communication. Given this fourfold division, one might expect French to be in a quite strong position vis-à-vis its competitors, and indeed it is so when it comes to its formal status. But as education remains so scarce, its speakers are few indeed. Lingala, on the other hand, has progressed and is by now the language with the highest Q-value. In many respects this reflects the widening presence of the state at the grass-roots level. In Congolese society, at least during the Mobutu era, Lingala may have been 'slick' and 'cool', and it may still be, but it is a safe guess that it is still not nearly as 'chic' as French. Lingala at best gets you a job driving a car for someone else, French at best gets you a car with someone else to drive it for you. Much the same still applies to Wolof or Kinyarwanda versus French.

In the literature much is made of language as a marker of ethnic and class identity in these countries. But a great deal can be explained in terms of optimizing communication opportunities, wherever the choice presents itself: for immigrants, or job seekers. They tend to prefer the domestic language with the highest Q-value. If it is accessible to them, they will opt for learning the standard, written version of French. Those who speak French do not stand to gain from others learning it, since they can already communicate with them in a regional vehicular language, or even in the domestic language that has spread nationally. Moreover, they would rather not see too many people learn French, as it would dilute their privileges in the upper, francophone levels of the labour market, where they operate. In many respects, therefore, the expansion of extended education is not in the elite interest in countries where the better jobs are almost exclusively in the civil service, the military, the customs service and the police, or in a few import and export firms and large mining companies, and where there is not much other employment for middle and high cadres. It is the exclusive nature of the educational system, the restricted currency of the colonial language, and the group monopoly on the upper echelons of the labour market which determine the dynamics of these constellations.

6.3   Three English-centred constellations south of the Sahara

In this section, the two-by-three comparison will be continued: here, three 'anglophone' countries are compared with one another and with their French counterparts. In the three language constellations centred on French, the configuration of domestic languages to a large extent determines the position of French as the official language. Thus Rwanda, where everyone speaks Kinyarwanda, could – at least in theory – do without French in almost all domains. Congo/Zaire, on the other hand, where hundreds of languages are spoken, and which has no fewer than four vehicular languages, will continue to need French for national, official communication, unless it can develop the most widespread of the domestic vehiculars, Lingala, into a medium of national communication. But this is unlikely to happen any time soon. Senegal, where one domestic language has become the mother tongue or the linking language for three-quarters of the population, could in principle replace French with Wolof in many of the domains where the former functions at present. The major obstacle, however, is the reluctance of the other ethnic groups to confirm explicitly the position that Wolof already occupies in fact, to recognize it formally and grant it official status next to or even instead of French.

In this section three similar constellations, this time with English as the colonial inheritance, will be compared with one another and with the francophone constellations presented above: Botswana, Tanzania and Nigeria. Here too, the question is how the configuration of domestic languages, homogeneous or fragmented, shapes the position of the former colonial language, English.

6.3.1 Botswana

The first case in this second series, Botswana, represents the English-centred counterpart to francophone Rwanda. In Botswana, at least 80 per cent of the Batswana speak Tswana as their mother tongue and practically all others have learned it at a later age (about 100,000 people are native speakers of a rather different Bantu language, Ikalanga).[60] In this respect, the country resembles Lesotho and Swaziland, two former 'homelands' created by the South African Apartheid regime where respectively Sotho (or Sutu) and Swazi are the predominant languages. Tswana and Sotho are very similar, and often grouped together in the Sutu language group.[61] Both belong to the wider Bantu family of languages, as does the language of Swaziland, which is usually assigned to the Nguni group of South African languages with Xhosa, Ndebele and Zulu.

The predominance of a single language in Swaziland and Lesotho owes much to design on the part of the Apartheid regime, which wanted to promote separate, homogeneous 'homelands', where urban blacks were forced to have their domicile and which were meant to solidify the lines of ethnic division. Botswana, however, was a British protectorate which achieved independence in 1966. Its large territory (as big as France) borders on the Kalahari desert. In past centuries the area had been gradually colonized by Bantu pastoralists who drove out the hunting and gathering Khoisan peoples, better known in Europe as the legendary 'Bushmen' and 'Hottentots'.

The Khoi and San languages have well-nigh disappeared; only a few pockets remain. In northern Botswana some hunting and gathering peoples survive to this day.[62] In the first half of the nineteenth century Boers began to settle in the area, during a period of great upheaval, invasion and migration. The British tried to halt the influx of Afrikaners and established a protectorate. British civil servants ruled the country and English became the language of administration. After independence, it was designated as the 'official language', next to Tswana as the 'national language'. In fact, for a long time, even in parliament only English was used (although almost all members speak Setswana as their first language).[63]

As an independent country Botswana has steered its own course in politics, with some support from Western powers. All the while, the country remained economically dependent on South Africa, if only because it is landlocked and needs South African transport routes. Shortly after independence, diamonds were discovered and as a result the new capital, Gaborone, became something of a 'boomtown', home to more than 10 per cent of the total population.

Given the 'unimodal'[64] character of these countries, in theory, they could do without any foreign language for purposes of domestic communication. But in Botswana, as in Lesotho and Swaziland, English prevailed as the official language. In the case of the homelands this is adequately explained by their artificial and contrived character, as creations of Apartheid. They were stunted from the outset, never meant to function as viable and autonomous political entities. Botswana, however, did develop into a rather vivid democracy. In fact, politicians increasingly find it expedient to speak Tswana in parliament and in the House of Chiefs. Yet practically all printed matter is in English (except for some Bible tracts, booklets on traffic regulations and textbooks for the first classes of elementary school).

As in Rwanda, the domestic language, Tswana in this case, is spoken in adjacent territories, neighbouring Bophuthatswana (another South African artefact) and Lesotho. Yet this does not seem to add to the momentum of language planning. Apparently, the political systems are too separate to combine forces in this respect. In Botswana, too, the political and entrepreneurial elites were schooled from early on in the former colonial language. They exploited their skills to maintain an effective monopoly on jobs in the civil service and international business. The 'mystique' and 'chic' of English in these English-centred societies is no less than that of French in francophone constellations. But when it comes to the communication potential, the Q-value for Tswana approaches one, while English scores much less.[65] Hence, the predominance of English is an anomaly that can only be explained by the low level of formal education, which has kept English exclusive. It is a fair but paradoxical guess that as education spreads and English skills become more common, its monopolistic advantages will be eroded and Tswana will be used more frequently and in more domains of society, while English may increasingly be reserved for international communication, popular entertainment, advanced science and technology.

6.3.2   Tanzania

Tanzania is one of the few countries in Africa that have adopted an African language as their national medium, and that have spread the language among the vast majority of their citizens.[66] Today Swahili is spoken by 95 per cent of Tanzanians,[67] is also common in Kenya, and is widely spoken as a trade language in eastern Congo/Zaire, Rwanda, Burundi and northern Uganda.

More than one hundred languages are spoken in Tanzania, but none of them by more than a tiny minority. The language with the greatest share of mother-tongue speakers, Sukuma, is spoken by a mere 20 per cent of the population. On the coast, Arabic is widely spoken. About one in six Tanzanians speaks English, a proportion that has remained constant for some time.

The Swahili as an ethnic group inhabit the coastal area and some islands in the Indian Ocean. Swahili is hardly associated with *the* Swahili. Notwithstanding this dissociation, or rather precisely because of it, Swahili could become the well-nigh universal language of Tanzania. It has replaced English in elementary schools and in part at the secondary level; it has driven out all native tongues that were once current in the urban areas. After independence (in 1961) and the merger of Tanganyika and Zanzibar (in 1964), Swahili was the mother tongue of only 10 per cent of Tanzanians. Since then, it has expanded to 95 per cent. At present, it is used by almost all Tanzanians in practically every domain outside the home. All other domestic languages have remained strictly local and ethnic in scope. Swahili prevails in all domains of public communication, in parliament and in business, in churches and mosques, and even in the major part of radio and television broadcasts. English remains reserved for high science and technology, for the high courts of justice and for all international contacts.[68] In some domains the two languages continue to be used side by side, in a somewhat precarious coexistence. English and Swahili remain rivals and the vicissitudes of national politics have their impact on the chances of one or the other as the medium of national communication.

Tanzania is a three-tiered language constellation. First of all, there are the domestic vernacular languages, in a peripheral position, used almost exclusively in oral communication at the local or regional level. Second, there is Swahili, the lingua franca that links the speakers of all these mother tongues, like a planet surrounded by so many moons. Finally, there is a world language, *the* world language:

hypercentral English, which connects Tanzania with the continental and global language constellations and fulfils a number of 'high' functions that are mostly complementary to and quite often in competition with those of Swahili. It is especially in the domain of education that Swahili has rivals on both flanks: English in the more advanced reaches and the vernaculars in the lower sections of the educational system.

The number of Swahili mother-tongue speakers has also been on the increase for some time, partly due to urban immigration. Where the grandparents still spoke only the local vernacular, the parents learned Swahili as a second language, and the children acquired Swahili only, as their mother tongue. Ngonyani reports a dramatic rise in native speakers of Swahili: among people older than forty-five years only 6 per cent had learned it as their mother tongue, as against 47 per cent of those younger than 18.[69]

For almost two thousand years, some form of Swahili has been the language of trade between the East African interior, the coastal market towns and the harbours on the Arabian and Indian shores. The traders from the Middle East brought Islam and Swahili became the language of conversion (another parallel with Malay). Once the Christian missionaries arrived, they too used the language to spread their faith.

Once the area came under German colonial rule in 1885, the regime recruited its clerks mostly from the coastal zone, that is among Swahili speakers. The German officials, on their part, prepared for their mission by learning Swahili. After World War I, the British took over the German possessions in East Africa, known as Tanganyika; they adopted the dialect of Zanzibar as the standard version of Swahili.[70] The British administration continued the German policy of favouring Swahili as the lingua franca of the colony. Only after 1945 did the colonial regime begin to promote English and the other vernaculars, most probably, one suspects, in order to stymie the nationalist movement, which from the start had relied on Swahili.

On the rebound, Swahili gained speakers in all ranks and corners of society. After independence, it was Swahili, indigenous and widely shared, that became the very symbol of National Unity, Self-sufficiency and *Ujamaa*[71] – the ubiquitous slogans proclaimed by the great leader of the struggle for independence, Julius Nyerere.[72] And indeed, Swahili incorporated all these ideals at once. Moreover, during the first years of independence an egalitarian policy greatly broadened the opportunities for education and employment, reaching masses of Africans who until then had been completely excluded from access to schools and skilled jobs. It was no longer English but Swahili that opened these doors of opportunity. Of course, this contributed much to the popularity of the language.[73] The political leaders, on their part, Nyerere in the first place, insisted on the 'non-ethnicity' of Swahili and played down its origins in the coastal region or its traditional links to Arabic and Islam. Academic linguists obligingly attributed virtues to Swahili that were mostly ideological fabrications, meant to stress the profound African roots of the language. Swahili is indeed deeply rooted in Tanzania and beyond. It is the language of the streets, of everyday speech and casual conversation, constantly renewed and enriched by the inventions of its informal users: thus a street pedlar is grandly called a 'businessman', who risks ending the day as one of the 'walalahoi' – who go to bed on an empty stomach.[74]

As matters stand, Swahili must still compete with English when it comes to prestigious registers and long-distance connections. That is why English is still very much in demand.[75] In fact, sometimes English, at other times Swahili, is the language of choice for the intermediate domains according to the 'movements of the pendulum'.[76]

A brief excursion to Tanzania's northern neighbours, Kenya and Uganda, will help explain why in Tanzania Swahili could become the language of almost everyone in almost all domains, while it occupies only a secondary position in the adjacent countries, where it is nevertheless well dispersed.[77]

In Kenya, from the outset, large ethnic groups resisted the spread of Swahili. It is true that among the most numerous ethnic group, the Kikuyu, forceful voices did speak up in defence of Swahili as the national language, among them the president, Jomo Kenyatta himself, and the famous author Ngugi wa Thiong'o. But the majority of Kikuyus resisted the introduction of Swahili, just as the other large language groups did, for fear that it would reduce their own language to second-class status. In this respect they resembled the Hindus more than the Javanese. English continued to occupy the central position, remained the official language and usurped all high-prestige functions, while the domestic languages of Kenya remained in an inferior position. Something similar occurred in Uganda, where the Baganda in the south opposed the introduction of Swahili as the lingua franca or official language.[78] Of old, Swahili had been the language of the army and the colonial police, recruited in large part in the north. As a consequence, it was despised as the language of the colonial oppressors, strongly identified with the northern peoples. The tyrannical regime of Idi Amin did much to strengthen these negative associations.

Even this quick look at Tanzania's neighbours helps to identify two aspects of the constellation that favour the adoption of a domestic national language: the language should not be identified too closely with any particular group in the country, and there should be no large, influential language groups, jealous of the privileges that another language might obtain. And, it should be added, a powerful and determined nationalist movement must put its full weight behind the promotion of the new national language. The Tanzanian situation satisfied all three conditions.

In Senegal, the other country in the comparison where a large majority speaks a domestic language (Wolof), the Fulani and the Serer were numerous enough to block the adoption of Wolof, which, moreover, was closely identified with the Wolof people. Maybe also for that reason, the nationalist movement never flaunted Wolof as the language of a new, independent Senegal.

The other comparison is, of course, with Indonesia, where the nationalist movement at independence equally succeeded in transforming a popular bazaar language of relatively low prestige, only loosely associated with an ethnic group and spoken by a small minority, into the official, national language of the country, spoken by almost everyone in almost every situation. Between Tanzania and Indonesia there is, however, one major difference: in Indonesia the largest language group, the Javanese, had to abandon any claims to linguistic hegemony. Malay became for Indonesia (and South-East Asia) what Swahili became for Tanzania (and East Africa).

The rise of an indigenous national language requires the presence of a low-prestige, non-ethnic vernacular, the absence of a major language group that might oppose it, and a strong nationalist movement. Indonesia and Tanzania differ in the second respect (although the Javanese never put up much resistance), but both adopted a domestic language as their national medium. In Kenya major ethnic groups did resist the adoption of Swahili and it never gained the currency it acquired in Tanzania. A strong nationalist movement and weak opposition from ethnic groups thus greatly facilitate the rise of a domestic national language.

6.3.3 Nigeria

Nigeria is the most populous country of Africa, fragmented into hundreds of ethnic groups who speak some four hundred languages, distinct but for the most part rather closely related.[79] As in the Congo/Zaire, this constellation is dominated by a small number of very large language groups: the north is dominated by Hausa, a language that has spread quite widely beyond Nigeria as a lingua franca. Igbo (or Ibo) is the language most frequently spoken in the southeast. Yoruba predominates in the southwest. But in contrast to the Congolese constellation, the great languages of Nigeria are associated very closely with ethnic groups, whereas except for Kiluba, the widespread vehiculars of Congo/Zaire have no such ties. Hence, English holds its ground in Nigeria, not only as a language of administration and higher education, but also as a medium that is 'neutral' with respect to ethnic groups and therefore acceptable to all as a vehicular language. Nevertheless, there exists in Nigeria another vehicular language, spoken almost everywhere, nowhere held in much esteem, but yet one that could very well serve as the national lingua franca one day: Nigerian pidgin.

In the 1940s English became the official language of Nigeria. After 1947 it shared this status in the north with Hausa. Only in 1979 were Igbo and Yoruba, each in its region, also elevated to 'co-official' status, and duly admitted in the national assembly. However, for lack of interpreters, a large part of the representatives still find themselves excluded from parliamentary debate, which continues to be held in English only: 'Sadly, the initiative remained a dead letter.' (The very constitution that formally established the equal status of the four languages of Nigeria was itself never translated into the co-official languages.[80]) Yet there were some legislative attempts to curb English: schoolchildren were increasingly taught in Hausa, Igbo or Yoruba, according to the region, and a second co-official language was made a compulsory subject, while English could only be taught from the fourth year on. Nevertheless, English continued to monopolize the more prestigious domains, in the administration and the courts of law, in the universities, in commerce and in industry.

The constitution of 1989 contained roughly the same language regulations as that of 1979. Yet, when it came up for the vote, the representatives of groups whose languages had not gained formal recognition now demonstrated by staging a walkout.[81] In the preceding two decades, the number of constituent states had been increased so as to form more homogeneous ethnic entities. In each state the language of the most numerous group was recognized as the official language. Actually, about a dozen of these 'network' languages were 'certified', as the expression went.[82] Nigeria followed a programme quite similar to that of India, bestowing official status upon a dozen or more languages and designating three indigenous languages (rather than just one, Hindi) as 'co-official' with English. But once again, these lofty linguistic intentions were never realized. The language groups that found themselves excluded insisted on also being listed among the 'co-official' languages, and in so doing precipitated the fiasco of the new policy. Every attempt to strengthen the position of the three large languages mentioned in the constitution only provoked new claims in favour of the languages that so far had been excluded. As the paralysis continued, English remained in fact the only functioning official language. If, on the other hand, a great number or even all of the languages of Nigeria had been accepted as co-official languages, English, as the one common denominator for the vast majority of representatives and officials, would have remained the only working language just the same. The more languages are accepted, the more English will be used. Very much as in India, the representatives of the smaller language groups in daily practice tacitly favoured English, just to prevent the three co-official languages from gaining any further ground.[83] The Nigerian parliamentarians played their game as accomplished rational-choice theorists.

In its entirety the constellation displays an apparently insuperable paralysis, brought about by the mutual jealousies between the large language groups, made even worse by the fears and ambitions of the smaller groups. Once again, also, it turns out that even when the authorities are finally converted to mother-tongue instruction, the parents oppose it because they want their children to be taught in English. In Nigeria, too, mixed couples often use English at home. Even when they do share a native language, they tend to teach their children English from the start, since that is considered 'chic' and helpful in improving the child's achievements in school. While the rate of school attendance increased seventeenfold between 1947 and 1987, the number of premature school leavers undid most of these gains. As a result, the percentage of Nigerians competent in English grew from 10 per cent to 20 per cent at most during the same forty years.

English may be held in great esteem in Nigeria, but its use remains mostly limited to written communications and formal encounters, and to contacts between people speaking different native languages. If the parties do share a domestic language, they will quickly resort to it in their more personal exchanges, where English would be considered aloof and presumptuous. Or, as the saying goes, with only slight variations, in so many tropical countries: 'English is the language for the airco, the native tongue is for the verandah.'

Hence, in Nigeria also, English remains the language of the elite. The laws that were adopted to promote the national languages embody –

in the words of Ayo Bamgbose – 'a policy conceived by the elite to benefit the masses'. And Bamgbose explains its failure as a consequence of the colonial past and the prohibitive costs of educational reform. But, he argues, the real reason for the fiasco is that the elites have an interest in announcing a policy that might benefit the great majority of Nigerians, but do not stand to gain from implementing it also.[84]

More than ten years ago, Ike Ndolo proposed introducing Nigerian Pidgin as the national language.[85] From his survey of local observers, Ndolo concluded that across the entire territory some 60 per cent of the population spoke Pidgin. It is used in popular radio programmes and in the most widely watched soap series on TV, and it is entirely void of specific ethnic connotations and would therefore not provoke the resistance that the national languages are bound to arouse. English, argues Ndolo, may well be the language of the law, but the laws are applied in Pidgin, in the street by the police, at the desk by the officials, in prisons by the guards and even in court by lawyers and bailiffs. What counts even more is that Pidgin does not provoke the shy hesitations in uneducated Nigerians that English does. On the contrary, the language is spoken everywhere, spontaneously, without embarrassment, with ease and confidence, also by educated Nigerians who prefer it to English in informal and homely encounters. F. Niyi Akinnaso, for his part, concludes: 'While English continues to perform "high" functions, pidgin has almost taken over the role of lingua franca in non-formal domains. Thus, it has become the most popular medium of intergroup communication in various heterogeneous communities throughout the country.'[86]

Apparently unaware of Ndolo's position, James Oladejo has proposed keeping English as the language of higher education and international communication and introducing Pidgin in all other domains of communication across Nigeria.[87] According to a survey he quotes, three-quarters of all respondents in 1989 opposed the replacement of English by a domestic language as the official medium. As to Pidgin, his data confirm that regional varieties are still mutually intelligible, that the language is not associated with specific ethnic groups or religions and that it is widely known (by at least 30 per cent, according to his sources).[88]

But the great weakness in all this strength is precisely the lack of prestige and pedigree: 'While everybody likes to use it to his own advantage, no one wants to be associated with its humble state.'[89] In fact, one may detect a certain sentimentalism – which I share – in this advocacy of Pidgin, a predilection for the folksy, the earthy, the spontaneous, and also a rather illusory expectation that social barriers and impediments will disappear once the language of the people is elevated to national and official status: the proponents argue as if differences now considered irrelevant would not then fuel disputes, as if a social embarrassment presently absent would not make itself felt as soon as more formal encounters had to be managed in the popular language. And yet there are the contemporary examples of Swahili and Malay and, in a much longer time perspective, the precedents of the vulgates such as Italian, French or Hindi which became folk languages and means of long-distance communication, then developed into vernaculars, and finally were elevated to official and national status. Such transformations, it appears, are brought about in the course of a few generations by writers first and rulers next, and above all, by the legions of talkative and creative users of the language.

This survey of six countries in Sub-Saharan Africa has first of all revealed how great are the impediments to the introduction of a domestic language for national communication in these societies. In fact, in all six of them a domestic vehicular language that could serve on a country-wide basis is available, current sometimes among a sizeable minority, such as the Congolese lingua francas or Nigerian pidgin, sometimes spoken by a large majority as in the case of Wolof in Senegal, or even by the entire population, as in Botswana or Rwanda. Yet only in Tanzania does a domestic language, Swahili, effectively function as the national language. The different language policies of the former colonizers do not make much difference. Most important is the opposition of an important language group to the introduction of another idiom as the national medium: 'language jealousy'. In the meantime the status quo continues and the former colonial language prevails, because it serves the interests of the administrative elites. The language is not freely accessible, since it requires formal schooling to master the written version. Education is not available for an important part of the population for lack of funds. The resulting group monopoly on the ex-colonial language safeguards the elite's exclusive hold on the better positions in the labour market. New cohorts of students prefer to learn the ex-colonial language, since they expect it to provide them with access to the most attractive jobs. This again strengthens the hegemony of the former colonial language.

South Africa: The survival of the old language regime

The road to English is paved with good intentions. So many countries adopt a liberal constitution and a pluralistic language policy regime, meant to strengthen the position of indigenous and immigrant languages, but in almost all of them, these policies only strengthen the position of English or another ex-colonial language: where previously so many languages were recognized, English comes to stand out as the one, indispensable linking language. This occurred in India and Nigeria, to mention just two examples which have been discussed earlier. The same is bound to happen in post-Apartheid South Africa. There too, and even more than elsewhere, language politics was always a politics of identity. Once again, a policy ostensibly aimed at promoting a diversity of languages will actually further the hegemony of English. That is the recurrent paradox of contemporary language politics: the more languages, the more English.

The more a proliferation of languages is encouraged for the sake of regional, ethnic or immigrant rights, as a move against 'language imperialism', 'linguicism' or the 'hegemony of English', the less of a chance the few viable alternatives stand in the competition with English. South Africa in the transition from the Apartheid era to a multiracial democracy represents a laboratory case of this perversion of well-intentioned policies into the opposite results.

South Africa was the last former colony to be liberated from a postcolonial settler regime. Apartheid was a large-scale experiment with the prolongation of colonialism after the severance of ties with the mother country. To complicate matters, the majority of white colonists were not of British but of Dutch origin. These Afrikaners found their common identity largely through a shared religion and a common language. It was a religiously pursued language policy that stood at the centre of the cultural politics of Apartheid.

7.1   The language regime under Apartheid

During the Apartheid era, South Africa was officially a bilingual society: English, the language of the British settlers, coexisted with Afrikaans, which evolved from the language that the Boers had brought from the Netherlands. The two initially had a roughly equal number of speakers and they were equal before the law. This in itself was an accomplishment on the part of the Boers, due to their dogged insistence on their language rights, an uphill struggle all along. But if Afrikaans after the demise of Apartheid is now losing its paramount position in the competition with English, this does not at all benefit the other languages of the land.

Next to English and Afrikaans, there are the many indigenous languages of South Africa. Most of them can be grouped under the broad denominator of 'Bantu languages', a subcategory of the widely dispersed Niger–Congo language family. Two other language groups, Khoikhoi and San, sometimes combined under one heading as 'Khoisan', were mostly spoken by surviving hunter gatherers and pastoral nomads. These are the original 'click' languages. While most of the few remaining Khoi have abandoned their mother tongues, these still survive through their influence on other languages.[1] Thus Khoisan 'click' sounds may have entered Xhosa and other Bantu languages in communities which practise *hlonipa* or 'syllabic avoidance': married women are compelled to avoid and replace the syllables that occur in the names of their husband's relatives: instead of these forbidden sounds they used clicks, which their children may have adopted next.[2] Even before the white settlers began to penetrate the interior from their Cape Town base, Zulu and Xhosa conquerors had made inroads into the territory of the Khoi and San peoples. The Khoisan were gradually ousted from the great plains into more arid, less fertile areas in the north.

In the course of the nineteenth century, the influx of white settlers into the Cape increased. Afrikaner explorers ventured ever further into the interior, into areas where they would be beyond the reach of the British colonial authorities. While the British immigrants mostly remained in the cities, the Boers moved on in search of land, edging into Xhosa and Zulu territory, and carving out their own autonomous zones in a series of bloody clashes with the original inhabitants.[3] Continually, they defended their new homesteads against raiding parties and coerced the natives to work as farmhands on the Afrikaner holdings.

Throughout, it was the Boers' religion – staunch Calvinism of the Dutch Reformed brand – that helped to keep their community together, each family on its own isolated homestead. The Netherlandish of the 'Staten' Bible translation (1637) provided them with a liturgical language and spawned a series of closely related dialects that evolved into 'Afrikaans'. The Malay slaves of the Cape added much to the vocabulary. Even today there exists a Cape Afrikaans, spoken by their descendants, the 'bruinmense' (literally 'brown people', that is, 'coloured'), as they were called during the Apartheid era. Even after the British rulers finally subdued the breakaway Afrikaners of Transvaal and the Orange Free State in the second Boer War (1899–1902), the Boers retained a considerable level of autonomy over their territories. During the war years, Afrikaans had become the hallmark of Afrikaner identity. No longer considered a folksy derivative of Dutch, Afrikaans now needed all the trappings of a modern, national language. Linguists wrote dictionaries and grammars, harmonized spelling and developed a standard version. The official Bible translation appeared in 1925.[4] Afrikaans became the 'official' language of the Boer provinces and in 1925 was finally adopted – side by side with English – as the co-official language of the national government.

The Afrikaner movement created a language completely equipped for the needs of a modern political dictatorship and a contemporary free market economy. Contemporary white Afrikaans is a highly codified language with a broad range of varieties and registers. It is equipped with all necessary linguistic resources, studied in academic departments and much enriched by a surprisingly vivid literature. Its vocabulary is continually expanded by new technological, scientific and administrative terms (which, however, usually enter the language through English as the 'source' language).[5] Afrikaans retains some features of seventeenth-century Dutch, such as the double negation: 'moe nie kijk nie [do not look not]'.[6] It has a simplified verb structure and lacks the twofold gender of Dutch. By the 1920s European Dutch had been abandoned as the standard. Written Afrikaans began to conform more closely to the spoken versions, while moving away from the language of the Low Countries. The break with Dutch as the 'holosystemic' language[7] also caused the written version of Afrikaans to drift further away from Dutch, and after World War II readers in the Netherlands increasingly read Afrikaans novels in Dutch translation.[8] Afrikaans students, on their part, no longer used Dutch textbooks but texts in Afrikaans. Conversely, full intelligibility was maintained all the while between British and South African English, both in writing and in speech, and this was in turn reinforced because South Africans continued to read unmodified American and British textbooks and novels.

The Boers assiduously cultivated Afrikaans for themselves, but also for others: during the Apartheid years, the government made a massive effort to impose it as the compulsory language of instruction for Africans.[9] This proved a tragic failure: the policy provoked mass protests among black secondary school students, which came to a head with the demonstrations of 1976. During one of the largest protest gatherings, in the Soweto township near Johannesburg, the police fired into a crowd of students, killing 150 of them. This ended whatever support there may have been among blacks for Afrikaans as a language of education.[10] Yet even today, the majority of people who speak Afrikaans as a second language are not of European stock: apart from the 'coloured' citizens, they are mostly black students who have learned it in school, or black farmhands who have picked it up on the job.[11] But these black Afrikaans speakers may be a dwindling group, as the language does not hold much attraction beyond the Afrikaner community and must now compete with English everywhere: 'To speak Afrikaans is to associate yourself with the oppressive regime and there is little economic advantage in knowing Afrikaans.'[12]

After their languages had gone separate ways, Apartheid caused a second rupture between the Netherlanders and the Afrikaners, this time of a politico-religious nature. After much soul-searching and debate, the Dutch Reformed Church condemned the policy of racial separation and finally broke off all relations with the South African 'kinfolk'. This severed the last remaining ties of Afrikaans with a closely cognate language and may well have weakened its position vis-à-vis English even further. As Afrikaans was the language of a religiously legitimated racist ideology, linguistic purism could come to full fruition.[13]

The emergence of Afrikaans as a separate language is unique in the history of Western expansion: Latin American Spanish, Brazilian

Portuguese, Canadian French or the numerous versions of (ex-)colonial English have not departed much from their metropolitan origins, not, that is, in the versions spoken by the 'European' or 'white' descendants of the colonizers.[14] Afrikaans is the only Afro-European language to achieve a distinct, national and official status. Indeed, all over the world creoles and pidgins emerged in the colonies, but not one of them was adopted by the colonial ruling strata, or by their postcolonial successors. And everywhere the settlers and their descendants maintained full intelligibility with the variety spoken in their mother country, except for the Afrikaners in South Africa.

To this day, however, the great majority of South Africans speak indigenous languages. Most of these belong to the 'eastern branch of the Niger–Congo family of languages'.[15] They are loosely designated as 'Bantu languages', a term that became tarred by the Apartheid brush and covers both the South African Nguni and the Sutu groups as well as languages as remote as East African Kikuyu and Swahili. In the north, many of the Khoikhoi and San languages disappeared as their speakers were massacred or enslaved and the survivors finally settled in the cities (mostly Cape Town).[16]

Under Apartheid, the 'native' tongues were not accorded much importance. They occupied an inferior position, except in the 'homelands', the quasi-autonomous enclaves that in the grand design of Apartheid were to become the domicile of the various African peoples. Since all black Africans would have their home in one of the homelands, it followed that they were only guests in the rest of South Africa, where they were required to carry a 'pass' and could be deported whenever they were no longer needed as miners, factory workers, domestic servants or farmhands. There, in their 'homelands', they were encouraged to speak their original languages, which even served as the medium of instruction at the elementary level. The Apartheid regime on the one hand grouped a dozen black African languages together under the one blanket heading 'Bantu' (excepting only the Khoisan group), with implicit connotations of inferiority, backwardness and primitivism, while on the other hand it strongly stressed the differences between the Bantu languages, and exaggerated their mutual unintelligibility.[17] This policy helped to harden the fluid transitions between the various indigenous languages and to contaminate them all with tribalist and racist connotations. Hence, for many South African blacks a return to the indigenous languages smacks of exclusion from mainstream society and of a fragmentation into so many tribes. Thus Apartheid succeeded in tainting Afrikaans and the indigenous languages at the same time: only English – much despised as it may have been by the Boer ideologues – came through unsullied.

The so-called 'Bantu languages' were relegated to second-class status, compulsorily taught in the 'homelands', but never meant to function in the more advanced sections of the economy and the more prestigious domains of society.[18] Janks quotes a nationalist politician in the 1950s: 'we should so conduct our schools that the native who attends those schools will know that to a great extent he must be the labourer in the country.'[19]

In order to grasp the Southern African language constellation it is necessary to deconstruct most of the distinctions that Apartheid linguists developed and to recognize the essentially 'invented' nature of many of these African languages. Throughout the colonial era English, Portuguese, Dutch and German missionaries, Catholics as well as Protestants, had been busy learning the indigenous African languages they encountered on their journeys. The most diligent and devoted among them devised an alphabet and an orthography, composed a lexicon and a grammar for the version of the language that their local informants presented to them. Usually they would start out with a rendition of the Lord's Prayer in the native tongue, and as they stayed on and became more proficient they might try their hand at the major books of the Bible. In so doing, they not only fixed a particular dialect (or their informants' version of it) but also helped to differentiate it from the nearest idiom.[20] A post-Apartheid advisory commission wrote:

> the missionaries managed to codify the African languages and to develop a Christian religious terminology and register. They managed to group the African community into different groups that were marked by 'different' languages and frequently by a different Christian Church. Although they produced orthographies and wrote texts in these orthographies they often did not manage to standardize the languages so that different orthographies were used even in the same community. This pattern was repeated in many African countries and was quite clear in South Africa.[21]

From the beginning of the twentieth century attempts were made to bring some unity to this bewildering variety of spelling methods and grammars, but the confusion continued.

7.2 Language policy after Apartheid

In many senses of the word, South African languages are 'invented traditions' not entirely unlike most European languages, except that the fabrication is much more recent and much less thorough and, except for Afrikaans, the resulting idioms never had a state to promulgate and support them.[22] The insistence on the official recognition of the regional indigenous languages owes much to educated and urbanized elites: 'it is precisely in the social turbulence of urban life that linguistic and cultural loss is registered, and conservative (or conservation) movements arise'.[23] The revival, maintenance and development of one or another indigenous language becomes the concern of educated city dwellers, teachers, lawyers, clergy. Their particular group language and culture allow them to distinguish themselves from their peers who belong to other language groups, and thus maintain a distinct identity in the surrounding urban 'mass' society; it also serves to tighten the bonds with their kinfolk in the village and, even at a distance, assume a position of cultural leadership among them. In many respects, this is an instance of what Anton Blok has discussed under a heading borrowed from Freud: 'the narcissism of minor differences'.[24]

The African National Congress was preoccupied most of all with maintaining unity within the ranks, and realized that the choice of a 'Bantu' language would almost inevitably provoke a quarrel about the choice of one among so many candidates. It therefore preferred to continue the use of English, which also stood for solidarity with other liberation movements in Africa and elsewhere, and for a connection with the white anti-Apartheid movement which spoke English inside and outside South Africa. The Apartheid regime, with its policy of general exclusion and a fragmentation of the black population in separate homelands, exploited the dialectics of black separation and tribal division that the concept of 'Bantu' implied.

'Language development became directly linked to political ideology': from the late 1950s on it became increasingly associated with the promotion of separate ethnic groups.[25] 'The linguistic balkanisation of South Africa was complete.'[26]

Some linguists in the anti-Apartheid movement have defended an approach that might help to overcome this proliferation of African languages. They proposed grouping the seven major forms of 'Bantu' speech in South Africa into two groups of languages that among themselves are quite similar and mutually intelligible: Nguni on the one hand, Sutu on the other. Nguni comprises the two largest black South African languages, Zulu and Xhosa, and also Ndebele and Swazi. Sutu combines Sotho, Pede and Tswana. Each category would have to be harmonized and standardized into a coherent and consistent language. The separate forms of speech in each group would remain acceptable as regional variations, for everyday, mostly oral use. The recombined languages, Sutu and Nguni, could then serve for school books at the primary and secondary school level, not demanding too much adaptation on the part of the pupils. The languages could be adopted for official purposes, for example in regional courts and parliaments, or for contacts with the bureaucracy, and as the idiom of the printed and broadcast media. Since there would be only two languages, instead of seven, they might be economically viable and sufficiently attractive to parents and pupils as a medium of instruction in the schools. Thus, the lip service that African politics pays to the many hapless native languages could be turned into true support for the two viable, recombined languages, Nguni and Sutu.

It is very hard for an outsider to judge the mutual intelligibility of the languages in each group. (And this intercomprehensibility is not an objective characteristic of any language pair, but depends on the skills and the willingness of the speakers, and the structure of the situation.) There is some evidence that the various African languages mix easily, as long as their official status is not at stake and hence no issues of group prestige intrude. In South Africa, pidgins and creoles spring up, popular speech forms that combine elements from various Nguni languages, or, as in Johannesburg, bring together lexical and morphological elements of both Nguni and Sutu languages. In popular entertainment (songs and TV comedies) these mixtures of indigenous languages are very popular, vivid and vital. But these are idioms of the street, hardly ever written down, used spontaneously and unselfconsciously for informal and everyday functions. The moment anyone proposed adopting these emerging languages as media of instruction or official business, a howl of protest would resound: the authentic forms of the indigenous language, the speech of the ancestors, the soul of the common heritage must be preserved, or so the cultural leaders would proclaim – in English – while the common folk would continue to use whatever dialect or pidgin they felt most familiar with or suited them best.

Neville Alexander, who became chairman of the transitional government's advisory board for language matters, strongly supported the solution of combining the Bantu languages into two groups, Nguni and Sutu. Kwesi Prah has defended the same proposal from a Pan-Africanist perspective.[27] Across the board, expert linguistic opinion seems to support the feasibility of the proposal. But apparently there is little sympathy for the idea either in government circles or at the grass-roots level, where other priorities prevail. Partly, this is a legacy of the Apartheid era, when these languages were rendered as essentially distinct. But our survey of language constellations in Africa and Asia has demonstrated that it does not take Apartheid to create jealous group relations and kindle the narcissism of minor linguistic differences. Moreover, parents have little confidence in African languages as career resources, even in a streamlined version. They much prefer English for their children. David Laitin points out that mutual intelligibility is explained more by the need to communicate than by the percentage of shared words or sounds. As a consequence, language policies that were aimed at standardizing a set of dialects into a common language have usually fallen on deaf ears.[28]

As a consequence, English is spreading rapidly; it is now spoken (with varying degrees of competence) by more than half of the population, even though it is the native speech of only 14 per cent.[29]

In 1993, South Africa adopted an entirely new constitution that stands as the very embodiment of enlightenment at the end of the millennium: universal suffrage, meticulous judiciary procedures, the abolition of capital punishment, vigorous guarantees of human rights and freedoms, and so on. Moreover, the Afrikaners' commitment to their language prompted black South Africans, including their representatives in the constitutional commission, to claim their linguistic rights with equal insistence. As a result, eleven 'official' languages were recognized: English and Afrikaans of course, and another nine indigenous languages, all on an equal footing, in principle. But the gap between the constitutional principle and the practice in government and administration remains immense.

Members of Parliament, representing the full variety of the peoples of South Africa, are entitled to use any one of the eleven 'certified' languages. As a matter of fact, every citizen has the right to address the central government in one of these languages. But there is not a chance that the eleven 'official' languages will function as equals.[30] Nevertheless, almost everybody acts as if they will one day. In fact there are no funds available in parliament to translate between English or Afrikaans and each of the nine indigenous languages, let alone to translate equally between each and every one of them.[31] When Members insist on speaking their home language and demand translation, the chair must dispatch an aide to find someone among the housekeeping staff who happens to be competent in that language and in English.[32] When ordinary citizens do indeed stand up for their linguistic rights and approach the authorities in one of the indigenous languages, they are unlikely to get any answer at all.

The constitution of 1993 promised equal status for English, Afrikaans and seven indigenous languages, Xhosa, Zulu, Ndebele and Swazi (the Nguni languages), and Northern Sotho, Pede and Tswana (the Sutu group) and, moreover, two languages from the northeastern area bordering on Zimbabwe were also recognized: Tsonga (rather close to Zimbabwean Shona) and TsiVenda.[33] The Khoisan languages of the indigenous foraging and hunting people of the great Karoo were not adopted as official languages.

In the Bill of Rights, which was adopted as part of the constitution of 1996, all individuals are expressly granted the right to use the language of their choice.[34] The 1996 constitution also provides for the promotion of the Khoi, San and (related) Nama languages, of immigrant languages and even of sign language for the deaf.[35] These formal rights must be considered mostly symbolic and may at best be interpreted as intentions for a distant future.[36] In fact, all the constitutional languages are indeed current in the Republic, but when it comes to their actual status, they occupy vastly different positions.

In terms of communicative potential, or Q-value, there is no doubt that English scores highest, not in terms of its native speakers alone, but because it is the language with the greatest number of second-language speakers. Afrikaans, too, scores quite high on centrality because it is the second language of considerable numbers. The Afrikaner movement had always promoted the language and once in power the Apartheid regime propagated it with all the means at its disposal. This preferential treatment is now held against the language by black Africans who resent its privileges.[37]

In the present constitution, Afrikaans is treated on the same footing as all other official languages. This implies an acute deterioration of its formal position, and it might damage its material position if the privileges and resources that have been promised to the other African languages were actually forthcoming. But, for lack of means, very little is done to promote them. Hence, Afrikaans continues to be a major language of politics, commerce and bureaucracy. Since the abolition of Apartheid, the position of English has been strengthened even more.[38]

7.3 The dynamics of the constellation

The underlying dynamics of the South African language constellation are best rendered by a survey of prevailing Q-values. Gerard Schuring's analysis of the 1991 census data allows us to estimate these values for the major languages. At the time, the census differentiated between South Africa proper and the 'Bantustans' (or 'thuislanden':

'homelands'). It also distinguished between 'urban' and 'rural' dwellers, and between 'whites', 'Asians', 'coloureds' and 'blacks'. The census registers the 'home language' of each respondent and contains some questions on competence in speaking, reading and writing other languages.

Schuring identifies eleven languages as having the greatest number of speakers and being the most significant, not entirely by coincidence the same as those that were later adopted as the 'official languages' of the 1993 constitution. As concerns the languages spoken at home in South Africa, *including the homelands* (and therefore coterminous with contemporary South Africa), Zulu comes first with 22 per cent, followed by Xhosa with 17 per cent, Afrikaans with 15 per cent, Northern Sotho with almost 10 per cent, English with 9 per cent and Tswana with 8.5 per cent (Southern Sotho scores 6.7 per cent, Tsonga 4.3 per cent, Swazi 2.5 per cent, Venda 2.2 per cent and Ndebele 1.5 per cent).[39]

Schuring's data allow us to estimate the Q-value for English and Afrikaans, since he quotes census data on the *'praatkennis'* (speaking knowledge) of these two languages and 'any African language', broken down for the different 'races' of the Apartheid era. Unfortunately, these figures pertain to South Africa without the homelands. However, on the basis of the figures as presented, the distribution of English, Afrikaans and African language skills in 'pan-South Africa' (that is, including the homelands) can be reconstructed.[40]

The population of South Africa in 1991 was 38.5 million (7.6 million of these lived in the homelands). There were 30 million speakers of an African language, about a third of whom also spoke English or Afrikaans or both.[41] The great majority of the remaining 8.5 million people spoke both English and Afrikaans.

When it comes to estimating the Q-values for the separate African languages, the attempt is frustrated by the lack of data on respondents who speak an African language as a 'second' language. Not only are census data lacking, but the very idea of distinct 'languages' is problematical. Among others, Neville Alexander and also Kwesi Prah proposed grouping together Zulu, Xhosa, Swazi and Ndebele as mutually intelligible versions of a single language: Nguni. According to the 1991 data, Nguni was spoken by 43 per cent of the population of South Africa (including the homelands). Equally, Northern and Southern Sotho may be grouped with Tswana in a single language, Sutu. Versions of Sutu are spoken by 25 per cent of the pan-South African population. Schuring confirms that the Nguni languages are 'usually' mutually intelligible, and so are the Sutu languages. Speakers of Tsonga and Venda, however, cannot understand one another, nor are they intelligible for those who speak Nguni or

Sutu.[42] The most realistic option, therefore, seems to be to analyse the four-language constellation of English, Afrikaans, Nguni and Sutu (table 7.1).

In 1991, just before the collapse of Apartheid, English (0.34) had a slight edge over Afrikaans (0.30). Both obtained higher Q-values than Nguni or Sutu, although Nguni speakers were the most numerous. The European languages, however, had a greater number of multilingual speakers. Sutu speakers preferred English over Afrikaans as a second language, Nguni speakers were indifferent between the two, but both Nguni and Sutu speakers ranked a repertoire with English or Afrikaans higher than one with an African second language. This alone may have been a brake on Africans learning an African language.

When all nine indigenous languages of the constitution are entered each on its own, none obtains a significant Q-value, and none is likely to entice language students. The present combination into two

Table 7.1   South Africa around 1991 (speakers in millions)

Native language	Sole or second language				Third language	Total
	AK	EN	NG	SU	LANG+ AFK&ENG	
AK	1	8	0	0	–	9
EN	0	1	0	0	–	1
NG	2	3	11	1	3	20
SU	1	1	0	7	2	11
Q_i:						41
AK	0.316	0.511	0.743	0.544	–	
EN	0.511	0.355	0.743	0.596	–	
NG	0.743	0.743	0.209	0.468	0.829	
SU	0.544	0.596	0.468	0.070	0.732	
Greenberg's A	0.452					

AK = Afrikaans; EN = English; NG = Nguni; SU = Sutu.
A dash – = Not applicable.

The rows show the native speakers of a language: speakers of that language only, and those who also speak a second (and third) language, as indicated by the column heading. The total number of speakers of a language may be found by adding to the row total of native speakers the entries in the corresponding column for foreign speakers of that language (avoiding counting monolingual speakers twice).

The prevalence p_i of a repertoire ρ_i is found by adding the entries in the columns and rows for the language(s) in ρ_i (while avoiding double counts) and dividing by N^s, the number of all speakers. The centrality c_i of a repertoire ρ_i is calculated by adding the entries for all *multilingual* repertoires that have a language in common with ρ_i and dividing by the total of multilingual speakers M^s.

In this procedure, the matrix for Q has been folded along the diagonal: in calculating p_i, c_i and Q_i, the numbers for, say, Afrikaans speakers who have learned Sutu have been added to the number of Sutu speakers who acquired Afrikaans, and vice versa. As a result, the entries in the lower left half of the matrix for Q are identical to the corresponding entries in the upper right half.

Figures have been rounded to the nearest million. Entries may therefore not always add up to the corresponding total.

categories makes it plausible that a harmonized and standardized Nguni and Sutu would at least stand a chance of holding their own against the European languages. The Pan-Africanist solution of creating an aggregate Nguni/Sutu language would improve the odds even further: this combination would obtain the highest Q-value by far. But mutual understanding would most probably demand some learning effort.

As matters stand, even the larger separate African languages, Zulu and Xhosa, cannot compete on their own with English or Afrikaans. And although in Johannesburg and other cities Zulu and Xhosa speakers quickly pick up the other language, no attempt is under way to achieve a more formalized version of an amalgamated idiom. Black Africans show a clear preference for English, which has the higher Q-value and is less tainted by memories of Apartheid than Afrikaans. The present analysis suggests that English will slowly but surely get the better of Afrikaans and that no single or combined African language is likely to replace it.

Just as the notion of 'Bantu' languages was introduced by Apartheid linguists to fit a political scheme, the concepts of Nguni and Sutu are proposed by linguists of the post-Apartheid era in order to create viable linguistic entities that might successfully coexist with Afrikaans and English. But there is no political entity that covers the Nguni or the Sutu area, nor is there an ethnic or national movement that might identify with the one or the other. As a result, black language activists tend to fall back upon the language labels that correspond with more familiar ethnic and political divisions: Zulu, Xhosa, Ndebele, Swazi, Pede, Sotho, Tswana and so on. The defence of these separate idioms no doubt strengthens feelings of group identity, but it also weakens the competitive position of each and all of them within the overall constellation, especially vis-à-vis English and Afrikaans.

These considerations are ignored in the discourse on linguicism and language rights: even if a group language is recognized and protected, its speakers may still want to learn and use another language, if only to improve their job opportunities; and outsiders may still not want to learn it, if it does not provide them with rewarding resources. At most, and this is important enough in its own right, legal protection and political recognition may help to persuade the speakers of a language not to abandon it, and to pass it on to their children. But still, growing up in a small language group, no matter what the legal safeguards are, tends to diminish one's educational and employment opportunities. Nor do these vernacular languages necessarily help to challenge the colonial and postcolonial frame of thought. Makoni argues: 'In fact, the exact opposite can happen: settler and missionary ideology can be remorselessly perpetuated under the guise of verna-cularisation.'[43]

In South Africa, as elsewhere, parents (and schoolchildren) sensed this as they opposed education in the regional or ethnic language only.[44] Marivate reflects: 'The mother-tongue principle in African education has always met strong resistance from most sectors in the country, particularly from the African community.'[45] In fact, there is a widespread preference for education in English. However, due to insufficient preparation in the schools, skills in the language are often woefully inadequate for pursuing higher education success-fully.[46]

The ANC has usually allowed the various language groups to plead their cause, without strongly supporting any specific proposal. The prospect that the proliferation of official languages will in the end favour English over all others may not entirely displease the leader-ship, which, after all, used English throughout the liberation struggle as the counterpoint to Afrikaans and the medium of national unity.[47] In fact, as Venter argues, following Laitin's argument on language hegemony, 'black political elites in the ANC have managed to estab-lish the hegemony of English (a strand from a previously dominant culture) in the language subsystem'. Nor were they interested in promoting their home languages, since to them 'linguistic identity is not a basis for mobilization'.[48]

7.4   Discussion

The question arises of why English always ends up on the winning side in the recent history of the world language system. In retrospect, this can only be a property of that system itself. What appears incidental in each separate narrative in the end becomes symptomatic of an underlying structure.

Dawid Venter has argued that the predominance of English in South Africa cannot be explained in the context of that society alone, but must be seen in the perspective of the world system in its entirety.[49] Colonization first integrated South Africa into the world system, by bringing it into the periphery mostly as a producer of raw materials. In the 1940s it became gradually more closely inter-twined with the global economy as a country in the 'semi-periphery'. It went into relative decline from the 1970s on, partly as a consequence of domestic turmoil. Not only the introduction of

English and Dutch, but also the disappearance of the Khoisan languages and the parcelling out of the indigenous languages, were the result of colonial policies as carried out by settlers, traders, soldiers and missionaries – the agents of early political and cultural globalization.

With the hegemony of Britain in the nineteenth century and the first half of the twentieth, and the hegemony of the United States in the second half of the last century, the 'ideology of English' spread across the globe.[50] This may also explain why the English-speaking South Africans preserved the ties of mutual intelligibility with British English (as did the Americans and the Australians),[51] while the Afrikaners – at a rather late point in their history – abandoned intelligibility between Afrikaans and Dutch for the sake of a separate national identity. Under the predominance of the British in South Africa, the Afrikaans movement was more in need of identity symbols such as its Dutch Reformed creed and its Afrikaans language. But the Afrikaners may also have realized that in the rest of Africa, and indeed in the rest of the world, the Q-value of Dutch was much less than that of English, and that may have prompted them to allow their Afrikaans to drift away from the home language to the point of mutual unintelligibility.[52]

Afrikaans is unlikely to maintain its strong position, as it is bound to lose much of its significance as a second language. Moreover, the purist Afrikaners will have to accept either multiple varieties of Afrikaans or an incisive change in the standard version, if the 'coloured' speakers of Cape Afrikaans are indeed to be accepted as fully fledged members of their language community. And the community will need them, if only to withstand the pressure of English. However, under Apartheid the 'coloured' were considered second-class citizens, though nevertheless privileged above blacks. This preferential treatment was one reason for the 'coloured' community to maintain Cape Afrikaans, so as to stress their closeness to white Afrikaners and their distance from black Africans. With the demise of Apartheid, this incentive has disappeared. Hence, 'coloured' South Africans may retain their own Cape Afrikaans, but increasingly learn English instead of Afrikaners' Afrikaans for use at work and in business. More or less the same applies to those rural blacks who learned Afrikaans. They may not need it any longer and quite a few probably never wanted it: Afrikaans was at times imposed at gunpoint and that is not easily forgotten.

Without a doubt, the spread and predominance of English is a consequence of developments at the global level, of British colonialism initially, of American military and economic hegemony later. But

this does not mean that there was or is an 'English-language imperialism' in the strong sense that authorities made a conscious and
organized attempt to impose English on distant nations and continue
to do so.[53] Rather, the spread of English is the mostly unintended
outcome of expectations held and decisions made accordingly by
hundreds of millions of people across the globe. And they considered
mostly what would maximize their communication opportunities,
especially with a view to employment chances. Their estimates
initially depended very much upon the choices of British colonial
administrators, of postcolonial politicians next, and more recently
on the decisions of multinational entrepreneurs, who orient themselves to national and worldwide markets.

Thus, English initially spread like so many languages before it in
human history, by conquest, conversion and commerce, but increasingly a fourth process added its momentum: collusion. Parents sent
their children to school to learn the language. People, not just in the
colonies and the former colonies, were and still are all too eager to
learn English for the opportunities they expect it to yield.

Even if English may not yet entirely predominate in the domestic
South African context, its apparent hegemony at the global level
works through the effects of hypercollectivity: expectations tend to
reinforce one another until a stampede ensues, slowed down only by
the costs, efforts and time required for foreign-language acquisition.[54]

If anything, the abolition of Apartheid in South Africa, with the
attendant termination of sanctions and the cultural boycott, has
meant further economic, political and cultural integration in the
world system. As a consequence, international contacts have greatly
increased and they are almost exclusively carried on in English.
Wherever different people speak different languages – for example
in business, in the mines and industry, in the schools, in the courts, in
government and in the churches – problems of communication are
almost unfailingly resolved by adopting English: 'language practice...converges in a way that suggests a developing hegemony of
English'.[55]

The language constellation of South Africa is somewhat reminiscent
of the Indian and the European system. In India, English and Hindi
compete as co-official languages of the Union, whereas a dozen others
have official status only at the state level, if at all. In the European
Union, English and French find themselves in competition as languages of the bureaucracy, while the other nine 'official' languages
are confined to domestic communication in the member countries

(although Spanish and Portuguese are of great importance outside the Union, in Latin America).

In fact, Hindi does stand a fair chance in the competition with English, by sheer dint of its vast numbers and the gradual spread of literacy throughout the Hindu heartland. It is much more doubtful whether, in the European Union, French will maintain its position vis-à-vis English in the years to come. As a rival to English, in South Africa, Afrikaans appears to be even more threatened.

The European Union: the more languages, the more English

With 370 million citizens, the language constellation of the European Union may not have the most numerous speakers, its economy may not even be the world's largest in terms of its gross 'subcontinental' product, and the few score languages that survive in the area may be easily outnumbered by the many hundreds found in some Asian or African constellations, but the EU certainly boasts the most polyglot institutions in the world. This is due to the emergence of the European Union as an integrating economy and body politic, with fifteen member states already, and another dozen waiting in the wings at the time of writing. At present, eleven languages are officially recognized by the Union, and an equal number may be added in the next decade. As a language constellation, the European Union already equals India or South Africa in complexity, and it may soon surpass them.

'The subject of languages has been the great *non-dit* of European integration.'[1] Apparently, it has turned out to be easier for the EU to settle upon a common currency than on a common language. But, in this case too, not taking decisions amounts to taking 'non-decisions' – and these will affect the European language constellation as incisively and lastingly as any explicitly adopted policy ever could.

In fact, there hardly is a language policy for the European Parliament, or for the Commission's bureaucracy, let alone for 'l'Europe des citoyens', for civil society in the European Union. Of course, from the start, the official languages of the member states were recognized as languages of the, then, Community.[2] But at the time, there were only four, at present there are eleven, and in a decade they may number more than twenty. Initially, without much discussion, French was accepted as the working language of the Commission's budding bureaucracy. In those postwar years, the Germans and the Italians did not insist too much on equal treatment and the Dutch and Flemish speakers were not numerous enough to make demands. But the same treaties and arrangements that governed the language regime at the time still do so today with only incidental alterations, while the Union has vastly increased in membership, population, competence, budget, scope and complexity. And the end of this expansion is not yet in sight.

Four levels of communication are to be distinguished within the European Union. The first is that of domestic communication within each member country. There, the official language is the mother tongue of the vast majority, used in every domain of society and protected by the national state in every way. Nevertheless, these 'central', official languages are increasingly confronted with regional and ethnic-minority languages at home, and with an invasive supercentral language for communication across borders. The second level is, accordingly, that of transnational communication between the citizens of Europe, where several languages compete for predominance in various areas of the Union and in many different domains of communication. At this level, English is paramount, no doubt, but it must still compete with French in southern Europe and with German in Central Europe, where Russian has well-nigh disappeared. These two levels both concern 'civil society', domestic and transnational, respectively.

The next two levels are those of the European institutions. The third is that of formal, public communication: the European Parliament and the European Council of Ministers in their official sessions, and the European Commission in its external contacts. Here, the founding treaty applies, which recognizes all official languages of the member states as languages of the Union, and, moreover, requires that decisions by the EU should be published in all its languages, since they affect the laws of the constituent states. And then, there is the fourth level, that of the Commission's internal bureaucracy, where the officials have more or less informally adopted a few 'working languages' in their everyday contacts and in-house correspondence.

The constellations discussed in the preceding chapters, all of them formerly colonized countries, resemble the EU in many respects, but with three major differences that strongly affect language policies: European societies are much wealthier than their overseas counterparts, their populations are far more educated, and the languages of the European states are without exception 'robust'. They have been under the protection of the central state for two centuries or more; they are imposed in the schools, the courts, and the bureaucracies, in the courts, in politics and government. That is why the supercentral languages will not easily dislodge them from the domestic functions in their 'home' societies. Thus, it is the European state system, even in the era of its transformation into a new supranational political entity, which continues to shape the dynamics of the European language constellation through the peculiar resilience each state has conveyed to 'its' language in the past. In the meantime, the process of European integration does entail the expansion of one, two or maybe three, languages as the chosen means of transational communication in the Union at large and in its institutions. In many respects, the languages that today compete for hegemony, or even for bare survival, as a means of pan-European communication are the battle-hardened veterans of an earlier rivalry for predominance in their respective national societies. Contemporary English and French are the most telling examples of languages that once won out over their domestic rivals and now must compete at the all-Europe level. The dynamics of this earlier period of national language unification will help us to understand the present process of linguistic accommodation at the European level.

8.1 Civil Europe (1): language unification in national constellations

In terms of our model of the world language system, national language unification occurs when a central language, surrounded by a number of more or less peripheral ones, gradually comes to predominate, as it becomes the second language of almost all citizens and the mother tongue of a growing majority, and finally succeeds in driving out the peripheral languages from practically all domains.[3] France and Britain represent typical cases of such a language constellation, but Spain and Russia could also provide illuminating examples. In early modern times, the constellation consisted of an arc of regional languages around a central language spoken in the capital and the court. There, ruling and commercial elites usually spoke only the central language. The regional populations were for the most part equally monolingual, but in one of the peripheral languages. Moreover, until late in the nineteenth century, they were mostly illiterate. In Britain, the peripheral peoples constituted the so-called 'Celtic fringe': Scots, Irish, Welsh (and until the nineteenth century Cornish, until the 1970s Manx). In France, the peripheral language groups included the speakers of Breton, Flemish, Alsatian, Occitan, Piedmontese, Corsican, Catalan and Basque.[4]

The regional elites in these constellations functioned as intermediaries between their respective clienteles and the political, economic and commercial centre. They tended to be bilingual in French (or English, as the case might be) and the language of their region. Extending markets, a growing political and administrative machinery, elementary education, compulsory military service, and increasing migration to the cities helped to spread the central language and forced the retreat of the regional languages. By the end of the nineteenth century almost everybody in the realm spoke the central language, while regional languages began to be abandoned, some of them already bordering on extinction.[5]

In these countries, due to the language-learning efforts of the peripheral populations, the Q-value of the central language steadily increased (the new speakers adding both to its prevalence, and – as bilinguals – to its centrality, too).[6] This greatly benefited the central elites without any learning effort on their own part. They just happened to have inherited the right mother tongue and reaped the matching linguistic 'position rent', as economists might call it. Indirectly, however, these elites did contribute to the spread of their central language, by promoting elementary education throughout the land. This entailed education in a national curriculum that conveyed to all children of school-going age the basic skills for communication with every citizen in the realm: a spatial definition of their habitat in relation to the capital and the rest of the national territory; a temporal account of how all of them had come to belong to one and the same nation; a series of routines for calculating and standards for measuring space, time and value that allowed them to traffic with anyone in the country; and finally a common language for the entire nation.

The bilingual regional elites, for their part, profited from the spread of the central language in regions other than their own, as its Q-value increased accordingly. But they did not gain from the spread of the central language in their *own* region, as they could communicate with their local clientele in the regional language anyway. Both the prevalence and the centrality of their bilingual repertoire remained constant.[7] The regional elites, accordingly, were not too eager to aid the spread of the central language in their region, since it did nothing to improve the value of their bilingual repertoire and actually eroded their group monopoly of mediation between their regional clientele and the political and economic centre of the land.

Those peripheral speakers who did learn the central language saw the Q-value of their new repertoire increase considerably.[8] The others in the periphery, who did not learn 'centralese' themselves and continued to speak their regional language only, might nevertheless profit indirectly as the centrality of their repertoire, c_j, grew with the increase of bilinguals competent in both their regional language and the central language. However, this effect might be reversed if central-language learning in other regions proceeded even faster.[9] Thus, while both the central elites and the regional clienteles stood to gain greatly in Q-value as the latter learned the central language, the regional elites benefited from the spread of the central language in other regions, but not in their own. On the contrary, as their clienteles became competent in the central language, these regional elites lost their relative advantage with respect to the central elites. In fact, they saw their mediation monopoly between the centre and their periphery dwindle. This may explain why these regional elites so often resisted the spread of elementary education, the major vehicle for the spread of the national, central language. The fact that they stood to profit from the spread of the national language in regions other than their own explains why their opposition was rarely united and why they lost out in the end.

In France and England, as in other European countries, this language rivalry was fought out as a conflict over the control of elementary schools. In general, established regional elites supported a relatively decentralized school system, run by the established churches, Catholic schools in France, Anglican schools in England. The metropolitan elites, on the contrary, tended to favour a national educational system under the direct control of the state. The language issue was a corollary of these notorious 'school struggles', since the churches were much more inclined to support instruction in the regional languages than was the central government, which championed the cause of the national language.

In the end, the regional elites could only carry the day if they closed ranks against lay education by the state and joined in a nationwide coalition to oppose it. But their collaboration at the national level then prompted them to agree upon a national curriculum as well. By the beginning of the twentieth century, the vast majority of children attended full daytime education for six years at least. Almost everywhere, elementary instruction proceeded in the national language.

Moreover, young males now had to go through compulsory military service, where they were further socialized in the standard idiom. Cheap, mass-produced newspapers popularized the national language for a growing readership that would soon also turn to the radio and grow accustomed to the standardized speech that was now broadcast throughout the country.

Political integration and, hence, language unification came later to Italy and Germany. But in these countries, clearly distinct languages were fewer than in France and England, even though the spoken dialects differed considerably from one another, both in Germany and in Italy. In due time, in these countries and elsewhere in Europe, the government imposed the standard version of the language throughout the territory.

Although most European states have adopted one language as the official medium, and this language is indeed spoken by almost all citizens, other mother tongues have survived, being spoken at home or in local communities. Outside of Europe and America, however, societal multilingualism is the rule rather than the exception, and since interaction between speakers of different languages is inevitable in these countries also, many citizens are necessarily multilingual. In fact, there may not be a single entirely monolingual country in the world.

In Europe, however, by the end of the nineteenth century, the state language had become closely identified with the nation, and it now constituted the major marker of national identity. The connection between the national language and the national state has become so intimate that one unwittingly attributes to 'language' the same permanence, the same omnipresence as inheres in the state, an equally strict and complete system of rules, and a demarcation from cognate languages as clear-cut as the state's borders. Whoever says 'language' has already tacitly thought 'state'. Clearly, this idea of language is a political construct, the outcome of a long-lasting symbiosis with the state.[10]

These historical antecedents have to a great degree determined the present process of language integration at the supranational level, by bringing about such a close association between states and languages, especially in the West. For centuries past, states have been the great protectors of languages in the modern world, but only of the officially adopted languages. First of all, every law and regulation is written in the official language, and this alone requires standardization of terminology and permanence of meaning over time. Second, all affairs within the administration and all contacts with citizens are transacted in this language of choice. Third, and most important in the long run, the official language becomes the language of instruction in the schools, usually from the first class on, compelling all citizens to acquire proficiency in it as they grow up. Fourth, private business must use the language in its dealings with central and local governments, forcing the middle and higher echelons to master it. Fifth, the language will be associated with the prestige of high office, extended education and economic wealth: for that reason alone it will be considered prestigious to be fluent in it. (But by the same token, others may consider it a mark of disloyalty to class, religious, ethnic or regional origins to affect the official speech. And equally, they may well believe that even if they master the language, they will still be excluded from the spoils by the elite for lack of connections.) Sixth, in so far as the state controls, or more informally influences, the mass media, this too will contribute to the use of the standard version of the language in newspapers and on radio and television. This impact in turn goes far to shape the canons of usage in the population at large. Finally, the state language will be further preserved by a cabal of appointed guardians, academic scholars, linguists, lexicographers and educators whose self-imposed task it is to describe and, as the case may be, to prescribe standards and see that they are adhered to.[11]

Since they are under the protection of states, the most demarcated and permanent institutions in the contemporary world, languages have become less fluent and shifting, and, parallel to the state's borders, their differences from adjacent languages have been emphasized and perpetuated, while within each society the language increasingly becomes a symbol, a cherished national and historical treasure, sometimes the only common denominator of the state's citizenry and itself constitutive of a sense of national unity from which the state takes its legitimacy. In short, languages partake in the robustness of the states that adopt them, and contribute to it. Where in the course of centuries a single language has spread throughout the territory of the state, growing from a court language into the most central language – that is, the second language of more multilingual speakers than any other – and then into the dominant language – that is, the language of a plurality or even a majority – and next into the general language – that is the speech, native or acquired, of all citizens – and finally into the only language in the realm, all its rivals having been abandoned, language and citizenship have become coterminous.[12] But this is by no means the general condition of affairs in the contemporary world. Even in those states where at first sight it appears to be the case, and where it is unthinkingly accepted as the normal situation, a second look will reveal many inconsistencies.

Nevertheless, it is the robustness of the official state languages of Europe that determines to a large degree the particular course of language rivalry and accommodation on the European subcontinent: it precludes from the outset a process of language unification through pidginization and creolization – the European languages are too robust to dissolve into new, intermediate idioms. Jealousy between established, state-supported language groups will also for a long time to come prevent the adoption of any single language as the sole official language of the Community.

The dynamics of the present European constellation of languages are not in the abandonment of the state languages for the sake of one European medium, or in their fusion into a single amalgam, but in the acquisition of additional, foreign languages. The question is which languages will gain most as a result of this process. The languages that the member states brought into the European Community have been forged for one or two centuries by a process of state-formation and nation-building. They may or may not hold out in the coming supranational competition, but on their own turf they will not recede easily.[13]

Within the countries of Europe, increasingly, a state of diglossia exists: in most domains of society, the national language continues to predominate, but in other spheres the supercentral linking language now prevails.[14] Quickly growing numbers of Europeans have learned English and speak it as their second language. They use it for international communication, in business and transport, science and technology. In some intermediate domains, English and the domestic language compete: in entertainment and advertising, in sports and fashion, for example. But as long as the state maintains its support of the national language, that will weather the pressures of the global language, in a precarious equilibrium of diglossia.

8.2   Civil Europe (2): *Q*-values in the European Union

For a long time, the language issue has been the dormant predicament of the European Community and the Union that has succeeded it. Of course, the EU is in the first place a common market, aimed at securing the free movement of goods, capital and people. It is based on a common human rights regime and a shared legal framework that is rapidly expanding. In recent years, a common currency has been established. The Parliament has gained in competence. The Commission generates a growing body of regulations, ranging from consumer protection, anti-monopoly decisions and social policy measures to environmental conservation, industrial standards and immigration controls. But the language in which all these activities proceed has rarely been a subject of discussion and reflection.[15] On the eve of the accession of half a dozen countries from Central and Eastern Europe and in the expectation that many more will join, the language problem seems more acute than ever. This prospect has finally begun to provoke some discussion, yet no reform of the language regime is in sight. But before we discuss the proposals and options for language policy in the European Union, the actual language constellation of the European Union must be investigated: it provides a most suitable test case for the theoretical concepts and a pertinent comparison for the empirical findings presented so far. Moreover, the distribution of first- and foreign-language skills in the European Union has been well documented, allowing us to calculate Q-values from quite reliable survey data.

On the face of it, matters in the Union are deceptively simple: the eleven official languages of the fifteen member states are the official languages of the European Union.[16] But a second look reveals a few irregularities. Letzeburgesch, the indigenous language of Luxembourg, has not been adopted by the EU. An official language of one member state, Gaelic for Ireland, is not a language of the Union: only some thirty thousand citizens speak it on a daily basis and half a million claim some knowledge of it as their second language next to English.[17] The European Parliament has recommended that Catalan, the language of some six million inhabitants of the 'autonomous community' of Catalonia, be accorded some of the rights granted to Gaelic.[18]

In fact, not all 'official' languages, but only two of them, are being used on a day-to-day basis in the actual working sessions of politicians and bureaucrats: French and English.[19] This fact goes a long way to explain the silence on the language issue in Europe and suggests what has been going on all along: a tacit rivalry between the great language groups of Europe for predominance within the Community.

From the outset, French had been in an especially privileged position: it was the sole official language of the precursor of the EEC, the European Coal and Steel Community. When the European Economic Community was founded in 1957, French lost its exclusive role, because the fundamental treaties of the Community and its binding decisions come before national law and therefore must be couched in the languages of all member countries. That was the reason why the four languages of the six founding members were all accepted as official media, and the same applied to the seven languages of the nine states that have joined since.

But in the Community, too, French remained privileged: the three cities where the EC had its domicile, Brussels, Strasbourg and Luxembourg, all straddle the age-old Franco-Germanic language border and all are partly francophone. In 1957, it was the common expectation that French would prevail as the EEC's vehicular language.[20] And even in 1986, out of 12,000 EC officials some 5000 were still French-speaking. Nevertheless, since the United Kingdom joined the Community, the use of English in the corridors of bureaucracy has steadily increased, and it is now the language used most often in the European Parliament. The French authorities certainly did not accept this development lying down: within the Community, as elsewhere in the world, they actively insisted on the use of French for the domains of international bureaucracy as well as science, the arts and diplomacy.[21] An Haut Conseil de la Francophonie permanently watches over French-language interests. For many years French scientists were pressed to demand the use of French in international meetings and to publish in French periodicals.[22] This *francophoniste* policy was not very successful. Even in Quebec, the position of French was threatened.[23] Whenever English and French collide head on in an international setting, French loses the competition.[24] Recently, the French government has reversed its course and it now encourages the schools to teach English, starting in the fifth year of elementary school. Scientists are no longer dissuaded from publishing in English. A strong purist current still runs against the adoption of English loan words or the use of English instead of French in domestic settings, but it finds little support among experts.[25]

English has become the predominant medium of international communication in the European Union. Although it is the first language nowhere on the European continent, it has become the most widely spoken second language everywhere. By 1980, Norman Denison could write: 'With regard to the role of English in Western Europe, a stage has now been reached, for a growing proportion of the population, in which a diglossia situation is rapidly approaching or already exists.'[26]

The reunification of Germany, in 1990, has increased the number of German native speakers in the EU by the 17 million teutophones of the former German Democratic Republic, considerably raising the communication value of repertoires that contain German. Beyond the eastern borders of the present Union, Middle and Eastern Europeans are acquiring Western languages en masse, having abandoned Russian at a spectacular pace: a true stampede *out* of a language. They opt for either English or German, whichever they consider the better bet. The prestige and attraction of English (and of the United States) is patent, but the reunited Germany in the heart of the new European area constitutes the economic core of the region and has regained much of its cultural and political stature in the past decade or so.

German cultural policy did maintain a low profile after World War II – it tried to convey the very opposite of hegemony and to suggest a kind of sober modesty.[27] The federal foreign policy establishment and the Goethe Institutes were quite successful in spreading this low-key message. Germans abroad were always ready to switch to English and at official occasions never insisted on the use of their own language. This policy of self-restraint and even self-effacement had some hidden, and maybe quite unintended, consequences. In quietly opting for English throughout the postwar years, the Germans certainly helped to weaken the most privileged position of their arch-rivals on the continent, the French.[28] From the outset, the tacit language rivalry in the Community was between French and German, with English on the sideline as the favourite for global communication and a looming threat as the language of a likely member of the Community. And yet, from the early 1950s until the mid-1970s, the prospects for French seemed so promising.

In the European Economic Community of 'the six', only four languages were current: German, French, Italian and Netherlandish (Dutch). The Belgians are divided into the French-speaking Walloons and the Dutch-speaking Flemish (and a very small German-speaking contingent). The Luxembourgers speak Luxembourg or Letzeburgesch and German, while almost 90 per cent learned French in school at that time.

The data in table 8.1 are rough approximations: there are no statistics on foreign-language skills for the population of the Community before the mid-1970s. However, various estimates yield the same conclusion: French scores highest, although it numbers fewer speakers than German (counting only native or both native and foreign speakers). There were, however, considerably more foreign-language speakers of French than of German in the Community, and that increased the centrality of French sufficiently to compensate for its smaller prevalence. Hence, German took second place. French may have been even more attractive than it appears here by dint of its

Table 8.1 The EC c.1970 (speakers in millions)

Native language	Sole or second language				Third language		Total
	FR	GE	IT	NL	FR&GE&NL	FR&GE&IT	
FR	41	5	7	2	0	0	54
GE	6	53	2	1	1	0	62
IT	1	3	45	0	–	1	51
NL	3	1	0	12	1	–	17
							183
Q_i:							
FR	0.292	0.692	0.600	0.378	0.757	0.935	
GE	0.692	0.232	0.586	0.358	0.757	0.935	
IT	0.600	0.586	0.143	0.309	–	0.935	
NL	0.378	0.358	0.309	0.030	0.757	–	
Greenberg's A	0.602						

Source: Data from Kloss and McConnell, 1989.

FR = French; GE = German; IT = Italian; NL = Netherlandish.

A dash – = Not applicable.

Only the four official languages of the Community at the time are considered. Knowledge of English is ignored. Belgian Walloons are included in the numbers for French, Flemish in those for Netherlandish, and Luxembourgers are classified as native German speakers. The figures for second and third languages are rough estimates, mostly derived from statistics on language learning by secondary school students quoted by Kloss and McConnell, corrected downward and extrapolated for the population at large. Speakers who reported a regional language as their mother tongue have been classified as native speakers of the official language of their country.

The rows show the native speakers of a language: speakers of that language only, and those who also speak a second (and third) language, as indicated by the column heading. The total number of speakers of a language may be found by adding to the row total of native speakers the entries in the corresponding column for foreign speakers of that language (avoiding counting monolingual speakers twice).

The prevalence p_i of a repertoire ρ_i is found by adding the entries in the columns and rows for the language(s) in ρ_i (while avoiding double counts) and dividing by N^s, the number of all speakers. The centrality c_i of a repertoire ρ_i is calculated by adding the entries for all *multilingual* repertoires that have a language in common with ρ_i and dividing by the total of multilingual speakers M^s.

In this procedure, the matrix for Q has been folded along the diagonal: in calculating p_i, c_i and Q_i, the numbers for, say, German speakers who have learned French have been added to the number of French speakers who have acquired German, and vice versa. As a result, the entries in the lower left half of the matrix for Q are identical to the corresponding entries in the upper right half.

Figures have been rounded to the nearest million. Entries may therefore not always add up to the corresponding total.

cultural prestige and its prevalence as a world language beyond the confines of the Community. Italian came third, at some distance, and Netherlandish ended up far behind, in fourth position.

An outsider wanting to communicate with the citizens of the EC would have done best to learn French, since it had the highest single-language Q-score. The Dutch and Italians were better off learning French than German as a second language, but it hardly made a difference. The repertoire with French and German gave direct access to two-thirds of the Community's citizens and to practically all its multilingual speakers. Clearly, the French and the Germans started out with a linguistic advantage in the Community of the Six.

It is hard to say what might have happened if this situation had endured and the tacit rivalry between French and German had come into the open. In the extreme case, France or the Federal Republic might have improved their relative position by scaling down the teaching of the rival language at home, thus lowering its Q-value. They might also have competed by offering to teach their schoolchildren Italian or Dutch in exchange for the promotion of their own language in Italy or the Netherlands (this is in fact the policy that the French later advocated – in vain – as an attempt to weaken the predominance of English).

But all the time a potential competitor hovered over the constellation: English. It was, as yet, not an official language in the EEC, but 'unofficially' it was already quite probably the largest second and possibly the most central language in the Community.

Once the UK, Ireland and Denmark joined the Community in 1973, the constellation changed drastically. German remained the native language of the largest number, but English now moved ahead of French as the language most widely spoken, when its foreign speakers were included (see table 8.2). Italian came in fourth position in the Community of the Nine, Netherlandish next, at a distance, and Danish remained well-nigh invisible (0.001).

Since English also scored highest on centrality (the number of multilingual speakers with English in their repertoire), English was the most attractive single language in the constellation. Outsiders would do best to learn English. The speakers of all other languages in the constellation preferred English as an additional language over any other, except the Germans, who were better off with French. Since speakers could reasonably expect most other language learners in the constellation to prefer English, each one had an incentive to choose English also. French, favoured by the English and the Germans, remained a strong alternative. The English should have preferred to learn French, but they might as well have refrained from learning any foreign language at all, confidently waiting until the rest of the constellation joined them.[29]

Clearly, from the moment that it become an official language of the Community, English gained the edge over the other languages. French, still a strong option, was already on the losing end, but remained ahead of German in third position.

The linguistic constellation did not change much when three Mediterranean countries joined: Greece in 1981, Spain and Portugal in 1986,

Table 8.2 The EC c.1975 (speakers in millions)

Native language	Sole or second language						Third language					Total
	EN	FR	GE	IT	NL	DA	LANG+EN&FR	LANG+EN&GE	LANG+EN&IT	LANG+EN&NL	LANG+FR&GE	
EN	44	9	2	1	0	0	–	–	–	–	3	60
FR	9	33	3	2	3	0	–	4	2	0	–	57
GE	13	2	40	1	1	0	4	–	0	1	–	63
IT	2	12	1	36	0	0	3	2	–	0	0	57
NL	2	1	5	0	4	0	3	3	0	–	2	20
DA	2	0	1	0	0	2	0	1	0	0	0	6
Total												263

Q_i:

	EN	FR	GE	IT	NL	DA	LANG+EN&FR	LANG+EN&GE	LANG+EN&IT	LANG+EN&NL	LANG+FR&GE
EN	0.278	0.578	0.525	0.513	0.382	0.297	–	–	–	–	0.828
FR	0.578	0.215	0.574	0.363	0.314	0.250	–	0.828	0.734	0.662	–
GE	0.525	0.574	0.165	0.406	0.234	0.179	0.828	–	0.804	0.586	0.753
IT	0.513	0.363	0.406	0.066	0.165	0.086	0.734	0.804	–	0.642	0.627
NL	0.382	0.314	0.234	0.165	0.023	0.035	0.662	0.586	0.642	–	0.600
DA	0.297	0.250	0.179	0.086	0.035	0.001	0.604	0.531	0.538	0.404	–

Greenberg's A   0.550

Source: Eurobarometer, 1976, pp. 4–7. Answers to the question, 'Which languages do you understand without difficulty?'

EN = English; FR = French; GE = German; IT = Italian; NL = Netherlandish; DA = Danish.

A dash – = Not applicable.

Trilingual repertoires are calculated by summing bilinguals and monolinguals; the excess over 100 per cent must be due to trilinguals (more extensive repertoires are ignored). This excess is attributed to trilingual repertoires in proportion to second-language skills among the language group concerned, and figures are rounded to the nearest million.

The rows show the native speakers of a language: speakers of that language only, and those who also speak a second (and third) language, as indicated by the column heading. The total number of speakers of a language may be found by adding to the row total of native speakers the entries in the corresponding column for foreign speakers of that language (avoiding counting monolingual speakers twice).

The prevalence p_i of a repertoire p_i is found by adding the entries in the columns and rows for the language(s) in p_i (while avoiding double counts) and dividing by N^s, the number of all speakers. The centrality c_i of a repertoire p_i is calculated by adding the entries for all multilingual repertoires that have a language in common with p_i and dividing by the total of multilingual speakers M^s.

In this procedure, the matrix for Q has been folded along the diagonal: in calculating p_i, c_i and Q_i, the numbers for, say, German speakers who have learned French have been added to the number of French speakers who have acquired German, and vice versa. As a result, the entries in the lower left half of the matrix for Q are identical to the corresponding entries in the upper right half.

Figures have been rounded to the nearest million. Entries may therefore not always add up to the corresponding total.

bringing the total number of languages to nine. English still had the greatest number of speakers on account of its popularity as a second language. French found support only in Spain. Spanish scored in Q-value just behind Italian, in accordance with their numbers of native speakers. Neither language attracted many foreign students, in Europe that is. In Latin America, of course, Spanish is a super-central language, with some 280 million speakers[30] (more than French), and Portuguese has roughly 160 million speakers, mainly in Brazil.[31] However, in Europe, Portugal is too small to make its mark, and so are Denmark and Greece.

In the former socialist countries of Central and Eastern Europe, German was traditionally the first foreign language, until it was superseded by Russian, which at reunification in 1990 began to disappear fast and without leaving much of a trace. Given the increasing German influence in these lands, on the one hand, and on the other the strong overall position of English among young East Europeans, this is the area where the two languages have been most competitive since.[32] The subsequent accession of Austria in 1995 further strengthened the position of German (by 8 million native speakers), and the membership of Switzerland may one day add to this potential and also increase the French and Italian contingent.[33]

English maintained the strongest communication value, and French continued to occupy second place even though German ranks had been so much increased. Q-values for the six smaller countries became negligible, due to the further fragmentation of the European language constellation. Among the three newcomers, English was, once again, the most important foreign language.

The accession of Sweden and Finland to membership of the Union in 1995 introduced two more languages to the constellation. The addition of Swedish and Finnish complicated already intricate matters even further. Yet it affected the dynamics of the language situation only slightly. Swedes and Finns (a minority of the latter speak Swedish) are few in number and their languages are hardly known beyond their borders. As a consequence, the Q-values of these languages on their own are as negligible as those of Danish, Greek or Portuguese. A large percentage of Swedes and Finns, however, do speak English (far fewer speak German), and in that respect their entry into the Union shifted the balance even further towards English. As their entitlement to equal status made the language predicament still more acute, the pressure for a simplified language regime increased accordingly.

The figures for table 8.3 are based on a *Eurobarometer* survey of 1998 which asked: 'Which languages can you speak well enough to

Table 8.3 The EC after 1995 (speakers in millions)

Native language	Sole or second language								Third language				Total
	EN	FR	GE	IT	SP	NL	GR	Other	LANG+EN&FR	LANG+EN&GE	LANG+EN&SP	LANG+FR&GE	
EN	**49**	8	2	1	1	0	1	1	–	–	–	1	63
FR	12	**34**	2	3	3	2	0	0	–	4	4	–	63
GE	31	5	**45**	2	1	2	0	0	5	–	2	–	92
IT	11	6	2	**33**	2	0	0	1	5	0	0	0	59
SP	5	1	0	0	**32**	0	0	0	2	0	–	0	40
NL	1	1	1	0	0	**5**	0	0	5	9	0	0	23
GR	4	1	1	0	0	0	**6**	0	0	0	0	0	11
Other	8	1	1	0	1	0	0	**13**	2	5	0	0	31
													383
Q_j:													
EN	0.352	0.559	0.537	0.510	0.463	0.391	0.374	0.398	–	–	0.668	0.734	
FR	0.559	0.120	0.427	0.224	0.200	0.165	0.144	0.189	–	0.734	0.668	–	

Table 8.3 (cont.)

Native language	Sole or second language								Third language				Total
	EN	FR	GE	IT	SP	NL	GR	Other	LANG+EN&FR	LANG+EN&GE	LANG+EN&SP	LANG+FR&GE	
GE	0.537	0.427	0.141	0.295	0.255	0.176	0.167	0.204	0.734	–	0.661	–	
IT	0.510	0.224	0.295	0.033	0.096	0.076	0.048	0.078	0.690	0.697	0.620	0.584	
SP	0.463	0.200	0.255	0.096	0.019	0.055	0.031	0.056	0.668	0.661	–	0.551	
NL	0.391	0.165	0.176	0.076	0.055	0.008	0.017	0.037	0.590	0.566	0.508	0.442	
GR	0.374	0.144	0.167	0.048	0.031	0.017	0.001	0.019	0.580	0.557	0.487	0.466	
Other	0.398	0.189	0.204	0.078	0.056	0.037	0.019	0.010	0.609	0.585	0.508	0.515	
Greenberg's A	0.599												

Source: Eurobarometer, 1999, annexes, p. B.80 (§6.9). Answers to the question, 'Which languages can you speak well enough to take part in a conversation, apart from your mother tongue?'

EN = English; FR = French; GE = German; IT = Italian; SP = Spanish; NL = Netherlandish; GR = Greek.

The category 'Other' consists of the languages Portuguese, Swedish, Finnish and Danish.

Trilingual repertoires are calculated by summing bilinguals and monolinguals; the excess over 100 per cent must be due to trilinguals (more extensive repertoires are ignored). This excess is attributed to trilingual repertoires in proportion to second-language skills among the language group concerned.

The rows show the native speakers of a language: speakers of that language only, and those who also speak a second (and third) language, as indicated by the column heading. The total number of speakers of a language may be found by adding to the row total of native speakers the entries in the corresponding column for foreign speakers of that language (avoiding counting monolingual speakers twice).

The prevalence p_i of a repertoire p_i is found by adding the entries in the columns and rows for the language(s) in p_i (while avoiding double counts) and dividing by N^s, the number of all speakers. The centrality c_i of a repertoire p_i is calculated by adding the entries for all *multilingual* repertoires that have a language in common with p_i and dividing by the total of multilingual speakers M^s.

In this procedure, the matrix for Q has been folded along the diagonal: in calculating p_i, c_i and Q_i, the numbers for, say, German speakers who have learned French have been added to the number of French speakers who have acquired German, and vice versa. As a result, the entries in the lower left half of the matrix for Q are identical to the corresponding entries in the upper right half.

Figures have been rounded to the nearest million. Entries may therefore not always add up to the corresponding total.

take part in a conversation, apart from your mother tongue?' The statistics for table 8.2 were based on answers to the question, 'Which languages do you understand without difficulty?', likewise posed by a *Eurobarometer* survey, in 1976. Since the 1976 survey asked about 'understanding without difficulty' and that of 1998 mentioned 'speaking well enough...', the two tables must be compared with some caution: 'understanding without difficulty' requires less competence than taking part in a conversation. Multilingualism may therefore appear more widespread in the earlier survey. On the other hand, the general level of education increased considerably in the twenty years between the two surveys, and this boosted the figures for foreign-language skills in 1998.

At any rate, English again scored highest on Q-value and by 1998 had become the favourite second language for every national contingent. But, in one major aspect, a change had occurred: according to the data, the communication value for French now lagged behind the Q-score for German. English speakers still preferred French to German as a second language, but the remaining language groups were better off with German than with French (with English remaining their first choice). This was due, for the most part, to the increase in native German speakers from the former East Germany and Austria: they now made up the largest group by far – 91 million as against 63 million for English (including the Irish) and 63 million for French (with the Walloons).

English has de facto become the connecting language of the European Union, and the present trends of growing secondary school enrolment and increasing instruction in English will only reinforce its predominance within the EU. At a considerable distance in table 8.3, Italian comes in fourth place, before Spanish; Netherlandish takes sixth position. These three languages make up the middle group of the European Union: all remaining countries end up with negligible Q-values (of 0.001 or less). Even the combined score of the category 'Other' (Danish, Finnish, Portuguese and Swedish) is only 0.01. Clearly, if the principle of equal entitlement were ever to be abandoned, English, French and German would be the serious contenders for a privileged position. However, Spanish, as a world language, and Italian and Netherlandish, as the languages of founding members of the Community, can also enter strong claims for inclusion in the basket of languages to be privileged.

The accession of Poland, the Czech Republic, Hungary, Estonia and Malta,[34] which is presently on the agenda of the EU, will not radically alter the prospects, much less will it simplify them. Each of these prospective members has its own official language, none of which has sufficient numbers of speakers to alter the overall distribution of Q-values perceptibly. English and German[35] are the most important foreign languages in these countries, and as young people attend secondary school in increasing numbers, the proportion of foreign-language speakers will continue to grow. On the whole, however, English, and German and French next, will continue to be the main languages of the Union, with Italian, Spanish and Nether-landish trailing in the second league. No other languages in the present or the future Union are of any significance beyond their borders.

8.2.1 The future of the Union

The data on the language skills of young people in the EC anticipate the distribution of foreign-language competence in the general popu-lation by two or three decades. Moreover, these statistics are more extensive and consistent over time than those of the overall surveys. In 1991, a sample of secondary school students and young adults was asked what language they spoke at home, which ones they had learned and in which they felt able to carry on a conversation.[36] On the average, European youngsters spoke one or two (or '1.5') foreign languages, with Luxembourger, Danish and Dutch adolescents speak-ing two or three, and their Greek and Irish peers averaging less than one.[37] The same survey shows that in the relatively short time span between 1987 and 1990 skills in foreign languages, especially English, increased across the board.[38] Young Europeans are also more fre-quently competent in foreign languages than those over the age of 25, another testimony to the rapid increase of these skills.

Ten years later, by the end of 1998, a third of *all citizens* of the EU felt able to converse in English, roughly twice the proportion in 1987, and about the same as the level of young people in that year. Know-ledge of French and German inched upward by a few percentage points at most, and the percentage for Spanish actually declined. Age cohort and length of education (with a strong correlation be-tween the two) are major determinants: while 45 per cent of all EU citizens spoke a foreign language well enough to hold a conversation, 77 per cent of students and 72 per cent of those who had been educated up to the age of 20 said they could do so, but only 26 per cent of retired persons and only 19 per cent of those who left school before the age of 16.[39]

Table 8.4 The EC in the future (speakers in millions)

Native language	Sole or second language								Third language					Total
	EN	FR	GE	IT	SP	NL	GR	Other	LANG+ EN&FR	LANG+ EN&GE	LANG+ EN&IT	LANG+ EN&SP	LANG+ FR&GE	
EN	**33**	17	7	1	3	0	0	0	–	–	–	–	1	63
FR	16	**16**	1	1	1	3	0	2	–	7	3	14	–	64
GE	55	8	**14**	2	1	1	1	1	8	–	0	1	–	92
IT	18	7	1	**17**	2	0	0	0	10	2	–	0	–	57
SP	16	4	1	1	**17**	0	0	1	0	0	0	–	0	38
NL	1	1	2	0	1	2	0	0	8	9	0	0	0	25
GR	7	1	1	0	0	0	3	0	0	0	0	0	0	12
Other	11	1	2	0	1	0	0	5	5	6	0	1	0	33
														384
Q_i:														
EN	0.562	0.733	0.696	0.678	0.658	0.609	0.582	0.611	–	–	–	–	0.833	
FR	0.733	0.146	0.467	0.252	0.243	0.186	0.171	0.217	–	0.833	0.824	0.818	–	
GE	0.696	0.467	0.144	0.298	0.288	0.183	0.169	0.209	0.833	–	0.807	0.791	–	
IT	0.678	0.252	0.298	0.033	0.115	0.070	0.046	0.081	0.824	0.807	–	0.765	0.621	

Table 8.4 (cont.)

Native language	Sole or second language								Third language					Total
	EN	FR	GE	IT	SP	NL	GR	Other	LANG+ EN&FR	LANG+ EN&GE	LANG+ EN&IT	LANG+ EN&SP	LANG+ FR&GE	
SP	0.658	0.243	0.288	0.115	0.028	0.062	0.041	0.069	0.818	0.791	0.765	–	0.616	
NL	0.609	0.186	0.183	0.070	0.062	0.007	0.015	0.037	0.764	0.733	0.724	0.703	0.484	
GR	0.582	0.171	0.169	0.046	0.041	0.015	0.001	0.020	0.751	0.714	0.695	0.680	0.508	
Other	0.611	0.217	0.209	0.081	0.069	0.037	0.020	0.011	0.777	0.735	0.726	0.700	0.548	
Greenberg's A	0.372													

Source: Eurobarometer, 1997, pp. 46–7. Answers to the question, 'Apart from your mother tongue, which of these languages can you speak well enough to take part in a conversation?'
EN = English; FR = French; GE = German; IT = Italian; SP = Spanish; NL = Netherlandish; GR = Greek.

Trilingual repertoires are calculated by summing bilinguals and monolinguals; the excess over 100 per cent must be due to trilinguals (more extensive repertoires are ignored). This excess is attributed to trilingual repertoires in proportion to second-language skills among the language group concerned.

The rows show the native speakers of a language: speakers of that language only, and those who also speak a second (and third) language, as indicated by the column heading. The total number of speakers of a language may be found by adding to the row total of native speakers the entries in the corresponding column for foreign speakers of that language (avoiding counting monolingual speakers twice).

The prevalence p_i of a repertoire ρ_i is found by adding the entries in the columns and rows for the language(s) in ρ_i (while avoiding double counts) and dividing by N^s, the number of all speakers. The centrality c_i of a repertoire ρ_i is calculated by adding the entries for all *multilingual* repertoires that have a language in common with ρ_i and dividing by the total of multilingual speakers M^s.

In this procedure, the matrix for Q has been folded along the diagonal: in calculating p_i, c_i and Q_i, the numbers for, say, German speakers who have learned French have been added to the number of French speakers who have acquired German, and vice versa. As a result, the entries in the lower left half of the matrix for Q are identical to the corresponding entries in the upper right half.

Figures have been rounded to the nearest million. Entries may therefore not always add up to the corresponding total.

People tend to feel more confident in one foreign language than another: while 47 per cent of EC students who reported in 1990 that they had learned French felt competent to take part in a conversation in that language, and only 35 per cent of students of Netherlandish felt the same about their conversational competence, the proportion of respondents who felt competent among those who had learned English was more favourable: 56 per cent. Not only do more people learn English than any other language in the Union, they are also more inclined to use it with confidence.

In 1997, *Eurobarometer* published the results of a survey on language skills among young citizens of the EU (table 8.4).[40] Respondents were asked which languages they knew sufficiently well to hold a conversation in. This, of course, is a stricter criterion than 'understand without difficulty' (*Eurobarometer*, 1976) and about equivalent to the criterion of *Eurobarometer*, 1999. The main difference between the surveys of 1999 and 1997 is in the age of the respondents: the young respondents of 1997 are the future voters, workers and consumers of the European Union.

The most striking result is the very high score of English, entirely due to the impact of the many young non-native speakers of the language. Surprising, also, is the position of French: ahead, even if only barely, of German. Apparently, young people still, or maybe increasingly, learn French in school. Again, there is a middle group, made up of Italian, Spanish and Dutch. The scores of all other official languages are negligible. After English, the best option as a foreign language is again German (except for the Dutch, who prefer French, by the slightest of margins). Hence, the outcome of the 1997 survey among young Europeans confirms the conclusions from the 1999 survey among all citizens of the EU and strengthens the expectations for the next ten or twenty years: English will predominate in European civil society, while French and German will continue to compete for the next-best position. Three other languages, Italian, Spanish and Dutch, to a lesser degree, may hold out in Europe as international languages of the second magnitude. And even this position is due more to the foreign-language skills of native Italians, Spanish and Dutch speakers than to the competence of foreigners in these languages. All other official languages of the Union remain almost entirely confined to their home society.[41]

This prognosis opens up a vista of a three-ring language constellation in the European Union. The first circle consists of the big three, used as lingua francas: English foremost throughout Europe, French mainly in the south, German mostly in the east. Italian, Spanish and (to a degree) Dutch are border-crossing languages in neighbouring countries. All other languages remain strictly limited to domestic use. But this recipe for civil Europe must match the language configuration of institutional Europe: the public ceremonial level of the governing bodies, the Parliament, the Council of Ministers and the Commission, on the one hand, and on the other the indoor practices of the European bureaucracy and the everyday committee sessions and informal meetings of the parliamentarians and their staff.

8.3 Institutional Europe (1): the public level

The European language constellation consists of four levels. Two have been discussed at some length: that of separate national societies, and that of civil society in the Union at large. So far we have dealt with 'l'Europe des citoyens'; now we turn to 'l'Europe des institutions'.[42] Two institutional levels must be distinguished. First, there is the level of the official, public, even ceremonial encounters of the Council of Ministers and, especially, of the European Parliament.[43] That is the topic of this section. The other institutional level concerns the routine, informal meetings and discussions of officials and politicians in the offices, corridors and committee rooms of the Union venues: the topic of the next section.

On the formal, public occasions, when the Council of Ministers or the Parliament are in session or when major committees meet, all official languages of the member states are to be treated on an equal footing. This is not just a matter of international courtesy or political accommodation; it touches the very foundations of the Union. First of all, the founding treaties stipulate the fundamental equality of all constituent states, and this also pertains to their languages. Second, the Council, the Parliament and the Commission can take decisions that directly affect the citizens of the member states, and it is a fundamental democratic principle that such laws are written in the languages of the states where they apply. Thus, the institutional multilingualism of the Union is not solely a result of some states refusing to give up outdated and inefficient privileges; it is deeply rooted in the constitution of the Community and the succeeding Union, an issue of equality between member states and of democratic governance. These basic considerations alone make it most unlikely that the principle of equal treatment for each official language will ever be abandoned. Therefore, all regulations that have a direct impact on the citizens of the Union must be written in the languages of all member states. But principles, no matter how lofty, do not exclude practical accommodations. The governing bodies of the Union might deliberate in only one or just a few languages. Under the given circumstances, such pragmatic, informal compromises are already current and will most probably extend their sway.

However, when it comes to official, explicit policy, a persistent immobilism prevails. In fact, no decision to change the language regime of the governing bodies has ever been agreed upon. It can be shown that such an agreement is impossible to achieve under the present conditions: a vicious cycle operates in the European Union, a latent 'voting cycle'. In principle, every proposal to limit the use of any one of the eleven languages of the Union would be supported by a large majority for reasons of efficiency and economy. Only the aggrieved member state would cast its vote against it. However, when after a series of votes the last proposal, 'use one language only' (English is the most likely), finally came to the ballot, it would be defeated by the counter-proposal 'use all languages': all members, except the one with the language that lasted till the end, would vote in favour of the new proposal. With all languages back on the roster, the Parliament would be back at square one and another round of voting might begin. It is this latent voting cycle that explains the paralysis, the inability to act, on the language issue in the EU: no solution to the language predicament is stable in the sense that it would win against every alternative proposal put to the vote.

Three assumptions underpin this argument: first, each member prefers a language regime that grants full status to its own language; second, each member state prefers a regime with fewer languages to one with more; third, languages will be put up for elimination in order of their decreasing Q-value. Under those conditions, if the language regime were put to the ballot, a voting cycle would ensue.

The language preferences of the respective member states may be inferred from table 8.5. It presents the Q-values of the official languages in the European Parliament, based on the distribution of language skills not among the population of the EU, but among the Members of Parliament. Interestingly enough, the figures for the Parliament of 1989 yield exactly the same order of Q-values as the data for Europe at large during that period: English, French, German, Italian, Spanish, Netherlandish, followed by the smaller languages (with some variation in sequence, but negligible scores).

English is the language with the greatest communication value, in the European Parliament also. Its position seems to be even stronger there than in the Union at large. More striking is the high Q-value of French, in second position, quite close to English. (This is in contrast

Table 8.5 The European Parliament 1989

	EN	FR	GE	IT	SP	NL	GR	PT	DA	(CA)	Others
Mother tongue (26 unknown)	95	87	81	72	54	34	24	23	16	3	3
Speaking skills	37	31	22	42	24	<10	13	<10	<10	<10	<10
Q_i	0.549	0.522	0.127	0.077	0.025	0.005	0.000	0.000	0.000	0.000	0.000
	EN&FR	FR&GE	FR&IT		EN&FR&GE	EN&FR&IT	EN&FR&SP		EN&FR&GE&IT	EN&FR&GE&NL	EN&FR&IT&SP
Speaking skills	48	15	13		37	13	14		11	18	16
Q_i	0.715	0.607	0.631		0.777	0.833	0.782		0.895	0.777	0.901

EN = English; FR = French; GE = German; IT = Italian; SP = Spanish; NL = Netherlandish; GR = Greek; PT = Portuguese; DA = Danish; (CA) = Catalan (not an official language of the EU).

Figures are based on 'speaking skills'. Only repertoires with more than ten speakers are included.

The German contingent does not include the German Democratic Republic.

Figures for representatives' language competence are based on Mamadouh, 1995, p. 106, who tabulated them from biographical data in *The European Companion*, 1993. (As this book went to press, the most recently published data was being processed.)

to the results for the Union at large in 1995, where French ranks behind German, in third position.) In fact, the number of bilinguals in English is barely higher than that for French. Also significant is the much lower communication value of German. Clearly, many MEPs have learned French, which might be expected from a generation presently in its forties and fifties, and from representatives who were probably in the education system for much longer than the average for their country. German ends up far behind French in the Parliament of 1989, partly because the 17 million East Germans were not yet represented, and also because, apparently, very few members had learned it as a foreign language. Italian and Spanish form a middle group with Netherlandish trailing far behind.[44] No other country obtains a significant score.[45]

Mamadouh has calculated the number of all representatives who lack a speaking knowledge of either English or French: 118 out of 528 (while for twenty-six no data are available).[46] Hence, almost three-quarters of the Parliament could speak (and understand) English or French. It should be noted that an Anglo-French language regime would exclude more than half the Greek and Italian delegate, and two-fifths of the Spanish. Nevertheless, the Q-values and second-language skills for English and French provide strong arguments for an Anglo-French regime in more informal, closed meetings. But given the latent dynamics of decision making on the language issue, this solution is unlikely to be selected in a plenary parliamentary vote, due to the operation of an implicit voting cycle.

Table 8.6 shows the preferences of the respective national delegations for a series of language regimes each with one language more (or less) than the next one. Under the present assumptions, there will always be a majority for the elimination of the next language, against the vote of the delegation whose language is to be dropped. When the language regime for the plenary parliamentary sessions or for the publication of binding decisions by the Union is at stake, decision making must be unanimous, and every proposal will be defeated by the veto of the country affected.[47]

Less momentous issues may be decided by qualified majorities. In that case, every proposal accepted by a majority would be defeated by the next, more restrictive proposal, until 'English only' remained, to be defeated next by the option 'all languages of the Union', with only the Irish and English vote against.[48] This also goes for quite viable options, such as 'English, French, German' (the German proposal for the Council and for the internal affairs of the Commission): it would be defeated over the votes of Germany, Austria and Luxembourg by 'English and French' (the present status quo in the Commission).

Table 8.6 The voting cycle in EU language choices

Delegations	Language repertoires						
	EN	EN&FR	EN&FR&GE	EN&FR&GE&IT	EN&FR&GE&IT&SP	EN&FR&GE&IT&SP&NL	EN&FR&GE&IT&SP&NL&Other
EN&IR	1	2	3	4	5	6	7
FR	7	1	2	3	4	5	6
GE&AU	6	7	1	2	3	4	5
IT	5	6	7	1	2	3	4
SP	4	5	6	7	1	2	3
NL	3	4	5	6	7	1	2
Other	2	3	4	5	6	7	1
BE	7	3	4	5	6	1	2
LU	7	6	1	2	3	4	5

EN = English; FR = French; GE = German; IT = Italian; SP = Spanish; NL = Netherlandish; IR = Irish; AU = Austrian; BE = Belgian; LU = Luxembourg.

The languages are eliminated from the repertoire from right to left, in order of increasing Q-value. The higher the entry, the lower the preference. It is assumed (1) that member states prefer a language repertoire that includes their language above one that does not; and (2) that among these options they prefer a repertoire with fewer languages to one with more languages.

The category 'Other' refers to all other delegations in the European Parliament, and their respective languages: Danish, Greek, Portuguese, Finnish and Swedish. Austria is assumed to vote like Germany, Ireland like the UK; Belgium supposedly prefers all combinations with French to those without it and all combinations with French and Netherlandish those with French only (combinations with Netherlandish and without French are not put to the vote). Similarly, Luxembourg prefers combinations with French and German to combinations with French only, and combinations with French to combinations without it. Figures for representatives' language skills are based on Mamadouh, 1995, p. 106, who tabulated them from biographical data in *The European Companion*, 1993.

Next, the Anglo-French regime would be rejected in Parliament in favour of 'English only' (against the votes of the French and the Belgians) with the familiar result: use the language of every land.[49]

The Union's mute immobility in matters of language is interspersed with an occasional conference or publication that must necessarily remain rather ineffectual. On the rare occasions when the European language issue is raised nevertheless, a cabal of experts in the relevant disciplines and of representatives for the affected interests will use the occasion for a high display of convictions and commitments, most of them as pious in their respect for the language rights of each and every party involved as they are pretentious in their ambitions for a grand scheme of European cultural rapprochement.

  The two do not go together. Clearly, there is a desire to square two circles: the vicious circle of mutually reinforcing expectations that lead to a stampede towards English, and the voting cycle that paralyses all policy at the Union level.

8.4   Institutional Europe (2): the bureaucracy

Just as in the United Nations bureaucracy, where French and English are the 'working languages', in the Union also French is slowly losing ground to English, and has been ever since Britain became a member in 1973.[50] Germany's increasingly insistent demands for the adoption of German as a third working language in the Commission have so far not been heeded. Apparently, the practice of using English and French (plus the language of the acting presidency) commands a solid majority against a proposal that would add German. In fact, candidates for a position with the Commission are required to be fluent in English and French (MEPs are expressly exempt from any language requirement).[51] Among the officials in the Commission's directorates, in 1991, more than 90 per cent were fluent in French, as compared to over 70 per cent in English, about 16 per cent in German and only 6–8 per cent in Italian or Spanish. Almost two-thirds of all internal communication went on in French, about a third in English and only a few per cent in German or Italian.[52] These figures are most likely to have shifted away from French and towards English in the past decade.

  At times, other European languages have been mentioned for inclusion under the Union language regime. The Irish did not press a claim for their language, and only the essential documents of the Union are published in Irish.[53] The Catalonians were partly successful in demanding recognition and their language was granted a status not unlike that of Irish.[54] The Luxembourgers never entered a claim for Letzeburgesch and use German (or French) instead.

The Union recognizes one and only one official language in every state,[55] a rather precarious position that threatens to become increasingly controversial as minorities in the member countries become more vociferous in their demands for recognition of their languages. In fact, as if to compensate for the exclusion of minority languages in official usage, the Commission and the Parliament have been quite active in this field.[56] Sue Wright comments: 'the activists in the regions had found a new ally'.[57] The Union has also financed programmes to encourage students to learn the smaller official languages.[58] But the impact of these schemes is dwarfed by the mostly autonomous growth of language instruction in the school system: 88 per cent of secondary school students now learn English.[59]

The major argument against the multilingual regime of the Union is of course its cost, in time but above all in money. In the expectation of another slate of member states, each with its own language, this prospect becomes only the more intimidating. The costs and the logistics of translation are indeed staggering. All external correspondence from the Commission must be drafted in the official language of the addressee, and all externally binding decisions must be translated into all eleven of the Union's languages (and in the case of major measures also into Catalan and Irish). During the official sessions of the Council and the Parliament every speech must be simultaneously interpreted into all the eleven minus one other languages: one hundred and ten interpreters' teams. And this is what actually happens, although many interpreters translate from more than one language, and quite often translation is indirect, via a more widely known intermediate language. Even in 1989, with only nine official languages, 'the European Community made use of 2,500 translators and 570 permanent interpreters, plus another 2,500 interpreters on temporary contracts'.[60] Expenditures have only increased since, with the addition of new member states and the considerable extension of the Union's regulatory activities. In 1999, the total translation and interpretation costs for the Commission alone amounted to 30 per cent of its internal budget, or 325 million Euros. Adding the expenditure for the other institutions of the Union, the total approaches 700 million Euros.[61]

And yet the costs of translation from and into all official languages of the Union, for correspondence, the publication of major decisions, and the interpretation of the full sessions of Council and Parliament, may be worthwhile. Its multilingualism is a visible and audible manifestation of the Union's respect for the equality and autonomy of the member nations. It allows the Union's citizens to have direct access, in their own language, to its missives, regulations and deliberations, as is their democratic entitlement. And finally, the formation of a corps of translators and interpreters, not just between the major languages of Europe, but between its minor languages, for example Finnish and Portuguese, or Greek and Swedish, is also an important investment in cultural rapprochement between these nations, which so far have rarely communicated directly with one another. These considerations may be highly abstract, but they are not any less vital for that. One only needs to imagine for an instant what might happen if they were swept aside, in terms of alienation among citizens, and recrimination between states.

Moreover, everyday practice does not conform to the full multilingualism that is the rule: the lower in the hierarchy, the more informal the meetings, the fewer the languages used.[62] Among themselves, the 'fonctionnaires' and the political insiders use French and English mostly. They have even come up with a 'curieux mélange' called 'franglais' or 'frenglish', like 'faire du stop and go'. The bureaucratic routine has given rise to a lingo of terms, titles, references and abbreviations that is comprehensible to the 'fonctionnariat' only, but shared by all officials alike, irrespective of nationality or mother tongue. Most 'eurofonctionnaires' have grown accustomed to thinking in a language other than their mother tongue and to switching incessantly between one language and another. But once the linguistic obstacles are overcome by an adroit combination of English and French, another layer of misunderstanding becomes apparent: the differences in administrative style, managerial habits and political custom become all the more patent and can cause frictions by themselves.[63]

8.5 Discussion

The European language debate, in so far as there is one, is governed by the dilemma between maintaining a multiplicity of languages and improving communication in the Union. The European languages acquired national hegemony in the course of the process of state-formation, and it was this process that also provided them with their particular robustness. For this reason, amalgamation among European languages is unlikely. Moreover, national languages will retain most of their functions in the domestic context. In this respect, the European constellation of state languages is quite different from the language constellation on the Indian subcontinent or in large parts of Africa: there English may indeed be more of a threat to the domestic functions of indigenous languages that are not as robust as European languages are.

Hence, at the first level of the European Union, within each member country, the national language will serve mostly for domestic interaction, while transnational functions will be fulfilled by the supercentral languages that ensure Europe-wide communication, again mostly English. As long as each state continues to act as the protector of its national language, it is in no immediate danger, even when a large majority of citizens have also acquired the supercentral language. A state of diglossia, a somewhat precarious equilibrium between two languages occupying different domains in one society, will prevail.

When it comes to the second level, that of civil Europe, statistics and survey data all concur that English is the first language of transnational communication, while French and maybe German play secondary roles in the corresponding regions and for a limited scope of cultural or commercial exchanges.

All official languages of the Union, eleven at present, are used at the third level, that of the Union's governing bodies, for public and ceremonial occasions, for externally binding regulations, and for correspondence with the member states and their citizens.[64] Only two languages, English and French, are used on the fourth level of internal communication in the meeting rooms of the Commission and the corridors of Parliament. German, in third place, lags far behind.

The position of French in the Community has been steadily eroded. German cannot spread enough to come anywhere near the Q-values for English, even in the unlikely case of the Central and Eastern European countries joining the EU and turning massively to German. Spanish, a major world language outside the EU, especially in Latin America, comes in fourth position within the EU. Like Italian it has few prospects for growth, since none of the candidate members uses either language, and they are not likely to attract great numbers of students.

English has in fact become the lingua franca of the European Union. In this respect, the European constellation resembles that of India, or for that matter South Africa or Nigeria, where English is also the linking language, as unwanted as it is inexorable, of the land. But there is a difference: robust as they are, the official languages of the EU member states are better protected and defended than those in the other constellations. And English is more widely and more equally spread in Europe than in Asia or Africa, due to the very high level of secondary education in the EU. The strong position of the official languages in Europe protects them in the unavoidable rivalry with English. The almost universal presence of English, on the other hand, makes it more of a threat in the uneasy equilibrium of diglossia that is now emerging throughout the European Union.

Conclusions and considerations

The global language system comprises the many thousands of language groups on earth in a single, strongly ordered pattern. It is one dimension of the modern world system, but one that so far has gone unnoticed. What does strike most observers right away is the astonishing multiplicity of languages. They tend to overlook the equally astounding fact that all these languages are connected to one another, linked by multilingual persons who hold the various groups together. The hierarchical, concentric pattern of these connections closely corresponds to other dimensions of the world system, such as the global economy and the worldwide constellation of states.

The present world language system is the latest stage in the millennial evolution of human language. After an initial period of dispersion, in which human groups spread all over the face of the earth and their languages grew apart, the main direction of development was towards increasing connectedness between language groups. At quite an early stage, pidgins and lingua francas must have developed between neighbouring groups. Under the early military-agrarian regimes, the language of the rulers came to occupy a central position, connecting the various languages of the subject communities. Ancient empires created a very extensive but very tenuous web of multilingual scribes, clerics and administrators who used the imperial language as a lingua franca all across the conquered territories. The formation of nation-states again entailed a process of language unification: a less extensive but much more intensive process of integration. The court language occupied the central position, connected to the peripheral languages of the territory by bilingual regional elites, initially. As state-formation and nation-building proceeded, compulsory schooling, a pervasive administration and military conscription compelled every citizen to learn the national language. In the process, regional languages were abandoned. This process of intensive integration at home went together with extensive integration overseas, as thin but far-reaching connections were established with the peoples of other continents. The colonial languages gradually gained ground in the overseas possessions and in most places they prevail to this very day. With hindsight, this early transcontinental web of colonial languages represents a preliminary stage of a truly worldwide language system. It thus anticipated the present globalizing process, which also entails the global integration of the language system.

9.1   Conclusions

Improved communications, expanding media entertainment, increasing international trade and travel, and a proliferation of international organizations all contribute to the spread of a few languages for continental and global exchange. Now, a single coherent world language system has emerged; at its core is hypercentral English, which is linked to a dozen supercentral languages; each of these in its turn serves a cluster of peripheral languages. The force that keeps the languages of this constellation together is multilingualism. Thus, the world language system now connects all known languages in a strongly ordered, strongly connected, hierarchical, four-tiered pattern. There are no isolated languages any more, since there are no longer any isolated societies. All human groups on the globe engage in relations of power, trade, migration and cultural exchange. These relations all involve verbal transactions; they are necessarily embedded in language.

The concept of a multi-tiered, hierarchical world language system provides the foundations for a political sociology of language. The dynamics of this emerging global system were generated by processes of state-formation, which led to language unification at home, and to transcontinental expansion of the language abroad. Within each constellation, group rivalry and accommodation, and elite attempts at closure, shape the division of functions between languages.

The concept of a global language system also provides the under-pinning for a political economy of language. In order to characterize the position of a language within this global system, the Q-value provides a measure of its 'communication value'. It is the product of the 'prevalence' of a language, that is the percentage of speakers of a language within the constellation of languages, and its 'centrality', that is the percentage of its *multilingual* speakers among all multi-linguals in the constellation. The prevalence provides a straight indi-cator of the number of speakers that can be directly addressed in a particular language. The centrality serves as a weighting coefficient that indicates the strategic position of a language within the network of multilingual links that constitutes the constellation. The centrality thus represents the connectedness of a given language in the constel-lation, either directly for people who speak several languages, or indirectly through the mediation of multilinguals.

It is assumed that people will choose to learn a language that adds more than another to the Q-value of their language repertoire. Thus, the Q-value provides an explanation of the frequently observed fact that languages with fewer speakers may still attract more learners than their counterparts with more speakers : that is because they are spoken by more people who speak more than one language. The Q-value provides a rough-and-ready indicator of the communication value of a language. In most cases it must be estimated from the available data, since figures on language skills are scarce and scanty in almost all countries. But whenever it can be assessed with some precision (as in India and the European Union) the results inspire confidence, since they match the impressions of expert observers. In all other cases the Q-value must be guessed from disparate sources, but even then, it yields persuasive rankings for the relative strengths of the various languages in the constellation.

The next component of this political economy is the definition of language as a *hypercollective* good, that is, one that both is a collect-ive good and produces external network effects. The most important implication is that a – slow – stampede may occur towards a language that is *expected* to gain speakers, and for that very reason; on the other hand, a language that is believed to be being abandoned by its speakers is therefore given up by an increasing number, who use it less and less and finally no longer pass it on to their children. In many cases, however, both languages survive. A certain inertia makes for an equilibrium between two languages in the same society, each func-tioning in different domains: diglossia. After all, a language is not quickly erased from memory. Moreover, the users of a language have a collective interest in maintaining it, if only in order to safeguard access to all the texts that have ever been recorded (or memorized) in it: this totality of texts constitutes the collective cultural capital of those who know the language. The collective cultural capital is language in its coagulated form. If the language disappears or dwindles into insignificance, access to the accumulated texts is lost. Professional producers of texts (writers, preachers, politicians) have a special interest in defending the collective cultural capital. They are usually the initiators of the movement for the conservation of the language and its culture.

Hence, the political economy of language provides the groundwork for a theory of language as a main determinant of identity: in many respects, having a 'national' or 'ethnic' identity means holding a stake in the collective cultural capital that in its totality defines the group and its members. In fact, language has become the most important denominator of national identities in the present world.

When it comes to an exchange of texts between language groups, the users and the authors of texts in the language with the higher Q-value enjoy all the advantages of their location in the language constellation – they reap 'position rents'. While they need make no effort to learn another language, others spend time, money and memory space to learn theirs. The authors in the big language enjoy a huge and growing audience, the readers and listeners a vast and increasing supply of texts.[1]

The authors in the small language groups face a dilemma: learn the language with the large Q-value and compete, with a handicap, in the big, global league, or exploit a given advantage by addressing a small, mostly captive audience in the home language. The economic theory of international exchange, of protection and free trade, provides some promising leads here. In many respects, translation costs resemble transportation costs, while acquiring another language is not unlike establishing a branch office in a foreign country.

The political economy and the political sociology of language provide the analytic framework for the discussion of specific language constellations, in India and Indonesia, in Sub-Saharan Africa, South Africa and the European Union. Regional specialists have depicted the variety and complexity of the language situation, each in his or her own field of expertise. Yet it takes a comparison across regions to reveal the striking similarities between them, or to highlight a feature, familiar in its home context, as an anomaly in the global setting.

The inexorable nature of language rivalries is amply demonstrated in the discussions of the formerly colonial constellations and of the European Union. Even after independence, neither India nor the new

African states could rid themselves of the languages of their former occupiers: only Indonesia and Tanzania succeeded in abolishing, entirely or mostly, the colonial language and introducing a domestic language instead. Both did so under the impact of a strong nationalist liberation movement and an intensely nationalist successor regime, and both chose a widely spread vehicular language, a popular lingua franca that was not associated with a particular ethnic group within the new nation. In Tanzania, there was no major ethnic group to claim national and official status for its language against the opposition of wary rival groups. In Indonesia, on the contrary, there was a predominant group: the Javanese. They did not publicly insist on the adoption of their language in an independent Indonesia. In the annals of language reform, this remains a unique instance of collective self-restraint.

Everywhere else, group assertion and language jealousies prevented the general adoption of a domestic language, because it was indeed perceived as the language of a specific group. The persistent opposition to Hindi in India provides the most telling example. The very effort of the Hindu nationalists (as opposed to the all-India nationalists of the Congress party) to purify and glorify their language made it unpalatable to the other ethnic groups on the Indian subcontinent. In the ensuing impasse, everything seemingly remained as it was, with English in the position of the linking language: the idiom of the central administration, of national politics, of higher education, science and technology, of big business and the elite media. Yet 'on the ground', things did change. As more people went to school and became literate, they acquired new language skills, learning the formerly colonial and still elitist language, English, and also the dominant indigenous language, Hindi, since both held the promise of better opportunities in the labour market. At the same time, migration to the cities enabled and compelled huge masses of people to learn the urban language, often 'in passing', in the streets, whereas the more successful immigrants sent their children to school, where they learned the formal versions of Hindi and English. Calculations based on data from the Indian census of 1991 show that Hindi has by far the largest Q-value, followed at a distance by English; all other languages remain far behind.

The example of India is by no means an exception. It closely parallels the pattern that emerged on a smaller scale in Senegal, with French as the persistent ex-colonial language and Wolof as the dominant indigenous one.

Nigeria and Congo/Zaire display a different type of constellation, where the ex-colonial languages, English and French respectively, compete with three or four large indigenous ones. In Nigeria the important indigenous languages are Yoruba, Hausa and Ibo, all three of them closely associated with a particular ethnic group. In Congo/Zaire the major indigenous languages are Kiluba, Kikongo, Lingala and Swahili, loosely connected to ethnic groups and widely adopted as popular lingua francas. In fact, in Nigeria, too, there is a popular and broadly used linking language, an English-based pidgin, that might have been adopted as the national language. Like Hindustani in India, Nigerian Pidgin is free of ethnic connotations. But this 'bazaar language' lacks any prestige and never found a Gandhi to elevate it into a medium of national liberation. As even Gandhi failed in his project to make Hindustani the national language, Pidgin never stood much of a chance in Nigeria. In Congo/Zaire the chances for the adoption of one of the indigenous vehicular languages as the national medium are even more remote, because there is an embarras de choix: there are four vehicular languages to choose from, and this frustrates any attempt to single out one of them as the national medium.

In these African countries, as in India, the historical moment of opportunity may well have passed once and for all. What proved to be impossible even during the brief period of nationalist enthusiasm at the time of independence may be even less feasible in times of 'normal' politics, interspersed with so many destructive episodes of ethnic rivalry and civil war.

South Africa after Apartheid seems to play out a similar scenario, notwithstanding all professions of good will towards the indigenous languages. In fact, it is precisely this apparent commitment of the leading elites to the promotion of a multiplicity of languages that paves the way for the further spread of English. A plethora of language rights is stipulated in the Constitution. But, in fact, only Afrikaans, barely, maintains its position in the new South Africa.

According to many linguists, seven indigenous languages could effectively be grouped under just two labels: Sutu and Nguni. They might even be combined into a single 'Bantu' (which again evokes bitter memories of the contemptuous relegation of all indigenous culture to a single denominator during the Apartheid era). Indeed, one or two amalgamated African languages might stand a chance against the onslaught of English, but the opportunity seems to have passed already. Once again, it was the payment of lip service to the ideals of ethnicity, variety and multiplicity that reduced the slight chance of actually achieving equal status which the indigenous languages might have had at some point. Even Afrikaans, the other 'indigenous' African language, albeit of European descent, now finds itself in a predicament. The close association between Afrikaans and the Apartheid regime has made the language unpalatable to the black majority, even though it is the language of many rural blacks and of the urban 'coloured' people of mostly Asian descent.

In fact, Q-values for English are slightly higher than for Afrikaans. Nguni comes third with a sizeable score and Sutu in fourth position. But the Constitution does not mention these amalgams and separately lists seven closely related languages instead. In South Africa, too, the paradoxical outcome is: the more languages, the more English. And since the black population is keenly aware of the avenues to opportunity, there is a clear preference for learning English. Here too, Laitin's apt reference to Mandeville's expression 'private vice and public virtue' applies. In public, most people will praise their ethnic language and defend its equal entitlement; in private, they will make sure their children learn English. This is true in India and Nigeria, in South Africa and in the European Union. In Congo/Zaire or Senegal things are not much different: there people opt for another colonial language, French. Even in Tanzania, Swahili must withstand the pressure of English. Only one colonial language, Dutch, the language of a small nation, was effectively driven out at independence, when *bahasa Indonesia* became the (indigenous) national language of Indonesia. If the Republic withstands the present upheavals, Indonesian may survive as the language of the land.

The most spectacular demonstration of the weakness of domestic languages vis-à-vis the colonial language is supplied by those countries where almost all inhabitants speak one and the same native language, such as Rwanda with Kinyarwanda, or Botswana with Tswana. Their linguistic homogeneity did not prevent French in the first case, or English in the second, from prevailing as the dominant language in commerce, politics, administration, law and higher education. And yet, in these two cases, language jealousies hardly came into play, since all citizens speak the same mother tongue. Again, in spite of their collective, public protestations, in their individual, private decisions they tend to favour the ex-colonial language which holds the promise of career opportunities.

But in these cases a third mechanism becomes more clearly visible: the Western languages serve as a means for elite closure. Although languages are hypercollective goods, and hence, by definition, 'nonexcludable', in these countries large masses of people are effectively prevented from learning them, as they have no access to the schools. As illiterates, they cannot acquire the written, standard version of the official language that is a requirement for the better jobs. Since they do not share in the distinction that comes with command of the 'high' language, they are disqualified as ignorant, uncouth and backward outsiders, unfit for the higher ranks of civil service and business.[2] Finally, the restricted elite languages also help to close the public space of political discussion and participation against the vast majority of the population, in effect keeping them out of politics, preventing them from controlling their rulers or competing for office. The elites, for their part, do not stand to gain if an outsider learns the official language, since it will not increase the Q-value of their repertoire, as they can communicate with everyone in the domestic language anyway.

The same dynamic operates elsewhere, too. In Senegal and Congo/ Zaire, French affords the elites a group monopoly of the most rewarding positions, while English shields them from competition in India, South Africa, Nigeria and Kenya (and, to some degree, even in Tanzania).

The recent history of Rwanda shows that it does not even matter which language the elite uses, as long as it is unintelligible to the population at large. A new Tutsi elite took power when the genocidal Hutu regime collapsed before the invasion by troops of the Rwandan Patriotic Front. The Tutsi rulers switched to English (the language of their long years of exile in Uganda), and French has been largely discarded since 1995. Yet the old Hutu rulers and the new Tutsi officials all speak the same language, Kinyarwanda, just like everyone else in Rwanda. But, apparently, the spoils of power are better managed with an exclusive language, whether it be French, the language of the old imperial allies, Belgium and France, or English, used by the new, American protectors.

Three mechanisms have been identified as instrumental in maintaining the former colonial language in place: ethnic fragmentation and the mutual language jealousies that go with it; private choices of the language that promises access to the upper echelons of the labour market; and, as a corollary, elite attempts at closure of their privileged positions by using a language that excludes (illiterate) outsiders. On the other hand, several conditions may help to replace the colonial with a domestic language: a strong nationalist movement and subsequent postcolonial regime, and the availability of a domestic, widespread and popular lingua franca, not closely associated with any particular ethnic group. On the whole, the absence of predominant ethnic groups furthers the acceptance of the indigenous linking language.

These are not exactly surface phenomena, easily superseded by language reform programmes, no matter how judiciously designed, eloquently advocated or elaborately put into law. In fact, even in the European Union similar mechanisms are at work: language jealousies and private preferences for the most rewarding language.

The European language constellation is in many respects very different from the former colonial countries. But in the Union, too, pious lip service is paid to the ideal of multilingualism, while, discreetly, only two languages are used in practice. However, the European Union does command the resources for elevenfold interpretation and translation and it can afford even larger numbers. Moreover, the citizens of the European Union are literate, hence they cannot be prevented from learning the elite language, or any other for that matter, in the formal, standard, written version.[3] That is why elite closure and mass exclusion do not occur in the Union as they do in the recently independent countries. The majority of Europeans are competent in at least one foreign language, generally English. European languages are indeed hypercollective goods. Third, the official languages of the European Union, due to long-standing protection by their respective states, are more 'robust' than their non-Western counterparts. Granting these major differences, there is much similarity in the dilemmas that multilingual constellations face.

   Like India, Nigeria or South Africa, the European Union recognizes a series of 'official languages', eleven at present. Everyone agrees that this is a completely unmanageable number, which moreover will only grow with the expected admission of new members. If only two, three or maybe four languages had been adopted for official use, they might all have been treated equally. Communication between the four languages of the founding members of the Community required translation in twelve directions. With eleven languages, one hundred and ten interpreters are necessary, and the addition of another dozen members will demand five hundred and six. If, as some language enthusiasts advocate, regional and immigrant languages are also admitted as equals, the number of interpreters will be proportionately disproportionate.[4]

   The formal analysis of the members' preferences for various language regimes has demonstrated that the Council of Ministers or the Parliament is quite unlikely to agree upon any limitation of the present number of official languages: a latent voting cycle operates in these decision-making bodies. All members, except the country that is affected, will support a proposal to abolish another language, until only one language is left (and that will be English). At that point, the proposal 'reinstate all languages' receives all votes minus two (the UK and Ireland). Next, the cycle may begin all over again.

In the Union, multilingualism to its fullest extent is reserved for public and ceremonial occasions, and for decisions that bind the citizens or the member states. In closed meetings and for internal correspondence, the Union's institutions are basically bilingual, in French and English. This informal, pragmatic solution is gradually being adopted for other occasions too. The more informal, the less public the meetings are, the lower in the hierarchy their participants, the fewer are the languages used. As the full round of interpretation becomes increasingly burdensome, MEPs will be more likely to waive their right to speak their own language and will revert to English or French as a matter of parliamentary etiquette, unless they wish to drive home a special point to their own voters.

In European civil society, English has already become the main all-Union language. Only secondary, regional roles are left for German and French as languages of border-crossing communication. The strong presence of English throughout the Union (and in the rest of the world) also manifests itself in domestic settings. In this respect, all continental countries of the Union are now the lesser parties in an unequal exchange of texts with the US and the UK, whether it concerns films, TV series, popular fiction or science. English is used in an increasing range of domains, also in the home society. Even so, the 'robust' nature of European state languages makes it unlikely that they will be driven out of their own countries by the hypercentral language. Rather, people will grow accustomed to dealing with their native language and English, according to the demands of the occasion.

Does the combined evidence point to English as the sole language to survive in the world system? Not at all. In fact, its expansion as a native tongue reached its zenith more than a century ago, with the settlement of North America, Australia and South Africa. Since then, English has spread in spectacular fashion, but only as a second, foreign language. It has expanded as an official language of government in the former exploitation colonies, and all over the world as a lingua franca of business, science, technology and transport, as a language of sports, media and entertainment. But it has not spread as a mother tongue or as the language for everyday, private, intimate use. English, people say in the tropics, is the language of the office during working hours, not of the home at leisure time. What does emerge is a state of diglossia, spreading rapidly in an increasing number of societies: one domestic language in the double sense of an indigenous language and a home language, another language of foreign origin for dealing with strangers; one language for spontaneous, informal contact, the other for official business in a formal setting. Of course, this division of functions is not so neat and clear. It will be contested, shifting this way and the other, with different domains falling to one language or its rival at different times and in different circles, varying from one country to another. Diglossia represents an equilibrium between competing languages, sometimes remarkably stable, especially in rather immobile societies where the domains have been assigned long since; for example, between the liturgical and the vernacular language in Islamic societies.[5] But the language constellations discussed in the preceding chapters are anything but stable. They exist in countries that became independent only a generation or two ago, or that have been for a few decades in the full swing of supranational integration into a European Union.

All societies in the contemporary world are being transformed by the spectacular increase of trade, transport and electronic communication. This 'globalization' proceeds in English. The attendant emergence of diglossia between English and the domestic language precludes for the time being a stable equilibrium, a solid separation of domains between the two languages. People will have to live with both English and their domestic language, and seek a feasible accommodation between the two. This is still the least complicated situation. In many parts of the world, another supercentral language competes with English for the functions of official and long-distance communication: Hindi in India, Turkish in Central Asia, Arabic in the Middle East, French and German (and Spanish) in the European Union. Moreover, quite often, several indigenous languages compete for the functions of informal and everyday usage in the domestic setting: Frisian and Dutch in the northern Netherlands, Tok Pisin and, say, Cimbu in the highlands of Papua New Guinea, or Berber and (Moroccan) Arabic in Morocco.

The world language system was not designed for efficiency. It was never designed at all. It just happened, as the mostly unintended consequence of a myriad of individual decisions (and non-decisions, resignation and compliance) which completely ignored the aggregate consequences for the larger language constellation. Thus, the distribution of languages across the earth occurred almost entirely as a blind process. In the long run, it turned out to be a process of continuous integration that greatly increased the coherence of the human species in its entirety.

9.2   Considerations

The hypercentral position of English at the hub of the world language system is not just self-perpetuating, it is self-expanding. People who want to learn a foreign language expect that others will opt for English, and that is why they themselves choose to learn it. Moreover, the adoption of available and viable alternatives to English is blocked by rivalries between language groups both in the European Union and in many former colonies, where, in addition, the elites seek to maintain their group monopoly on the official language.

Looking back at the constellations discussed in the preceding chapters, it appears that almost everywhere lip service is paid to the ideal of a multiplicity of languages. Yet, almost everywhere, actual practice favours one or at most two languages above all others. In fact, the more languages are formally assigned equal status, the less chance they stand of holding their own against the one dominant language, usually English, sometimes French. This result is not entirely unintended by the parties concerned: the administrative elite in India most probably wanted it that way, and the leadership of the African National Congress may not be entirely innocent of the growing hegemony of English. The leading circles in Nigeria or Botswana did not engineer the dominance of English, they just perpetuated it, much to their advantage. And yet, in all fairness, even if they had been sincere about their commitment to the introduction of a domestic language, the ruling strata in the formerly colonized countries never commanded the resources to fund mass language education or multiple translation between all the languages they had formally recognized. Since they were in no political position to make a choice between rival language groups, they could do little else but grant them all formal recognition and continue their business as usual, in the colonial language that served them so well.

With hindsight, it might be argued that postcolonial elites could have opted for a different rhetoric: they could have proclaimed that the colonial language was part of the spoils of the victorious independence movement. When the European rulers were forced out, they could not take their language with them, but had to leave it for the newly liberated to use as they pleased. Why, indeed, should Africans and Asians forever complain in the most florid and eloquent English about their continued use of the language? They might as well appropriate it as rightfully theirs and enjoy its many advantages.

Sociolinguists and other experts on language policy at present consider the persistence of the colonial languages an unfair and undesirable state of affairs. They plead the cause of the domestic languages, and especially of the – endangered – small, indigenous languages. When it comes to Western societies, until the mid-twentieth century, most language experts supported the promulgation of the national language, the standard language of the state and its political and entrepreneurial elite. The language experts themselves sincerely believed in the superiority of this standard variety (which was partly of their own making) and it must have seemed to them that their advocacy was inspired purely by intrinsic, linguistic considerations. Since then, the mainstream has reversed its course: the majority of language experts now plead the cause of the 'smaller languages', the languages of immigrants, of ethnic and regional minorities. This is partly due to advances in general linguistic theory, which have refuted the arguments for the superiority of one language over another, and in part to the progress of sociolinguistics, which has demonstrated that local dialects and popular sociolects may be less prestigious, but are no less complex or rule-governed than the standard version.

There is a third motive for the defence of the smaller languages: many peripheral languages disappeared and many more are in danger of extinction, not only in remote, exotic areas, but also in the very heartland of the world system. These threatened languages deserve to be protected, very much like endangered animal species. Linguists are to language what ecologists are to nature. But at this point the metaphor runs away with the similarity: species can survive if people will just leave them alone; languages die precisely because people abandon them. In other words, for a language to survive in any real sense of the word, hundreds, nay thousands, of people must be persuaded to go on using it and teaching it to their children. They may not want to do so for very good reasons of their own. On the other hand, they may be mistaken, poorly informed or demoralized, intimidated into believing that their language is worthless. In those cases, language experts might try to convince them of the uniqueness of their language and remind them that their collective cultural capital will be lost with their language. But there is no good reason why people should not switch to another, more viable language, if, all things considered, that is what seems best to them.

The great majority of language experts feel prompted to defend the peripheral languages against the central, and the central languages against the supercentral. However, since people tend to learn the language with the greatest communication value anyway, regardless of expert admonition, this stance is mostly irrelevant. Moreover, because a proliferation of languages actually favours the one predominant language, which then appears the only remaining solution to an increasing confusion of tongues, the experts' stance is also counterproductive.[6] What would be both pertinent and instructive is expertise and advice on how to cope with the precarious coexistence of peripheral or central languages with an increasingly dominant hypercentral language.[7]

Many arguments that are mustered against this predominance of a single vehicular language are downright silly. Thus, the cognoscenti will argue that words in a foreign language are often not what they seem; they may be *faux amis*, seemingly familiar but in fact quite treacherous (like 'faux ami', for example). Or they will point out that certain sentiments and experiences cannot be conveyed in any foreign language at all. They may stress that most people are much less competent in the other language than they think they are. But these observations, valid or not, make no valid arguments against the adoption of a single vehicular language. On the contrary, if transmission from one language to another is so tricky and troublesome, and inevitable nevertheless, then it had better be restricted to the native language and one widespread lingua franca. Between Finnish and Portuguese there may be no more pitfalls than between Finnish and English, but the problems with translation to and from English are much better known, superior dictionaries and textbooks are available, and a vastly greater amount of research is accessible.

It has been argued that the adoption of a single vehicular language affords an unfair advantage to its native speakers and an equally undeserved disadvantage to those with a different mother tongue. In fact, native English speakers enjoy a 'location rent'. The learning efforts of total strangers only add to this advantage. On the other hand, students of English also share the advantage. They acquire access to many more people than any other language could ever afford them. The Q-value of their repertoire grows spectacularly when English is added.

Nevertheless, many proposals have been tabled to compensate for this unfair distribution. Thus, the Danish delegation, on taking its place in the European Parliament, proposed that representatives with English as their mother tongue would henceforward speak French, while the native francophones would counter by speaking English, just to level the playing-field.[8] If everybody cannot be equally proficient, then let everyone be equally deficient. Hence, two Dutch representatives suggested that the Parliament speak Latin.[9] Quite a few authors have advocated Esperanto.[10]

Some language pundits (mostly French) do not so much worry about the fate of the small languages as affect concern for the fate of the global lingua franca: it is bound to degenerate, as so many foreign speakers abuse its grammer, syntax and vocabulary. Sour grapes. Indeed, when speaking to foreigners of limited competence, native speakers may revert to a childlike, simplified version of their language, but they will never use this broken speech with competent strangers, let alone among themselves. Several varieties of English, and French, have in fact emerged. But surprisingly, these 'Englishes' and 'Frenches' have remained mutually intelligible. They do not appear damaged or damaging in any way.

Linguists tend to celebrate the multiplicity of languages and they have gladly suggested that every schoolchild should learn two or even three foreign languages.[11] This could deprive English of its monopoly. Indeed, young children pick up languages seemingly without effort, but most adults who have neither the gift nor the vocation of the polyglot find it hard to master even one foreign language well enough to avoid the many traps and tricks that it holds in store for them.

In a book on the European language predicament, Zapp stressed the equality of all languages in the European Community. He then proposed that each secondary school student in the EC learn at least one out of three or four foreign languages (the other European languages were not that equal after all). This would allow every secondary school graduate to communicate directly with a sizeable proportion of young Europeans abroad.[12] The proposal is, however, somewhat unfair to the students. If they would all learn one and the same foreign language, they could speak with each and every one of their peers in the European Community. In fact, at present almost all of them do learn the same language: English.

So as to increase the variety of languages that young Europeans learn, the Union subsidizes exchange programmes for students to follow courses in other member states. In fact, in order to attract foreign students, many of those courses are taught in English, even in non-anglophone countries.[13]

There is a hopeful expectation that computers will soon solve the present predicament, by providing automatic translation. The European Union has invested massively in the development of translation software. So far, the result has been somewhat disappointing. At present, translation programs seek the equivalent of a phrase to be translated into another language, using a huge and expanding database of standard sentences. In many fields where a finite number of standard phrases are used, such as law, administration and science, the procedure works. If only people would speak and write more like machines, machines would succeed better at translating their words. In fact, many scientists and officials are trying hard.[14]

Only ten years ago, chess buffs were completely certain that no machine would defeat an accomplished player in the foreseeable future. Now, a chess computer has beaten the reigning world champion. Chess lovers deny that the machine plays chess: it just crunches numbers. But it wins.

So far, an accomplished translator still beats the best machine with ease.[15] But there is no doubt that automatic translation will improve. This will increase the chances for other viable languages to function next to English.

In the meantime, several language experts have proposed making better use of passive language skills, understanding rather than speaking, reading rather than writing, as they are so much easier to acquire. In this 'polyglot dialogue', conversation partners each speak their own language, and understand the other one.[16] The 'stratégie de l'intercomprehension' works best between closely related languages, such as Norwegian and Danish, Dutch and German, or French and Spanish. It may also work between, say, English and French, since so many British children have learned some French, and so many French students a little English.

So far, the strategy has not been practised much, and even less documented or investigated. No doubt, in this setting, the many pitfalls of multilingual exchange will work with a vengeance. Moreover, widespread languages, especially widely taught ones, will still remain privileged, since members of smaller language groups – the Danes, for example – are likely to develop a passive grasp of a widespread language – German for the Danes – while the reverse remains improbable. Yet this proposal may help to introduce and safeguard alternatives to English for international use.

One argument against the use of a multiplicity of languages and in favour of a single vehicular language meets broad agreement in all multilingual constellations: the costs of translation and interpretation from and into all recognized languages are prohibitive, not only in India or South Africa, but also in the prosperous European Union, which faces the accession of another dozen members. In the Union, these expenses already represent the largest item on the institutional budget.

Nevertheless, this argument, which seems so realistic, is mostly mistaken. For a body politic in the course of integration, the training and employment of highly skilled intermediaries between the various cultures that must somehow be brought closer together seems to be a vital investment. The expenditure yields many invisible, mostly external effects that are bound to pay off in the long run and in unexpected ways. Money spent on producing well-trained and knowledgeable interpreters should not be evaluated only in a narrow cost–benefit approach that remains restricted to the immediate institutional context. It should also be judged as a contribution to the recruitment of a corps of cultural and linguistic mediators, in Europe as well as in the other multilingual constellations.

This wider viewpoint has immediate implications for the ways in which interpreters and translators should be recruited and educated. Ideally, the European Union should establish its own language academies, where translation is taught not merely as a technical skill, but as the core of a linguistic, cultural and intellectual vocation of bringing together different languages, nations and cultures. The European Union can afford the necessary outlays; in other areas, where wages are lower, the expense will be proportionally less.

While one accepts English as the hypercentral language of transnational and transcultural communication, it might be prised loose from its native speakers. 'Il faut désangliciser l'Anglais', Pierre Bourdieu exclaimed in a public debate on European language policy:[17] English should be de-anglicized. Europeans might develop their own variety, the way Indians did, for example. Native speakers of other European languages, trained in English at the language academies of the Union, could become authoritative editors and judges of style for an emerging European English.

What matters more is to separate the hegemonic language from the hegemonic world views that it transmits. Almost every conceivable opinion, almost any human sentiment, is expressed in English; there is no language that more fully reflects the variety of human experience. The danger of global uniformity is not in the language. It is in the power relations that prevail in the global constellation, where English is the hypercentral language. Thus, the adoption of English as the universal language of science has gone together with the adoption of American models and standards, since mostly American editors and American referees judge contributions to professional journals.[18] As publication in 'international' and 'refereed' (read 'American') journals is a requirement for appointment and promotion in many countries in the EU, American criteria now tacitly decide the selection of European scholars. If English is now widely adopted as the language of transnational communication, it should all the more be used in a critical vein, with a keen ear and an alert eye for the hegemonic messages that the hegemonic language seems to convey so naturally.[19] But, as the language of global communication, English also allows dissident voices to make themselves heard all over the world. If English is the language of the powers that be, it is also the language of empowerment.

The contemporary world language system has evolved over the past centuries according to a dynamics of its own, the aggregate outcome of countless mutual expectations and innumerable individual choices. Everywhere people must cope with several languages, at distinct levels, from the peripheral to the hypercentral. The language at the higher system level increases their opportunities for communication; the language at the lower level embodies their specific cultural capital. Hence, they have a stake in several levels at once.

People have every right to use whatever language they please, most of all their mother tongue. The right of free speech implies not only that people can say whatever they want, but also that they can say it in the language they prefer.[20] They are also entitled to learn the languages of wider communication, if only as a matter of equal opportunity. Within the domestic context, the central, national language enables them to follow extended education, seek employment, deal with the bureaucracy, take part in politics; in sum, to gain access to society at large. On the next level, in multilingual and multinational constellations, and in the transnational context, access is provided by the supercentral language, most of all through hypercentral English. It allows them to attend university, seek the most rewarding jobs at home or abroad, choose from the full supply of global media culture, and keep abreast of advanced science and technology: it opens the world to them.

The complex language constellations that at present prevail in so many parts of the world make for a variety of registers, for code switching, mixing of genres and contamination of vocabularies; they demand the navigating, bridging, ignoring or manipulating of cultural differences and divergent traditions; they allow us to adopt loan words and foreign sayings, to create ambiguity and *double entendre*, to exploit jokes, ruses and slights. In short, they both enable and compel people to alternate between different levels. A wealth of tongues is an embarrassment of riches.

Notes

Chapter 1   Introduction: the global language system

1   Cf. De Swaan, 1991b.
2   Karl Deutsch, 1966 [1953], pioneered a global and systemic vision of communication networks in his *Nationalism and Social Communication*.
3   There are precursors in formal and quantitative theory. Greenberg, 1956, proposed a 'diversity index', elaborated by Lieberson, 1964; Laitin, 1992, 1993, 1994, and others applied game theory; Pool, 1986, 1996, and others discussed compensation proposals; Church and King, 1993, analysed bilingualism in terms of network externalities. See also chapters 2 and 3 for further sources.
4   See Cavalli-Sforza, 2000; Deacon, 1997; Jablonski and Aiello, 1998; Lieberman, 1984; Pinker, 1994; Ruhlen, 1994.
5   Thus, the number of bird species has been revised regularly, from 19,000 in 1900 to some 9,000 in 1945 and since then upwards again (science supplement to *NRC/Handelsblad* 29 August 1999, p. 5).
6   Thus, for example, Netherlandish (or Dutch) is a 'Co-Sprache' (co-language) of German, as are Yiddish, Afrikaans and Frisian: the product of economic and political rather than linguistic needs having grown apart (Décsy, 1973; cf. also Goossens, 1976; Ammon, 1991).
7   See Goody, 1986; Ong, 1982.
8   Of old, peripheral languages were often connected by unwritten indigenous, vehicular languages, and also by pidgins, creoles and sign languages. See also Wurm et al., 1996.

9 The French sociolinguist Louis–Jean Calvet, 1999, pp. 75–99, has devoted the better part of a chapter to the presentation of the world language system. After an initial reference and a faithful, at times almost verbatim, summary of my 'galactic model', he rebaptizes it a 'gravitational model'.

10 See the atlas of the world's languages by Moseley and Asher, 1994.

11 Cf. Genesis 11:1–9.

12 See Goudsblom et al., 1996.

13 See Parker, 1983; Pollock, 1998.

14 Gensini, 1985.

15 'The divisions of linguistic continua and homogeneous space into vernacular languages and heterogeneous places accordingly constitute a cultural act, not a natural fact ... Language and place were becoming mutually constitutive' (Pollock, 1998, 63).

16 For a description of the spread of the great languages of the world, in mutual competition, see among others Calvet, 1999; Laponce, 1987; Wardhaugh, 1987; for English see Crystal, 1997; Graddol, 1997.

17 See Collins, 1986.

18 See Ramsey, 1987. Figures have been taken from the monumental study by McConnell and Kerang, 1995. The authors mention that 'Han language has big differences among its dialects between some of which communication is difficult' (p. xxvi). Compare this to Cheng, 1979, p. 541: 'Whether or not Taiwanese, Hakka, Cantonese, and Mandarin, etc. are different languages or different dialects of the same language is a problem. Western linguists have regarded them as different languages on the ground that they are not mutually intelligible. Some Chinese patriots view this to be an attempt by imperialists to divide China. I use the term "variety" here to cover "language" as well as "dialect".' See also Barnes, 1982, p. 264: 'The amount of difference which obtains between these speech groups [namely of North Chinese (Mandarin)] has been obscured by the tradition of referring to them as "dialects," and there is compelling evidence that speakers of these groups are not as a rule capable of intercommunication.' Cf. also Ramsey, 1987, p. 7.

19 McConnel and Kerang, 1995, p. li.

20 They are classified as Balto-Slavic languages in the index of Crystal, 1987, p. 300.

21 See Cheng, 1979.

22 Chartier and Corsi, 1996, esp. the contribution by Weindling.

23 For comparative statistics on scientific publications in various languages, see Laponce, 1987; Ammon, 1998.

24 McNeill, 1976.

25 See Crosby, 1986.

26 Zolberg, 1999.

27 See Veltman, 1996; Putzel, 1996; Vaillancourt, 1996.

28 See Benrabah, 1999.

29 Casanova, 1999.

30 It is usually associated with the work of Immanuel Wallerstein, 1974, and his school.

31 Or, as Elias, 1978, called it, a 'figuration'.
32 De Swaan, 1988.

Chapter 2 The political economy of language constellations

1 Thus, for example Domínguez, 1998, discusses 'language' as a 'product' with a 'price' that can be 'sold to consumers', but as the metaphor is elaborated, all specific meaning is lost.
2 See Pinker, 1994.
3 E.g. Kindleberger, 1983.
4 Coulmas, 1992, presents a very informative overview of the costs involved in language learning, multilingualism, interpretation etc., but never looks at language as an economic good per se.
5 E.g. Katz and Shapiro, 1986.
6 Kindleberger, 1983, p. 377, remarks with respect to standards of measurement: 'In fact they are a strong form of public good in that they have economies of scale. The more producers and consumers use a given standard, the more each gains from use by others through gains in comparability and interchangeability.' Accordingly, it may be argued that these standards create communication networks with respect to some measurement. Kindleberger presents as examples measures of time and of value (i.e. money). Language remains entirely unmentioned! It is, however, referred to in passing by Arthur, 1990.
7 The languages themselves are not produced and marketed, but language courses and textbooks are. There are languages that have been 'produced' by someone: the 'artificial' languages such as Volapuk or Esperanto (cf. Eco, 1993), and computer codes called 'languages', such as FORTRAN, C or BASIC. Since their value is so much dependent on their spread, the inventors tend to leave the languages at the free disposal of everyone, while textbooks or courses on CD-ROM etc. may be sold for a price.
8 See Olson, 1965, p. 5. See also De Swaan, 1988, p. 5.
9 The notion that no one can be prevented from learning (and using) a language often implicitly presupposes that people are literate and can teach themselves from books. Poor and illiterate people can easily and at low cost acquire the languages they hear at work and in the streets (including low versions of the official or colonial language), but they are effectively excluded from learning the 'high' version in a way that bestows its cultural capital upon them too.
10 Domestic attempts at exclusion do occur, such as the Turkish government's effort to prevent Kurds from using or learning their language. Since language acquisition mainly occurs in the bosom of the family, such policies are notoriously costly in human terms and in policing efforts. Unless they are coupled with physical deportation or even

annihilation, as in Nazi Germany and in the Soviet Union under Stalin, they remain mostly ineffective and may even provoke a counter-movement for the preservation of the threatened language.

11 Of course, some 'artificial' languages were created by a single author; the most successful case is that of Esperanto. But even its creator, Zamenhof, could not on his own assure that the language would be used and 'maintained'; that is, he could not 'impose' it (or, for that matter withdraw it, once it had gained acceptance; cf. condition two). There is some evidence that languages that have come into existence in the relatively recent past, such as creole languages, were indeed 'created' by a relatively small number of people, possibly very young children, in a very brief span of time; see Pinker, 1994, pp. 32–9; cf. also Mintz, 1985. In the case of a 'secret' language, as with any secret, it takes only one 'traitor' to give it away. But even in that case, one might argue that the language continues to exist, although no longer in secret.

12 For most collective goods, there is a limit to this condition: when too many people want to enjoy them at the same time, 'crowding' occurs. But no such effect manifests itself in the case of languages; they cannot be 'overused'.

13 Schelling, 1978, pp. 99–102, discusses this notion of 'tipping' as it applies to neighbourhood migration. Laitin, 1993, pp. 229–31, adopts this concept of a 'tipping game' for the analysis of foreign language learning.

14 Church and King, 1993, have shown that in a system of two languages, learning costs being equal, and individual gains increasing with the number of users, all efforts will be directed towards learning the language that had more users to begin with, unless quite outlandish learning-cost curves are assumed.

15 See the proposal by McConnell, 2001, for an agency that would collect data on the distribution of languages across the world.

16 The foreign speakers of language B are those in column B (4 + 2; excepting the 60 B-only speakers in the (B:B) cell), plus the speakers of A&B&C (1) who are not native B-speakers.

17 Cf. Greenberg, 1956.

18 Cf. Lieberson, 1964.

19 The probability that the first speaker of a pair is picked from language group i, with repertoire ρ_i and numbering f_i speakers, is indeed f_i/N^S. The odds that the second speaker is selected from group j with frequency f_j is $f_j/(N^S - 1)$. The odds of forming a pair of speakers from respectively ρ_i and ρ_j is therefore $(f_i \cdot f_j)/(N^S)(N^S - 1)$. If language repertoires ρ_i and ρ_j have a language in common (the intersection of ρ_i and ρ_j is not empty, $\rho_i \cap \rho_j \neq \varnothing$), their speakers can communicate directly. In that case, for a given language repertoire ρ_i, the sum of all the products $(f_i \cdot f_j)/(N^S)(N^S - 1)$, or $\sum (f_i \cdot f_j)/(N^S)(N^S - 1)$, defines the odds that a speaker with repertoire ρ_i will be randomly paired with another speaker with whom direct communication is feasible. Summing these sums for

all ρ_i produces the odds that any pair will be formed which has a language in common. Subtracting this value from 1 yields the complementary probability that a pair *without* a common language will be selected – Greenberg's *A*, or diversity index:

$$A = 1 - \sum_{i=1,k} \sum_{j=1,k} \left(\frac{f_i}{N^S} \cdot \frac{f_j}{N^S - 1} \right) \text{ for } \rho_i \cap \rho_j \neq \varnothing; \ k = 2^n$$

where n is the number of languages in the constellation and 2^n denotes the number of repertoires.

Since $\sum (f_j / N^S)$ for all repertoires ρ_j such that $f_i \cap f_j \neq \varnothing$ is by definition identical to the prevalence ρ_i of ρ_i, the expression for Greenberg's *A* may also be written as:

$$A = 1 - \left(\sum_{i=1,k} \frac{f_i}{N^S - 1} \cdot p_i \right); \ k = 2^n$$

Chapter 3 Language, culture and the unequal exchange of texts

1 'Netherlandish' and 'Dutch' are here used as synonyms, denoting the language spoken in the Netherlands and Flanders (i.e. the Flemish part of Belgium). In the literature one sometimes also encounters the term 'Netherlandic'. The spelling and vocabulary of Dutch are standardized under the auspices of the joint *Nederlandse Taalunie*.

2 Dorian, 1989; Hindley, 1990; the brief contributions on 'Endangered languages' in *Language* 68.1, March 1992, pp. 1–42; and Uhlenbeck, 1994.

3 See Phillipson, 1992. Cf. also Clayton, 1999, who points out that not only the imperialist strategy of imposing the conqueror's language, but also the 'pragmatic' strategy of mobilizing domestic languages in support of imperial rule, may bolster the conqueror's position.

4 The most vivid and interesting discussions occurred in India and in anglophone Africa. Cf. for the latter Omotoso, 1994, p. 28: 'If the cultural imperialists imposed their languages in the past, why have these Africans now, either as individuals or as states, not gone back to the restoration of their own languages? Or are the imperialists still at work?' Omotoso heaps especial scorn on Ngugi wa Thiong'o, a Gikuyu author who after much international success declared that he would write no longer in English but in his native language only. Omotoso 'could only smile and wonder for how long this decision would hold'. Wa Thiong'o's Gikuyu writings were immediately translated into English and from there into other languages. Cf. Ngugi, 1986. Omotoso quotes Caliban from Shakespeare's *The Tempest* (I, ii):

> You taught me language; and my profit on't
> Is, I know how to curse: the red plague rid you
> For learning me your language.

Omotoso then (p. 33) cites the Nigerian novelist Chinua Achebe on English: 'I have been given this language and intend to use it.' Appiah, 1992, p. 60, comments 'few things, then, are less native than nativism in its current forms'.

An early, frank statement in favour of europhone languages from a Nigerian minister visiting India in 1953 is quoted in Whiteley, 1971, p. 189: 'We are not keen on developing our own languages with a view to replacing English. We regard English as a unifying force.' For two authoritative and opposing voices from India, cf. Kachru, 1986, and Dua, 1994.

5 A similar effect operates in the multinationalization of firms: cf. Carnoy, 1993, p. 71: 'The greatest pressure on automobile firms to become global, however, is still protectionism – the power of national political aims imposing themselves on comparative prices.' Since duties and other trade restrictions make it more costly to import or export, 'the general effect will be to increase the costs of using external markets relative to multinational control' (p. 60). That is, it will probably pay to open a branch office or subsidiary plant in the protectionist country.

6 To readers, the advantage of learning a highly central language may reside in the opportunity not only to read its literature but also to read the translations that have been made into it from a multitude of other languages.

7 Hoskins and Mirus, 1988, discussing the popularity of TV drama, take as their central concept the notion of 'cultural discount': 'A particular programme rooted in one culture, and thus attractive in that environment, will have a diminished appeal elsewhere as viewers find it difficult to identify with the style, values, beliefs, institutions and behavioural patterns of the material in question.' Cf. also Biltereyst, 1992, p. 533: 'A country-by-country analysis shows that own-language drama is successful', and on p. 536: 'the popularity matrix...in those countries is dominated overwhelmingly by domestic and US fiction, with a clear stress on home made drama. Fiction from other countries is virtually non-existent.'

8 One must not, of course, underestimate the value of 'an unhappy childhood: a writer's goldmine', according to Connolly, 1961.

9 Cf. www.censusindia.net.

10 As long ago as 1980, almost two-thirds of all chemical and almost three-quarters of all medical articles were published in English. Adding five other languages would account for well over 90 per cent of publications in these fields; cf. Laponce, 1987, pp. 66–8. Except in the USA, television entertainment is almost all imported, and imports come overwhelmingly from the United States; cf. Varis, 1984; Biltereyst, 1992, p. 523.

11 For statistics on translations from Netherlandish, see Heilbron, 1995.
12 On the aversion to dubbing and subtitles among English-speaking television audiences, see Hoskins and Mirus, 1988, p. 500.
13 Heilbron, 1995, and Casanova, 1999, have applied the notion of a world language system to the network of translations. Casanova has shown how Paris functions as the hub of a network that elevates literary works from peripheral and central languages to the supercentral level of French belles-lettres, while Heilbron has demonstrated that literary works from the smaller languages enter world literature by being translated into English and other world languages and from there being introduced into smaller languages. Similar movements have been observed for popular music, films etc.
14 In 1990, 93 per cent of young people in Europe speaking some foreign language had learned it at secondary school; cf. *Eurobarometer*, 1991.
15 There is a counter-tendency: as the cultural elites, fluent in the foreign language, are familiar with these foreign texts and performances, their prestige may convince others that these products are indeed desirable, and the demand for translated versions may increase accordingly among those sections of the public that have not learned the foreign language. The relative impact of the two tendencies is a matter for empirical investigation.
16 'Dumping' refers to the practice of selling goods at marginal cost or lower on separate – that is, usually foreign – markets (so that on the home market the goods may still fetch the full price).
17 For an even-handed but sceptical discussion of the defence of protective trade measures, see Bhagwati, 1988.
18 Import quotas on foreign films and TV productions were strenuously propagated by the French and only recently dropped by the EU in favour of production subsidies for domestic films and television productions. See 'EU ministers pick funding over quotas', *International Herald Tribune*, 22 June 1995. Cf. also Forrest, 1994.
19 This is the briefest possible summary of the position taken by Pierre Bourdieu, 1984, and by many of his predecessors.
20 I am well aware that this is, or should be, a most controversial consideration, since the substantive criteria of cultural 'merit', or contribution to collective cultural capital, can in no way be inferred from generally accepted principles. Nevertheless, there is an empirical finding that deserves mention in this context: both Pierre Bourdieu, 1984, pp. 33–4, and, in a replication study, Van Calcar and Koppen, 1984, found that people who are not at all interested in or knowledgeable about 'high culture' agree that it is more meritorious, or that it is something for other, 'better-educated' persons to enjoy. This is an aspect of what Bourdieu calls 'cultural hegemony'. Cf. also De Swaan, 1991a.
21 For a brilliant and early exposé of this practice, see Van Bruggen, 1925. See Goudsblom, 1988, for a lucid essay on the self-constraints that the 'civilized' or high version of the language imposes on its users. Cf. also Bourdieu, 1991.

22 These are affective bonds in the first place, but they also represent a form of social capital: claims to peer support in times of need.

23 Cf. Muth, 1968.

24 Translators usually translate into their native language.

25 For brevity's sake I have limited this discussion to the case of English; however, Arabic and Spanish – both growing international language communities – and French – a stagnant one at best – would provide interesting cases on their own.

26 This again is a tenet of classical international trade theory since David Ricardo and John Stuart Mill; cf. Bhagwati, 1988, pp. 24–33.

27 Nevertheless, economic, political and military dominance do not always translate into cultural hegemony: the former Soviet Union tried hard to introduce its language and culture in the satellite countries, but without much success. Young East Europeans swear that they know no Russian, even after six to nine years of intensive instruction (cf. Vogel, 1994).

28 Cf. Skutnabb-Kangas and Phillipson, 1994.

29 'En Afrique, chaque vieillard qui meurt est une bibliothèque qui brûle [In Africa, when an old person dies, it is as if a library went up in flames]': Hompate Bâ, quoted in Diongue, 1980, p. 53.

30 The effort need not be a sacrifice; it may be pleasurable in itself.

31 The term is a variation on an expression coined by Ferguson, 1959: 'diglossia', a concept he restricted to the coexistence of two 'varieties' of the same language for different domains in the same society. Later the term was used in a broader sense for the coexistence of two languages rather than registers of a single language.

32 The prevalence $p_{\{i,j\}}$ of a two-language repertoire $\rho_{\{i,j\}}$ is defined as the proportion of all speakers in the language constellation S who have either the language i or the language j or both in their repertoire. When all j-speakers have learned the language i, $p_{\{i,j\}} = p_i$. Equally, the centrality $c_{\{i,j\}}$ is defined as the proportion of *multilingual* speakers who have either i or j or both in their repertoire. Unless there are speakers of a third language in the constellation who also speak j but not i, or speakers of j who also speak some third language but who do not speak i, which is rare in the actual constellations under study, it is the case that $c_{\{i,j\}} = c_i$. As a result:

$$Q_{\{i,j\}} = p_{\{i,j\}} \cdot c_{\{i,j\}} = p_i \cdot c_i = Q_i$$

Competence in the language j no longer adds to the Q-value of a speaker of i.

33 It is customary to argue that no one is individually motivated to contribute any effort to this collective objective. However, in this case also, many of the activities required are not just a 'sacrifice', but may well be rewarding in themselves; for example, admonition, rebuke, scandal, ostracism, even joining demonstrations, participating in riots or collaborating in terrorist attacks may generate individual satisfaction. In

general, informal, negative social sanctions are quite often a pleasure to apply. Cf. De Swaan, 1988, p. 5.

34 Cf. Laitin, 1987, 1989b.

35 Cf. Schelling, 1978; Laitin, 1993.

36 No one has depicted these dilemmas more starkly than David Laitin, 1992, 1994.

37 The public is much concerned with the appearance of foreign, mostly English, loan words in the vocabulary. But such additions to the lexicon leave the morphological 'hard core' of the language, its grammar, syntax and pronunciation, mostly unaffected; cf. Hagège, 1987, pp. 27–89. The resilience of many European languages is demonstrated by the adoption of English verbs, such as 'delete' or 'save' in computer speech, which are then conjugated according to the rules of the borrowing language, e.g. in Dutch: '*Ik heb de file geseef*' – i.e. 'I saved the file'. Surprisingly, both the tense and the word order are spontaneously transformed into perfectly correct Dutch, a feat that students often fail at in formal translation exercises.

38 This programme comes very close to what Norbert Elias used to call the '*Menschenwissenschaft*'; cf. also Goudsblom, 1992.

39 See De Swaan, 1999.

Chapter 4   India: the rivalry between Hindi and English

1 Cf. *India Today*, 18 August 1997, 'State of the Nation' (quoted from website). To the question 'Do you think there should be one language across the nation?' 61 per cent of respondents answered in the affirmative, and 77 per cent believed this one language ought to be Hindi (as opposed to 8 per cent for English).

2 Originally the Vita Schedule contained fourteen languages: Assamese, Bengali, Gujarati, Hindi, Kannada, Kashmiri, Marathi, Malayalam, Oriya, Punjabi, Sanskrit, Telugu, Tamil and Urdu. Sindhi was added later. In 1992, with the seventy-first amendment to the constitution, Konkani, Manipuri and Nepali were added to the list. Cf. *Manorama Yearbook*, 1996, p. 464.

3 See *Census of India*, 1991, Series I, Question C-7, p. 9. In the 1971 census the speakers of scheduled languages made up 88 per cent, but as three languages were added to the list they added another 0.6 per cent. The other 7.4 per cent comes from the increase in speakers of the other fifteen scheduled languages.

4 The census lists forty-eight varieties 'and others'. It could be argued that the numbers for closely related Urdu ought to be added, or even those for other cognate languages, swelling the numbers for Hindi to well over 50 per cent; cf. Krishnamurti, 1979, p. 681ff. Beyond the Indian subcontinent there may be some 50 million or more Hindi speakers.

5   The most important being Telugu, Tamil, Kannada and Malayalam, comprising together some 22 per cent of all Indian mother tongue speakers.

6   India consists of twenty-five states and seven Union territories: website of the Indian Bureau of the Census, 'India at a glance'. Cf. also Laponce, 1987, p. 61.

7   Krishnamurti, 1988, pp. 54–64.

8   Grant McConnell has developed a composite index of 'language vitality' and applied it to India, where each of these languages displays considerable vitality in the area where it is an official language. Cf. McConnell and Gendron, 1993.

9   Laponce, 1987, counts publications in scientific journals of chemistry and medicine in various languages: 65 per cent and 73 per cent respectively are in English, Hindi is barely visible, and except for a single article in Punjabi, the other Indian languages do not appear in the statistics.

10   Although Hindi newspapers and periodicals outnumber and outgrow those in English, when it comes to advanced culture or science, technology, commerce and industry, the complementary function of English has remained stable; cf. Dua, 1996b.

11   Website of the Indian Bureau of the Census, 'India at a glance'. Illiteracy in rural areas is 55 per cent on the average and 60 per cent for women; in large Hindi-speaking states such as Bihar and Rajasthan it is well over 60 per cent.

12   It was pointed out to me by Prof. Satish Saberwal that this analogy with the distinctions made by Basil Bernstein, which I applied to early modern Europe, also holds for contemporary India. See Brass, 1974, ch. 1, esp. pp. 25–6 *et passim*.

13   These gradual transitions, compounded by the tendency to report a language one wishes to be identified with rather than the language one actually uses, make it difficult to define census categories and assess the results. The expressions 'fluid zone' and 'stable zone' convey this lack of linguistic robustness, especially in the central part of India. Cf. Khubchandani, 1979, 1986.

14   Pandit's example of 'a citizen of Bombay' who in the course of a single day uses five different languages is not typical but highly exceptional (Pandit, 1979, pp. 176–7). On the other hand, India's population is so large that even an extraordinary exception may still number many millions. Not surprisingly, according to the 1991 census, bilingualism (overall 19.44 per cent) was lowest (11.01 per cent) among Hindi speakers, who on account of their numbers and their position in the Indian heartland need it least, and highest among Konkani (74.2 per cent), Sindhi, Kashmiri and Sanskrit (51.59 per cent) speakers (*Census of India*, 1991, Series 1, Question C-8, p. 7). Bennett, 1980, p. 236, complains that 'It is a continuing disappointment that in India, where plurilingualism is widespread, the census should be as ineffectual as it is in compiling the relevant evidence' – only the first additional language

mentioned by respondents is recorded. Tri- and quadrilingualism, let alone quinquelingualism, accordingly disappear from the statistics. Nevertheless, Indian census data on language are more detailed and more complete than those for almost any other country.

15 See Hobsbawm, 1990, esp. pp. 51–63.

16 See Deutsch, 1968; Guxman, 1968; Jakobson, 1968.

17 Cf. Joshua Fishman's conceptual pair 'nationalism' and 'nationism' respectively (Fishman, 1972).

18 The title of a collection of essays (Vermes and Boutet, 1987).

19 Cf. Pollock, 1998, p. 46, who, too, maintains: 'the primary site of vernacular production everywhere at its commencement was the site of political power, namely, the royal court'.

20 Ibid., p. 58.

21 Or like petals around the heart of a flower: the 'floral model' that I used to describe this constellation in my *In Care of the State* (De Swaan, 1988).

22 See Gopal, 1966, p. 157. It should be added that English, and the English, initially spread through India from the margins inward, from the seaports towards the centre.

23 See chapter 3 for the derivation of the Q-value of communication and its application to the 'floral' constellation.

24 On the position of the Indian civil service in this language game, see Laitin, 1989a. See also De Swaan, 1997b.

25 See Scotton, 1982, p. 84: 'At present, access to the official language via formal schooling is restricted by the horizontal communication network made up mainly of the elite.'

26 Hans Dua, 1996a, has discussed the issue in terms of a 'Language of Wider Communication' (LWC), usually a former colonial language, and, the 'national language', the largest domestic language (e.g. Hindi): 'The use of the LWC is not only perceived as a unifying force but also as a means to reject the imposition of one indigenous language over others. Thus the LWC can serve as a double-edged political weapon cutting across linguistic diversity on the one hand and preventing the prominence of another indigenous language or language group on the other. Secondly, it is pointed out that the LWC is equally disadvantageous to all language groups as opposed to the national language which puts its speakers in an advantageous position as compared to other native language groups ... the LWC is neither neutral nor equally disadvantageous in the sense that the political and social elite are generally highly educated in it and have a better access to it than other groups. They have a great stake in its propagation and domination.' And also: 'the developed nations have a stake in the prolonged hold of the LWC in the developing countries'.

27 See Lieberson, 1982, p. 56, who concludes: 'the role of a language, once established, will tend to be perpetuated long after the disappearance of conditions which were initially necessary for its generation'.

28 '[T]o rule effectively, one must love India, to love India, one must communicate with her people; and to communicate with her people,

one must learn her languages': Kopff quoted by Rahman, 1996, p. 96, who discusses the controversy between Orientalists and Anglicists.

29 See Mehrotra, 1993.

30 See Sridhar, 1987.

31 See Mallikarjun, 1986, p. 18, who quotes Gandhi: 'We should use Hindi for the work that we are today doing in English.' For a characteristic nationalist rejection of English, see Dwivedi, 1981, p. x: 'continuing with the status quo would surely result in loss of face before the community of nations as no self-respecting nation would brook the ignominy of carrying on with a foreign language as its official language'.

32 See Sridhar, 1987, pp. 302–3. Cf. also Gopal, 1966, pp. 180–92.

33 On the complex relations between the Hindu nationalist and the Indian nationalist currents in the Congress movement, cf. Jaffrelot, 1996.

34 See Das Gupta, 1970.

35 Dua, 1990.

36 For a history of these movements, cf. Srivastava, 1979, and Misra, 1979; see also Brass, 1974.

37 See Ramaswamy, 1997, a book rich in textual analysis and strangely devoid of historical fact; see also Dua, 1996a, 1996b.

38 Section 3 of the Act as quoted by Gopal, 1966, p. 224.

39 See Dua, 1985, pp. 203ff.

40 See Brass, 1974, pp. 16–19, who points out that neither demands for secession, nor claims to form a state based on religious bonds, have ever been accepted. States based on specific languages or language groups have, however, been created.

41 See Schwartzberg, 1985, esp. p. 160.

42 See ibid., p. 177.

43 *Census of India*, 1991, Table C-8. This volume alone counts 1070 pp. of tables.

44 Only scheduled languages with more than 10 million speakers have been included. Together they are spoken by 798 million speakers out of a total of 807 million for all scheduled languages, and out of 838 million for all languages (scheduled or not). The languages represented in table 4.1 accordingly represent 98 per cent of all Indians in 1991.

45 According to the website of the Indian Census Bureau, just over half of all Indians are literate, and illiteracy is higher among rural than urban dwellers, among women than men, and in the north than the south.

46 See Dua, 1985; Laitin, 1989a.

47 'Urban in-migrants recognize that there is a necessary configuration of societal elements – the right certificates, the right contacts – which they must have in order for them to be benefited by learning the main official language': Scotton, 1982, pp. 86–7; cf. Inglehart and Woodward, 1967.

48 Cf. McConnell and Gendron, 1993, p. 315.

49 As Dua (1991, p. 114) points out (and this agrees with the floral model): 'it was not the bureaucrats alone who had a vested interest in the perpetuation of the colonial language. Even the politicians had an interest in that the control of the elite and the bureaucrats through a

reward system conducive to their self-interest strengthened their hold on them as well as [on] the government.'

50 Since almost all multilinguals speak either Hindi or English or both, the sum, M^s, of all multilinguals in the constellation roughly equals the sum of all multilinguals with Hindi, English or both in their repertoire. Accordingly, $C_{h\&e} \approx M^S$ and $C_{h\&e}/M^S = c_{h\&e} \approx 1$.

51 Cf. *India Today*, 18 August 1997, 'State of the Nation' (quoted from website). Asked which languages they 'speak', 66 per cent mentioned Hindi, 19 per cent English, and when it came to 'reading' and 'writing' the respective percentages were 47 and 49 for Hindi and 34 for English. This last is more than the percentage of those who 'understand' or 'speak' it! Clearly, English is a language one learns at school, while Hindi is frequently picked up in informal settings and through the media. Moreover, the fact that the percentage of those who understand or speak Hindi is so much higher than that of those who read or write it may well be a consequence, at least in part, of the high incidence of illiteracy in the Hindi belt (roughly 50 per cent). Cf. www.censusindia.net.

52 Dua, 1996a, p. 17.

Chapter 5   The triumph of *bahasa Indonesia*

1 On Kenya, see section 6.3; on India, see chapter 4. The Philippines are a most complicated case. Tagalog is the most widely spoken language, but English the official language, along with Pilipino, a stillborn version of Tagalog into which elements from other languages of the archipelago were incorporated in the hope of mitigating language jealousies among outlying groups.

2 See Hoffman, 1973, esp. pp. 19–22.

3 Geertz, 1968; Siegel, 1993, pp. 15–21.

4 Abas, 1978, pp. 99–101. See also Anderson, 1990, p. 199.

5 Groeneboer, 1993, p. 412.

6 Cf., however, ibid. pp. 332, 412.

7 De Josselin de Jong, 1976, esp. pp. 16–17.

8 Groeneboer, 1993, p. 421, quotes the nationalist author Abu Hanifah, who estimated that, as late as 1940, less than 5 per cent of Indonesian intellectuals spoke Malay, and even if they did speak it they thought in Dutch and silently translated what they had to say into Malay.

9 www.britannica.com.

10 See Steinhauer, 1994, for a survey of statistics.

11 These numbers are based on the response to census questions: respondents (over 4 years of age) were asked what their mother tongue was, and also which language they used most often. The percentages are only marginally different (Chambert-Loir, 1996, p. 33).

12 For the distribution of Javanese and Malay, see the map in Poedjosoedarmo, 1982, p. viii.

13   Cf. Anderson (1990, pp. 142–4): *bahasa Jakarta* is to Indonesian what *ngoko* (low Javanese) is to *krama* (high Javanese).
14   Based on Steinhauer, 1994, p. 5; Biro Pusat Statistik, 1991, table 13.
15   Steinhauer, 1993, p. 4.
16   Biro Pusat Statistik, 1991, table 11.
17   Moeliono, 1986, p. 37. Steinhauer, 1997, p. 25, reports that Indonesian is the language of instruction from the third year on.
18   For a similar family situation in Senegal, cf. Calvet, 1987, p. 97, who cites a research report: 'Ce n'est donc pas l'influence de la famille, mais *l'influence du milieu* que subissent les élèves [It is thus not the influence of the family but of the *social environment* which the pupils experience].' Cf. also Steinhauer, 1997, p. 25: 'Nearly all regional languages in Indonesia, including the very large ones, are losing ground, at least percentually, to Indonesian.'
19   Steinhauer, 1994
20   See Omar, 1996, p. 530; cf. also Omar, 1998.
21   Cf. Fullante, 1983; Gonzalez and Bautista, 1986; Sibayan, 1986.
22   The most important monograph is Groeneboer, 1993.
23   The Netherlands continued to claim and occupy New Guinea until it was transferred to Indonesia in 1962 on the condition that a plebiscite be held to determine its future. This resulted in New Guinea's definitive incorporation into Indonesia in 1969.
24   Groeneboer, 1993, p. 447; Halim, 1986, p. 101.
25   In fact, in 1957 President Sukarno banned all Dutch books and publications, and forbade the use of Dutch in education (Groeneboer, 1997, p. 79).
26   Van Doorn, 1994, p. 101.
27   Groeneboer, 1993, p. 311, quoting a contemporary educationalist writing in 1902.
28   See Anderson, 1990, pp. 135–7.
29   Among the 'ultraprogressives' the opposite concern existed: education in Dutch language and culture might alienate the 'inlanders' from their peers and from their origins. Cf. Geschiere (as quoted in Van Doorn, 1994, p. 101).
30   Groeneboer, 1997, p. 69.
31   Van Doorn, 1994, p. 27.
32   Poedjosoedarmo, 1982, p. 4, who settles the matter in a footnote (3).
33   See, however, for an early Javanese objection to Malay, Steinhauer, 2000, p. 7.
34   Moeliono, 1993, p. 136.
35   'The oath of the young': one country, one nation, one language.
36   Anderson, 1990, pp. 138–9.
37   Anderson, 1990, p. 194.
38   Ibid., p. 197.
39   Ibid., p. 207.
40   Ibid., pp. 130–46.
41   Ibid. pp. 215–18.

42 Ibid. pp. 210–11.
43 For a similar argument, see Steinhauer, 2000, pp. 7–9.
44 See Dieckhoff, 1993.
45 Gensini, 1985, p. 363.
46 Javanese in different versions was spoken by roughly half of the population of Indonesia ($p_j = 0.5$), but only a small number among them spoke another Indonesian language. A rough guess would be around 10 per cent ($c_j = 0.1$), yielding an estimated Q-value for Javanese: $Q_j = 0.05$. Malay was spoken by about 15 per cent of the Indonesian population, by some two-thirds as a second language: $Q_m = (0.15) \times (0.66) = 0.099$.
47 Moeliono, 1993.

Chapter 6 Africa: the persistence of the colonial languages

1 Fabian, 1986, pp. 81–2.
2 Curtin, 1984, pp. 42–3.
3 Ibid., p. 138.
4 The felicitous expression is again Curtin's, p. 38.
5 Wesseling, 1978, p. 6.
6 See, however, Walter Ong's chapter on the 'psychodynamics of orality' (1982, pp. 31–77). Cf. also Jack Goody on the administration of (African) states without writing (1986, pp. 99–113): 'For writing was in principle available to the states of the West African savannahs since the beginnings of the second millennium AD, just as it had been used by Europeans on the coast since 1500' (p. 99). The question remains, however, why they did not use it.
7 Cf. Eisenstein, 1981, p. 61, on the malleability and flexibility of non-codified languages.
8 Fabian, 1986, pp. 82–3.
9 Cf. Goodman, 1968, pp. 724–5: 'The rediscovery of the various national languages in the Soviet Union came as a mixed blessing to the national minorities, since it often had the curious effect of increasing the importance of Russian among the non-Russian peoples... Soviet policy elevated dialects into languages, even at the cost, if need be, of inventing new, written alphabets. This conscious policy of fragmentation might be explained, in large part, by the fear that large, cohesive blocs of non-Russians, speaking a common tongue, would present a formidable threat to the centralized, Russian-based dictatorship.'
10 Indeed, the famous multilingualism of Africans may to a large extent be exaggerated due precisely to the overaccentuation of differences and to the fact that very few Western linguists are able to check their claims, since one is hard pressed to find scholars who can match the alleged knowledge of their informants with their own expertise in the many languages in question.

11   This leaves out of consideration the lusophone countries, formerly occupied by Portugal, where Portuguese has remained the official and vehicular language: Guinea-Bissau, Cape Verde Islands, Mozambique and Angola. As mentioned earlier, North Africa, with its arabocentric constellation, is also ignored in this chapter.

12   The situation is very similar to that in neighbouring Burundi. Since the successful invasion in 1994 by the troops of the Rwandan Patriotic Front, who had been based in Uganda, English has become the second official language of Rwanda (www.britannica.com).

13   All figures taken from www.britannica.com.

14   Cf. Manessy quoted in Chaudenson, 1991, p. 35: 'La proportion de ces derniers [les locuteurs qui ont une connaissance suffisante de français pour participer à la vie publique] est évaluée à 10% par M. G. Anson ...au Togo où le taux de scolarisation est proche de 58% [The proportion of the latter [those who have sufficient knowledge of French to participate in public life] is estimated at 10% by M. G. Anson ... for Togo where some 58% attend elementary schools].' Manessy comes up with similar proportions for Senegal and Mali. The great disparity is explained in terms of overcrowded classes and poorly skilled teachers.

15   Laitin, 1992, pp. 152–3.

16   Officially, it is called the 'Organisation Internationale de la Francophonie'.

17   Flaitz, 1988, pp. 103–13.

18   Crystal, 1997, p. 56. Couvert, quoted by Queffelec in Chaudenson, 1991, p. 104, mentions that roughly 90 per cent of the population speak no French.

19   Crystal, 1992, pp. 338–9.

20   Nkusi, 1991, p. 134.

21   It is worthwhile to quote Manessy, 1994, p. 72, at some length: 'les raisons qu'ont les Africains d'apprendre le français ne sont que très partiellement analogues à celles qui motivent habituellement l'acquisition d'une langue seconde; ce qui est en jeu n'est pas l'extension du champ de la communication, mais l'accès à un statut social privilégié [the reasons why Africans learn French are only to a very limited extent analogous to those which usually motivate the acquisition of a second language; what is at stake is not the broadening of one's communicative potential, but the access to privileged social status]'. And on p. 77, apropos of Sango: 'Le fait le plus banal, le moins contestable, est que, sauf exceptions, le français est la langue maternelle d'aucun de ses usagers et qu'il est principalement transmis par l'école [the most banal and least contestable fact is that, exceptions notwithstanding, for none of its users is French their mother tongue and that it is mostly transmitted through education]'.

22   Katesi, 1988, p. 202.

23   Alexandre, 1967, p. 122.

24   It is of course Pierre Bourdieu, 1984, who has stressed this point of 'hégémonie', that is, the acknowledgement by the dominated of

their own inferiority, and especially the function of language as a core element of the cultural capital that they lack. See also Bernstein, 1974.

25 Manessy, 1994, mentions this repeatedly in his book, referring, however, to Senegal. See also Dumont, 1983, pp. 196, 202.
26 Kazadi, 1991, p. 147.
27 Ibid. p. 98.
28 Oral communication from Ms Madeleine Mukamabano, *Radio France Internationale*, 'Echo d'Afrique', Paris.
29 On processes of inclusion and exclusion along ethnic rather than linguistic lines in Rwanda, see De Swaan, 1997a.
30 Figures taken from www.britannica.com.
31 See Diouf, 1994, p. 15.
32 Chaudenson, 1990. See for example Swigart in Chaudenson, 1990, p. 546, for a related observation on the capital city of Dakar. Even couples sharing a minority language tend to speak Wolof with their children. Similar observations are reported for Indonesia; cf. chapter 5.
33 This figure is considerably lower than the estimates made earlier, which generally hover around 80 per cent. Cf. Dumont, 1983, p. 25 *et passim*, who estimates the percentage of 'l'ethnie Wolof' at 36 per cent and the number of all Wolof speakers at more than 80 per cent, while this latter number is 'expanding vigorously'. On p. 216 Dumont also mentions that as late as 1963 the percentage of Wolof speakers was only 68. Cf. also Daff, 1991, p. 146, who reports that Wolof '[est] parlée par plus de 80% de la population [is spoken by more than 80% of the population]'. Diouf, 1994, p. 62, states that: 'il est rare de trouver des Sénégalais qui ne parlent pas, ou qui ne comprennent pas le Wolof [One only rarely encounters a Senegalese who does not speak or understand Wolof]' and that (p. 63): 'La Wolofisation est surtout un phénomène urbain [The spread of Wolof is in the first place an urban phenomenon]'. This may well explain the overestimation of Wolof as a second language: the researchers collect their material above all in urban settings. Moreover, the census they refer to dates from 1964 (Calvet and Wioland, 1967): the forms had to be filled out in the classroom and the teachers – for the most part convinced nationalists at the time – helped their students answer the questions. Cf. Calvet, 1994.
34 Calvet, 1994, p. 98.
35 Cf. Dumont, 1983, p. 325, who quotes figures that would amount to at least 10 per cent, at most 20 per cent, of males at the time being competent in French, and at most 1 or 2 per cent of females. Cf. also Diouf, almost thirty years later (1994, p. 62): 'moins de 20% de la population [less than 20% of the population]'. See also Daff, 1991, p. 146: 'Actuellement nous ne disposons pas de données statistiques fiables pour déterminer le nombre réel de locuteurs du français. On ne peut pas davantage déterminer le degré de competence en français des Sénégalais. A notre connaissance, aucune enquête de ce type n'a été faite [At present we have no reliable statistics that allow us to assess the level of French

skills among the Senegalese. To our knowledge, no survey of this sort has ever been undertaken]'.

36 There are, to be sure, exceptions at the local level: the majority of inhabitants of Dakar are said to speak Soninke as a second language, and in Ziguinchor a majority have apparently learned Mandingo, according to the census data of 1989 as presented by Calvet, 1994, p. 90.

37 Calvet, 1994, p. 101 (my translation). This is, of course, the economic and symbolic power that Bourdieu, 1991, refers to. Although Calvet adopts many of Bourdieu's ideas, Calvet criticizes him for ignoring the issue of multilingualism.

38 Calvet, 1994, p. 101.

39 Swigart, 1990, p. 547.

40 Ibid., p. 548.

41 Daff, 1991, p. 157.

42 Dumont, 1983, p. 196.

43 Ibid., p. 206.

44 This is what David Laitin has called, invoking Mandeville's expression, 'private vice and public virtue'. Cf. note 15.

45 Mandingo, in several variations, functions as a vehicular language throughout the West African region and as the major domestic language of Mali. Like Wolof it must compete with French, and it is identified with the Mandingo-speaking peoples of Mali. Therefore, it has never been accepted as a lingua franca for the region (Calvet, 1982, p. 192).

46 Nyunda ya Rubango, 1986, pp. 253–4.

47 Ibid., p. 253.

48 Ngalasso, 1990. See also Ngalasso, 1986.

49 See Goyvaerts, 1997, pp. 34–5.

50 Ibid., p. 41.

51 Sango is a dialect of one of the Adamawa-Eastern languages. It shows the result of contact with French, as well as its usage by many tribes in trade along the Ubanqi river. It is the lingua franca of the Central African Republic and is extremely widespread as a second language in Central Africa. Many other trade languages based on an African vernacular are also spoken in this central area of the great rivers; for example, a pidgin dialect of Swahili, a pidgin form of Kongo (Kikongo) and Lingala.

52 See Samarin, 1989, p. 244.

53 Goyvaerts, 1997, p. 30.

54 Fabian, 1986.

55 Kashala Mwepu Kashadidi and Bwantsa Kafunu Obonobon in Chaudenson, 1991, p. 165.

56 Cf. De Swaan, 1996, p. 18.

57 Chaudenson, 1991, p. 194, schema 3. Chaudenson, pp. 23–4, uses the term 'corpus' for the distribution of language skills and the frequency with which the language is used; 'status' refers to the functions it fulfils in a given society. According to his indices, the corpus of French in Senegal is roughly equal to that in Congo/Zaire; in Rwanda it is indeed smaller. The status of French is slightly higher in Congo/Zaire.

58 Nyunda ya Rubango, 1986, p. 261 (my translation).
59 The oppressed have a fine sense for the gradations of prestige in the ranks of the oppressors; the Congolese soon suspected that the Flemish were less regarded than the Walloons at the time, while Dutch was just a Nordic planet circling the French sun.
60 Nyati-Ramahobo, 1998.
61 Herbert, 1992, pp. 2–3, on the 'fiction' of the distinction between Tswana and Northern Sotho.
62 Fardon and Furniss, 1993, p. 153.
63 Most of the facts in these paragraphs have been taken from Janson and Tsonope, 1991, esp. pp. 18–22. Cf. also Van Binsbergen in Fardon and Furniss, 1993, esp. pp. 153–65.
64 'Unimodal' countries (the expression is Fishman's) are those which are torn between the desire to respect their national tradition and maintain their native language as the national language on the one hand, and the desire to meet the demands of the modern time by adopting an international language on the other; Verdoodt, 1979, p. 510.
65 Well-nigh all Batswana speak Tswana ($p_t \to 1$), and almost all bilinguals therefore also have Tswana in their repertoire ($c_t \to 1$); accordingly, $Q_t \to 1$. As roughly 10 per cent of the population speak English, and practically all multilingual citizens do, $Q_e = p_e \cdot c_e = (0.1) \cdot (1) = 0.1$.
66 Crozon, 1996, p. 19.
67 Ngonyani, 1995, p. 72, quotes a survey in which more than 90 per cent of all respondents considered themselves competent, or even very competent, in Swahili. Cf. also Fasold, 1994, pp. 265–77, on Tanzania.
68 Cf. Rwezaura, 1993, pp. 33, 35, 40, 45; Ngonyani, 1995, p. 70.
69 Ngonyani, 1995, p. 80, table 6.
70 Whiteley, 1969, pp. 80–1.
71 Freely translated as 'family feeling' or 'solidarity'.
72 Whiteley, 1969, pp. 64–5.
73 Crozon, 1996, p. 20.
74 Ibid., p. 27.
75 Ngonyani, 1995, pp. 70, 90.
76 Cf. Yahya-Othman and Batibo, 1996, who entitled their article on English in Tanzania 'The Swinging Pendulum'.
77 Cf. Ryanga, 1990; Rwezaura, 1993.
78 Ngonyani, 1995, p. 87. Cf. also Mazrui and Mazrui, 1996, p. 295.
79 Akinnaso, 1989, pp. 134–5; Ajulo, 1990, p. 516.
80 Ajulo, 1990, p. 518.
81 Ajulo, 1995, p. 171.
82 Brann, 1993, p. 640; Arasanyin, 1997, p. 63.
83 Oladejo, 1991, p. 259.
84 Bamgbose, 1996, p. 370.
85 Ndolo, 1989, p. 681.
86 Akinnaso, 1989, p. 136.
87 Oladejo, 1991.

88 Cf. Oladejo, 1991, p. 262.
89 Ibid., p. 263. There have been other proposals for an all-Nigeria lingua franca: Wazobia, a mixture of Ibo, Hausa, Yoruba and Swahili (championed by the well-known author Wole Soyinka), or Guosa, another mixture of indigenous languages, after the example of Esperanto, or Hausa, which is rejected for its close association with the peoples of the north and Islam. Cf. Fakuade, 1994. Cf. also Ayo Bamgbose, 1996, p. 367, who mentions the huge pressure exerted on children to speak the correct version of English, rather than Pidgin.

Chapter 7   South Africa: the survival of the old language regime

1 Cf. Van Rensburg, 1997, p. 23: 'Hoewel die Koi hulle moedertaal afgeleer het, leef die taal nog op 'n manier voort in ander tale wat deur die Koitale beïnvloed is [Although the Khoi have abandoned their language, it still somehow survives in other languages influenced by it]'. Only the Nama of southern Namibia represent a sizeable population (83,000) of speakers of a Khoisan language (www.britannica.com).
2 Cf. Finlayson, 1995. Initially, it was assumed that women of Khoi or San descent who married into Xhosa families had imported these click sounds.
3 Cf. Thompson, 1995, pp. 70–109, 112.
4 Cf. Thompson, 1995, p. 160.
5 Webb et al., 1992, pp. 33–4.
6 This is the title of a – Dutch! – novel by Henk van Woerden, *Moenie kyk nie*.
7 The expression comes from Van der Plank, 1971, p. 68.
8 Thus, Afrikaans authors such as Etienne van Heerden and André Brink are published in Dutch translation in the Netherlands. The Cape Town version as spoken by 'white' Afrikaans speakers is, however, intelligible to native Dutch speakers with a little effort after some exposure.
9 'This decision did more to harm Afrikaans than all the previous attempts to mock it or to classify it as a language with limited expressive capability': Cluver, 1993, p. 25.
10 Cf. Janks, 1990, pp. 254–5; see also examples of Bantu education's aims of keeping blacks as second-class citizens (ibid., p. 250).
11 Cf. Ridge, 1996, p. 22: 'more than half the mother tongue speakers of Afrikaans are not white'.
12 Cluver, 1993, p. 28.
13 On the nationalistic and moral–religious implications of linguistic purism in the case of Afrikaans, see Kriel, 1997.
14 In this case, too (as in Indonesia), the Dutch language did not maintain itself as effectively as other colonial languages did. This appears to be a

function of the weak position (Q–value) of the Dutch language in the world language system, while, in contrast to the Portuguese in Brazil, Dutch settlers never became a majority in either South Africa or Indonesia.

15 LANGTAG, 1996, p. 71.
16 Some related languages are still spoken in the marsh district of northern Botswana and by the Nama in Namibia.
17 For a recent survey of 'the black languages' of South Africa, cf. Wilkes, 1995.
18 Marivate, 1993, pp. 97–9, presents a brief survey of Afrikaner opinion in the mid-1940s.
19 Janks, 1990, p. 250.
20 The LANGTAG report, 1996, p. 72, quotes Doke, 1961, pp. 3–4: 'For the sake of argument, let us suppose England to be a heathen country. Four distinct Missionary Societies commence work, one among the Cockneys, one among the university class, one in Yorkshire and one in Devonshire. Each produces a translation into the "local" vernacular, each further uses a different orthography and some split up their words into their component parts. What an enormous difference there would be between the four literary efforts: they would not be mutually understood.'
21 LANGTAG, 1996, p. 72.
22 Formally, the homelands were entrusted with the mission of promoting the language of their territory. Cf., for Lesotho, Matsela, n.d., *c*.1992.
23 Ridge, *c*.1999, p. 3
24 Cf. Blok, 1997.
25 LANGTAG, 1996, pp. 78–9.
26 Ibid., p. 79, quoted from Msimang, 1992.
27 Alexander, 1992; Prah, 1998. Several scholars had already proposed linguistic consolidation of cognate South African languages in the 1930s, and Jacob Nhlapo defended the proposal again in the 1940s; cf. Ridge, *c*.1999, p. 11.
28 Laitin, 1992, pp. 19–20.
29 Ridge, 2000, p. 5, puts the proportion of native speakers of English at 9 per cent of the population and estimates that 56 per cent are able at least to understand it; see also, however, Webb, 1996, pp. 178–9: 'It is far more likely that, in reality, less than 25% of the black population of South Africa know English well enough to be able to become empowered through it, i.e. obtain meaningful access through it to educational development.' Cf. for a sceptical account also Phetoana, 1993. Some authors (e.g. Janks, 1990) have stressed the inadequacy of English-language skills among most blacks: some have concluded that therefore English should be assigned a less pivotal position, others that education for blacks, and not only in English, must be improved.
30 Webb et al. 1992, p. 59, quote Alet Kruger, published version 1995, who, among some hundred and thirty 'registered' translators, found only one who translated from an 'African' language and one who translated into an African language.

31 Ridge, 1996.
32 Oral communication from the Deputy Speaker of Parliament, Ms Baleka Mdete Kgositsele.
33 In naming the scheduled languages of South Africa I shall adhere to the terminological suggestions put forward by Mesthrie, 1995. I will also follow his ethnic classifications ('coloured', 'black', 'white').
34 Paragraphs 30 and 31; cf. Ridge, 1996.
35 Moreover, provincial legislatures have the right to decide (with a two-thirds majority) which of these official languages will be the official language(s) of the province; Ridge, 1996, p. 5.
36 Ibid.
37 Van Rensburg, 1997, p. 54: 'Die bevoordeling was egter ook skadelik vir Afrikaans [This preferential treatment, however, also damaged Afrikaans]'.
38 After sanctions were lifted, South Africa was better able to participate in world trade, cultural and political exchanges and the like. Needless to say, English is the lingua franca of these domains. Thus, South Africa's opening up only served to strengthen further the role of English within South Africa itself.
39 Schuring, 1993a, p. 4. It is quite likely that the many hundreds of thousands of 'illegal' residents in South Africa, who were registered in the homelands but lived in the townships, were not counted anywhere, hence the speakers of indigenous languages may be underreported in the census. When the former homelands are excluded and only the population of the Republic of South Africa at the time is considered, Zulu still scored highest (27 per cent), Afrikaans came second (18 per cent) and English third (11 per cent), while Xhosa was in fourth position, since its 4 million speakers in the homelands of Ciskei and Transkei were ignored, and Tswana ended up in seventh position (with 5 per cent), as almost 2 million Tswana speakers in another homeland, Bophuthatswana, were ignored. For the present purposes, these figures are mostly significant as evidence of the effective exclusion of the population in the homelands. This, of course, increased the relative importance of Afrikaans and English in South Africa (without the homelands).
40 For this purpose it is assumed – realistically – that all inhabitants of the homelands speak an African language, and that knowledge of English and Afrikaans in these rural areas is half as frequent as it is in South Africa without the homelands.
41 In the 'old' South Africa, 22.2 million people spoke an African language, and all 7.6 million citizens of the homelands may be added to this number: 29.8 million. In 'pan-South Africa' 18.5 million spoke only an African language. It follows that (29.8 million − 18.5 million =) 11.3 million speakers of African languages could also speak English or Afrikaans or both (Schuring, 1993a, table 16, p. 17). Of all African-language speakers in the 'old' South Africa, 30 per cent spoke Afrikaans and 32.5 per cent English (Schuring, 1993, table 14, p. 15). It is assumed

here that in the homelands the percentages for those who spoke either language are one half of that, that is, 15 per cent for Afrikaans and 16.25 per cent for English. This yields 0.3×22.2 million $+ 0.15 \times 7.6$ million $= 7.8$ million African-language speakers who also speak Afrikaans and 0.325×22.2 million $+ 0.1625 \times 7.6$ million $= 8.5$ million who also know English; together 16.3 million. Since there were only 11.3 million African-language speakers who also knew English or Afrikaans, it follows that 5 million must know both Afrikaans and English. Hence, 7.8 million $- 5$ million $= 2.8$ million African-language speakers also know Afrikaans, but no English, 8.5 million $- 5$ million $= 3.5$ million also know English but no Afrikaans, and 5 million know both English and Afrikaans.

Schuring mentions that 12.5 million people in 'pan-South Africa' spoke English and Afrikaans: since it has just been calculated that 5 million inhabitants were trilingual in Afrikaans, English and an African language, it follows that 12.5 million $- 5$ million $= 7.5$ million must be bilingual in Afrikaans and English. The figures for Afrikaans only and English only can now be calculated from Schuring's table 16. Since there are 16.3 million Afrikaans speakers and 12.5 million Afrikaans and English speakers, there must be 16.3 million $- 12.5$ million $= 3.8$ million people who speak Afrikaans but not English: among these 3.8 million, as has just been established, there are 2.8 million Afrikaans and African-language speakers, which leaves 3.8 million $- 2.8$ million $= 1$ million monolingual Afrikaans speakers. Equally, as Schuring reports that there are 16.4 million English speakers in South Africa (including the homelands), the same method, by subtracting the Afrikaans and English speakers, and next the trilinguals in Afrikaans, English and an African language, yields 16.4 million $- 12.5$ million $- 3.5$ million $= 0.4$ million monolingual English speakers. In table 7.1 here, these figures for Afrikaans only and English only have been set at 1 million each. The last step is to split up the category 'African' for every combination into 'Nguni' on the one hand, and 'Sutu' on the other. Since the overall percentages of the two language families are known, this is done proportionally. Table entries are obtained by rounding to the nearest million.

42 Schuring, 1993a, pp. 12, 13, 14 respectively.
43 Makoni and Kamwangamalu, 1998, p. 162.
44 Schuring, 1993b, pp. 17–18, presents figures on the preference for English-language education among black parents.
45 And the author continues (p. 91): 'What made this policy even more deplorable was its connection with the Bantu Education Act no 47 of 1953, the Christian National Education Manifesto, the Homelands policy and the ideology of apartheid in general.' Cf. Marivate, 1993.
46 Cf. Jacobs, 1993; Leibowitz, 1993; Webb, 1996; De Klerk, 1996. See also Amuzu, 1993, a contribution that openly promotes the use of English at all levels of education.
47 This has been the case since the foundation of the ANC in 1912. Ridge, c.1999, p. 3: 'Their [i.e. the leadership's] return from exile brought back into South Africa a group of highly competent leaders, most with a high

level of proficiency in English and a tendency to use it to avoid any ethnic taint in their engagement with a multi-ethnic reality...The preferred language of the oppressor was Afrikaans, so using English was an oppositional gesture.'

48 Venter, in press. English is also considered as a means of access to equal opportunity. In 1993, the ANC published a position paper (the 'NEPI document'), advocating 'that all South Africans have access to English (because it is currently the language of access to further education, and because it is an established *lingua franca* in South Africa and further afield), without jeopardizing the rise of African languages'. The last phrase seems a pious afterthought. Peter Titlestad, 1996, p. 171, cites this passage and comments: 'Here English is privileged by hints rather than by the open statement.'

49 Venter, 1999.

50 Flaitz, 1988.

51 The option of a distinct 'South African English' standard has been advocated, if only for pedagogical reasons. But Titlestad, 1996, p. 168, argues: 'A standard other than the international standard would help nobody', and black parents would be cheated out of the advantages they expect from standard English.

52 A similar willingness to abandon Dutch was demonstrated by the Netherlandish-speaking Javanese elites after 1945, when the nationalist regime made no effort to reinstate Dutch, discarded by the Japanese occupiers, but adopted Malay as the official language of the new Republic and chose English as its foremost foreign language. For the educated Javanese this meant surrendering at one stroke the two languages they knew best, Javanese and Dutch. After the decolonization of Indonesia the Dutch did hardly anything to salvage the last remnants of Dutch in the archipelago.

53 Cf. Phillipson, 1992, who takes, however, a less personified view of 'imperialism'.

54 This global domination of English is in turn used as an argument against the domestic adoption of Afrikaans (which the Suid-Afrikaanse Akademie vir Weetenskap en Kuns advocates), since the latter's international function is 'doubtful' (Titlestad, 1996, p. 170).

55 Venter, 1999, p. 2.

Chapter 8   The European Union: the more languages, the more English

1 This has not changed at all, as the sentence that follows this quotation shows. 'There was much talk of milk pools and butter mountains, of a unitary currency, of liberalizing movements for EC citizens and restricting access for outsiders, but the language in which these issues were dealt with remained itself a non-issue' (cf. De Swaan, 1993, p. 244).

2 The European Community became the European Union on 1 November 1993.

3 Cf. De Swaan, 1988, ch. 3, where communication opportunities are also formalized, but in a different manner. That chapter also contains a more extensive discussion of language unification in Western Europe.

4 Cf. Balibar, 1987.

5 Dorian, 1989.

6 A constellation in which all bilinguals speak the central language, a, and one of a series of regional languages, i, is a 'floral figuration' (De Swaan, 1988). In this constellation, $C_a = \sum C_{a\&i} = M^s$, and $\sum C_i/M^s = C_a = \sum C_{a\&i} = 1$. For the central monolingual speakers the prevalence of their language, p_a, increases as speakers of the peripheral language learn their language, a, and $Q_a{}^s$ increases with it. For the regional monolingual speakers p_i decreases (as some of them become bilingual) and c_i increases if their regional language gains bilingual speakers at a faster rate than the overall increase of bilingual speakers M^s in the land.

7 In this floral constellation, the prevalence $P_{j\&a}$ (where j is some regional language and a the central language) remains constant, since for every bilingual gained, a monolingual in that regional language is lost; the centrality remains constant, $C_{j\&a} = C_a = 1$, since all bilinguals have a in their repertoire.

8 As they learned the central language, a, the communication value of their repertoire increased from Q_j to Q_{ja}, that is, the repertoire with their regional language and the central language.

9 Since the Q-value, Q_j, of regional language j would shrink whenever the total number of bilinguals, M^s, in the denominator increased faster than the numerator with the number of bilinguals, C_j, in their own region. Apparently, regional languages may lose in Q-value as their population lags in learning the central language.

10 On the role of the state in the emergence of national languages in Europe, see also Wright, 2000.

11 Cf. Haas, 1982.

12 There are some parallels here with the terminology adopted by Mazrui and Mazrui, 1993: the 'hegemonic' or 'dominant' language has the largest number (plurality) of speakers, the 'preponderant' language is spoken by the greatest number of multilinguals (centrality) and the 'imperial' language is in a position akin to that of the 'court' language before its spread.

13 In fact, when asked which language they speak at home, young Europeans overwhelmingly – that is, more than 97 per cent – mention the national language, except in France, Spain and Luxembourg, where the percentages are still 94, 88 and 87, respectively; cf. *Eurobarometer* 1991, table 3.6.

14 Fasold, 1994, p. 42. Originally the term 'diglossia' referred to the coexistence of distinct varieties of the same language for different domains of the same society. Fishman also uses the term for the presence of two languages in different domains. Cf. Fasold, 1994, p. 4.

15 See however, Mamadouh, 1995, and Wright, 2000, for discussions and regulations.

16 A discussion of the Community's 'language regime' may be found in most introductory texts on the Community. See Labrie, 1993. The eleven official languages of the member states are equal in every formal respect; in practice, French and, increasingly, English are the media of administrative deliberation and political consultation. Luxembourg has French, German and Letzeburgesch as official languages, Belgium French and Dutch (and German), Ireland English (and Gaelic), and the official language of Austria is German.

17 These figures, and most others, are from Kloss and McConnell, 1989. For a specification of the – ambiguous – status of Irish in the European Communities, cf. 'Answer to written question no. 896/86 by the Commission of the European Community' of 14 November 1986. The major treaties of the Communities have been translated into Irish, it may be used in the European Court and Parliament, and decisions modifying major treaty texts and general information to the public at large are also published in Irish. See also O'Riagáin, 1991.

18 But Catalan cannot be used in the European Parliament: cf. resolution A3 169/90 adopted by the European Parliament on 11 December 1990. See also Barrera i Vidal, 1991.

19 German is used in the Commission, but only rarely, since it is the foreign language of very few, mostly Dutch, officials.

20 E.g. Friedrich, 1969, pp. 204–5: 'and with French having become the unacknowledged *lingua franca* of the Commission (all languages are supposed to be on an even footing) this [the most widely spoken] second language is apt to be French'.

21 Cf. Flaitz, 1988; also Wardhaugh, 1987.

22 The Conseil publishes a yearly report on the state of the French language: *État de la francophonie*, 1986–date. That informal pressure was exerted upon French scientists to use and promote French in international meetings was confirmed in oral communications by P. Birnbaum and Y. Hersant. Ammon, 1996, p. 263, mentions similar pressure by the president personally on French diplomats. For a discussion of French language policy, cf. Durand, 1996.

23 Cf. Strevens, 1987.

24 See for example Cestac, 1987; Goffin, 1987. For statistics on the use of French, English and other languages in the EC bureaucracy, see Haselhuber, 1991; Gehnen, 1991; Mamadouh, 1999.

25 E.g. Étiemble, 1973, and the riposte by Hagège, 1987. Cf. also Durand, 1996.

26 Denison, 1980; see also Conrad and Fishman, 1977.

27 Cf. Ammon, 1996, p. 262.

28 German pressure to improve the stature of its language in the EU first became public in 1992. 'Chancellor Kohl has asked the European Community to give the German language equal weight with English and French in EC affairs': *International Herald Tribune*, 3 January 1992.

The request had been submitted in preceding years, without, however, having been made public. The *New York Times* of 2 February 1992 added: 'The campaign coincides with Germany's new assertion of its political strength...But one prominent German, Helmut Schmidt, the former chancellor, warned...that if the effort is perceived as too aggressive, it could stir bad feelings.' See also Ammon, 1991, p. 83, for earlier initiatives in this matter. In subsequent years the German government quietly continued to insist on the use of German on a par with English and French and finally, in the autumn of 1999, demanded from the Finns, who chaired the Commission at the time, that German be used in committee sessions along with English, French and the host language. This provoked a vivid discussion in Germany and induced the Spanish to warn that, if Germany had its way, they too would demand equal status.

29   Native English speakers *as a collectivity* would do better not to learn the individually most rewarding option, French, since that would only add to the numbers of a rival language. Collectively they would be better off spreading their second-language learning over the smallest and least central languages, which would never become a rival option for foreign-language learners elsewhere, while the speakers of English plus one of these small languages would still add to the centrality of English. On the other hand, individual English students, of course, obtain a much better Q-value by adding French or, second best, German to their repertoire.

30   See, for a discussion of language policies in Spain, Hoffman, 1996; Brassloff, 1996.

31   Cf. Crystal, 1987, p. 453.

32   Among Budapest gymnasium students to whom the notion of central languages was explained, 89 per cent (of 170) answered that they thought that at present the most central language in Europe was English, and 9 per cent named German. Asked which language would be most central in Europe around the year 2010, 81 per cent thought that English was likely to be most central, 14 per cent German. Russian, French and other languages were hardly mentioned at all: Jannes Hartkamp, unpublished paper. Ammon, 1991, p. 77, asked the opinion of seventeen sociolinguists from Eastern Europe in 1989 and concluded that, all in all, German was still the most widely used lingua franca in Eastern Europe, even though for the younger generation English already played a larger role than German (and so, at the time, did Russian).

33   Cf. Dürmüller, 1991.

34   The official languages of Malta are English and Maltese. The latter is a dialect of Arabic written in the Latin alphabet.

35   Except in Malta.

36   *Eurobarometer*, 1991, pp. 70–90.

37   Both statistics are consistent with rational language learning: the anglophones can afford to wait and see others learn their language, but speakers of the less widespread languages must invest in learning the highly central languages, and in doing so gain a great increase in Q-value. Clearly, native English speakers reap 'position rents' from their

mother tongue at the expense of those who grew up with less prevalent and less central languages. Like so many advantages, this one too is undeserved. Although the issue of compensation arises in Union politics at every turn, to my knowledge it has never even been mentioned in this context. On the theoretical possibilities of fair compensation as a solution to language conflicts, see Pool, 1991.

38   Between the polling years 1987 and 1990 the percentage of young Europeans who felt competent in at least one official EC language increased from 50 per cent to 60 per cent, and among the young the percentage that estimated itself competent in English rose from 34 per cent to 42 per cent in the same period (*Eurobarometer*, 1991).

39   *Eurobarometer*, 1999, pp. 109–14. This tendency continues.

40   *Eurobarometer*, 1997, pp. 40–1.

41   It is hard to reconstruct from the data the impact of immigrant languages on the 'foreign'-language skills in their home society, since the surveys do not distinguish between native citizens, naturalized citizens and 'resident aliens'.

42   For a thorough discussion of the treaties and regulations governing the language regime for the various institutions of the European Community, and the subsequent Union, see Labrie, 1993.

43   The European Court of Justice uses the defendant's language in the proceedings, the 'deliberations' are held in French as the unofficial working language, and the findings are published in all official languages of the Community (plus Irish); see Labrie, 1993, pp. 130–2 (Catalan was added later; Mamadouh, 1995, p. 16).

44   This once again confirms the position of the Netherlands as what the French ambassador to the country aptly qualified as 'the smallest of the large and the largest of the small countries in the EU': Bernard de Montferrand, interview in *De Volkskrant*, 15 July 2000.

45   Mamadouh, 1995, presents the repertoires that are reported by more than ten MEPs. Hence, the figures for the smaller languages are much underestimated: the repertoires with, say, Portuguese (e.g. EN&FR&PT or FR&GE&PT) must be small, because the relatively small number of Portuguese representatives may well be distributed over several repertoires, none of them big enough to be counted in the present results. Hence, repertoires containing one or more of the smaller languages (PT, GR, DA), as they remain under the ten-member limit, are ignored by Mamadouh, 1995.

46   Mamadouh, 1995, p. 99.

47   Article 217 of the Treaty of Rome (1957) stipulates that the language regime of the Community's institutions is determined unanimously by the Council of Ministers. The Treaty leaves it to the institutions to determine how this regime shall be applied. The Treaty of Nice (2001) may imply that the present unanimity requirement will be replaced by a qualified majority from the year 2005 on. The use of French and English within the Commission is based on customary law. Cf. Truchot, 2001.

48 Schlossmacher, 1994, p. 118, reports that a majority of MEPs preferred a restricted number of working languages, even though such a proposal had just been defeated in Parliament at the time. See also Wright, 2000, p. 164, on the failure of proposals to reduce the number of languages used, typically at the eve of the accession of new members, that is, in 1982 and 1994: the Parliament's 'commitment to the equality of the official languages and working languages of all the countries of the union' was affirmed again (Wright, 2000, p. 167) – as the present model would predict.

49 The European Patent Office was instituted with a five-language regime: English, French, German, Italian and Spanish. After the vote, the Dutch representatives were criticized for not having been sufficiently alert. In the end, applications were nevertheless allowed to be submitted in any official language of the Union – an outcome that should no longer surprise (Mamadouh, 1995, p. 16).

50 Cf. Cestac, 1987.

51 Mamadouh, 1995.

52 Figures quoted by Ammon, 1996, p. 262.

53 Cf. O'Riagáin, 1991; Irish may also be used in the Parliament.

54 But Catalan may not be used in the Parliament; cf. Barrera i Vidal, 1991; Labrie, 1993, p. 249.

55 Belgium indeed has two official languages (or even three, with German), but these are all also official languages of neighbour states and do not add to the polyglossia of the Community.

56 The European Parliament has voted to support the European Charter for Minority Languages, adopted by the Council of Europe in 1992 (Wright, 2000, pp. 188–9). For a survey of decisions by the European Parliament, see Labrie, pp. 1993, pp. 213–54. A European Bureau for the Lesser Used Languages, created in 1982, acts as an advisory body to the Commission (Labrie, 1993, p. 239).

57 Wright, 2000, p. 187.

58 Examples are the student and teacher exchange programmes Erasmus and Lingua. However, in the smaller countries, courses for visiting students are taught mostly in English; 50 per cent of the teachers visit an English-speaking member country, another 25 per cent go to a francophone one (Truchot, 2001).

59 European Commission, 1996, pp. 54–5: 32 per cent learn French, 19 per cent German and 9 per cent Spanish.

60 Gubbins, 1996, p. 126, quoting Baratta and Clauss, 1991.

61 Truchot, 2001, p. 10: even higher estimates (1.8 billion Euros) circulate, but cannot be confirmed, 'as the subject remains taboo'. Gubbins, 1996, reported a total expenditure of 1.4 billion ECU (about 1 billion pounds), as early as 1989!

62 Truchot, 2001.

63 Cf. Bellier, 1994, pp. 56–7. Bellier, Abélès and McDonald collaborated in a fascinating anthropological study of the Commission.

64   In the correspondence with citizens and authorities outside the Union, initially French was used, but by now English has surpassed it by far.

Chapter 9   Conclusions and considerations

1   Henry Ford, with his keen but economistic eye, as long ago as 1925 proposed the abolition of all foreign-language education in the USA, since people in other countries would choose to learn English anyway (*International Herald Tribune*, 31 July 2000).

2   On the 'umbilical cord' that ties Africans to the former colonial language and makes for a disregard of indigenous languages, see Adegbija, 2000.

3   This does not rule out the opposite strategy: instead of preventing others from learning English, the elite may reproduce itself by making sure that the next generation learns English even better and from an earlier age. Cf. Dronkers, 1993; Weenink, 2000. A cultivated mid-Atlantic accent, a rich vocabulary and elegant phrasing help to distinguish the 'right people' from the other folk.

4   In fact, adding m languages to the n languages already in use requires increasing the number of interpreters by $(n + m)(n + m - 1) - n$ $(n - 1) = m(m + 2n - 1)$.

5   How precarious such an age-old and seemingly immutable equilibrium may be in fact is demonstrated by the abolition of Latin mass in the Catholic church.

6   In South Africa, however, linguists like Alexander, 1992, have defended the amalgamation of African languages into two major groups, so as to limit the proliferation of languages and bolster the chances of indigenous alternatives to English.

7   Thus, Van Parijs, 2000, has advocated a strict application of the linguistic territoriality principle: 'Cuius regio, eius lingua [The language is that of the people whose region it is]'. This should safeguard linguistic diversity across the globe as the firmest protection of cultural diversity and the firmest brake on the mobility of people (so as to maintain domestic social justice).

8   Wright, 2000, p. 174.

9   The delegates Patijn and Van der Hek in 1974; cf. Wright, 2000, p. 246; Coulmas, 1991, p. 31.

10   Labrie, 1993, p. 342; cf. also Gubbins, 1996.

11   Thus, one expert proposed that German schoolchildren should learn Turkish compulsorily – one sure recipe for ethnic animosities.

12   Cf. Zapp, 1979.

13   Wright, 2000, p. 222.

14   Cf. Weber, 1998, p. 59: 'It is generally acknowledged that MT [machine translation] works best (relatively spoken [*sic*]) with informative, factual, descriptive text in a matter-of-fact (functional) style, on scientific or technical topics with "invariance of content".'

15 Ibid., pp. 49–50: 'In fact, linguistic quality achievable by fully automatic translation was and is by no means comparable to that of human translation for publication and distribution.'
16 Cf. Posner, 1991a, 1991b, esp. p. 130; Ammon, 1994.
17 Bourdieu, 2001.
18 Cf. De Swaan, 2001.
19 Pennycook, 1994, final chapter: 'Towards a critical pedagogy for teaching English as a word language'.
20 And, as with other aspects of free speech, there are limitations. For example, authorities may require that people provide information and register (or refuse) consent in one or a few 'official' languages. There is no need, however, to construct language rights as a separate category of human rights, as in Skutnabb-Kangas and Phillipson, 1994.

References

Abas, Husen, '*Bahasa Indonesia* as a Unifying Language of Wider Communication: A Historical and Sociolinguistic Perspective' (Diss., Manila University). Manila (1978).

Adegbija, Efurosibina, 'Language Attitudes in West Africa', *International Journal of the Sociology of Language: Sociolinguistics in West Africa*, ed. Ayo Bamgbose, 141 (2000), pp. 75–100.

Ajulo, Sunday Babalola, 'Reflections on Sections 51 and 91 of the 1979 Constitution of the Federal Republic of Nigeria', *African Affairs* 89.357 (1990), pp. 511–22.

Ajulo, Sunday Babalola, 'The Nigerian Language Policy in Constitutional and Administrative Perspectives: Theory and Practice', *Journal of Asian and African Studies* 30.314 (December 1995), pp. 162–80.

Akinnaso, F. Niyi, 'One Nation, Four Hundred Languages: Unity and Diversity in Nigeria's Language Policy', *Language Problems and Language Policy* 3.2 (summer 1989), pp. 133–46.

Alexander, Neville, 'South Africa: Harmonising Nguni and Sotho', in N. Crawhhall (ed.), *Democratically Speaking: International Perspectives on Language Planning*. Cape Town: National Language Project (1992), pp. 56–68.

Alexandre, Pierre, *Langues et langage en Afrique Noire*. Paris: Payot (1967).

Ammon, Ulrich, *Die Internationale Stellung der Deutschen Sprache*. Berlin/New York: De Gruyter (1991).

Ammon, Ulrich, 'The Present Dominance of English in Europe. With an Outlook on Possible Solutions to the European Language Problems', in Ulrich Ammon, Klaus J. Mattheier and Peter H. Nelde (eds), *Sociolinguis-*

tica: International Yearbook of European Sociolinguistics. Vol. 8: *English Only? in Europe*. Tübingen: Max Niemeyer Verlag (1994), pp. 1–14.

Ammon, Ulrich, 'The European Union (EU – formerly European Community): Status Change of English during the Last Fifty Years', in Joshua A. Fishman, Andrew W. Conrad and Alma Rubal–Lopez (eds), *Post–imperial English: Status Change in Former British and American Colonies, 1940–1990*. Berlin/New York: Mouton de Gruyter (1996), pp. 241–67.

Ammon, Ulrich, *Ist Deutsch noch internationale Wissenschaftssprache? Englisch auch für die Lehre an den deutschsprachigen Hochschulen*. Berlin/New York: Mouton de Gruyter (1998).

Ammon, Ulrich, 'Grundzüge der Internationalen Stellung der Deutschen Sprache – Mit Hinweisen auf der Neueste Entwicklungen', *Zeitschift für Anglistik und Amerikanistik*, 47.2 (1999), pp. 99–119.

Amuzu, Koko, 'The Role of English in Education in the New South Africa', *Language Matters: Studies in the Languages of South Africa*. Pretoria: University of South Africa, 24 (1993), pp. 129–41.

Anderson, Benedict R., *Language and Power: Exploring Political Cultures in Indonesia*. Ithaca, NY, and London: Cornell University Press (1990).

Appiah, Kwame A., *In my Father's House: Africa in the Philosophy of Culture*. New York: Oxford University Press (1992).

Arasanyin, Olaoba, 'Learning from India's Experience: The Quest for Unilangue in Nigeria', *Journal of the Third World Spectrum* 4.1 (1997), pp. 37–69.

Arthur, W. Brian, 'Positive Feedbacks in the Economy', *Scientific American* 262 (1990), 80–5.

Balibar, Renée, 'Préface: la langue de la France exercée au pluriel', in G. Vermes and J. Boutet (eds), *France, pays multilingue. Tome I: Les langues en France, un enjeu historique et social*. Paris: Éditions l'Harmattan (1987), pp. 9–20.

Bamgbose, Ayo, 'Post-imperial English in Nigeria', in Joshua A. Fishman, Andrew W. Conrad and Alma Rubal-Lopez (eds), *Post-imperial English: Status Change in Former British and American Colonies, 1940–1990*. Berlin/New York: Mouton de Gruyter (1996), pp. 557–88.

Baratta, M. and J. U. Clauss, *Internationale Organisationen*. Frankfurt: Fischer (1991).

Barnes, Dayle, 'Nationalism and the Mandarin Movement: The First Half-century', in Robert L. Cooper (ed.), *Language Spread: Studies in Diffusion and Social Change*. Bloomington, IN: Indiana University Press (1982), pp. 260–90.

Barrera i Vidal, Albert, 'Le Catalan, une langue d'Europe', in Ulrich Ammon, Klaus J. Mattheier and Peter H. Nelde (eds), *Sociolinguistica: International Yearbook of European Sociolinguistics. Vol. 5: Focus: Status and Function of the Language in the Political Bodies of the European Community*. Tübingen: Niemeyer (1991), pp. 99–110.

Bellier, Irène, 'Une culture de la Commission Européenne? De la rencontre des cultures et du multilinguisme des fonctionnaires', in Yves Mény, Pierre

Muller and Jean-Louis Quermonne (eds), *Politiques publiques en Europe*. Paris: Éditions l'Harmattan (1994), pp. 49–60.

Bennett, Charles J., 'The Morphology of Language Boundaries: Indo-Aryan and Dravidian in Peninsular India', in David Sopher (ed.), *An Exploration of India: Geographical Perspectives on Society and Culture*. London: Longman (1980), pp. 234–51.

Benrabah, Mohamed, *Langue et pouvoir en Algérie: histoire d'un traumatisme linguistique*. Paris: Séguier (1999).

Bernstein, Basil, *Class, Codes, and Control. Vol. 1: Theoretical Studies Towards a Sociology of Language*. London: Routledge & Kegan Paul (1974).

Bhagwati, Jagdish, *Protectionism*. Cambridge, MA: MIT Press (1988).

Biltereyst, Daniël, 'Language and Culture as Ultimate Barriers? An Analysis of the Circulation, Consumption and Popularity of Fiction in Small European Countries', *European Journal of Communication* 7 (1992), pp. 517–40.

Biro Pusat Statistik, *Sensus Penduduk*. Jakarta (1991).

Blankart, Charles B. and Gunter Knieps, 'Path Dependence, Network Externalities and Standardization', *Memorandum from Institute of Economic Research* (memorandum no. 439), Faculty of Economics, University of Groningen (August 1991).

Blok, Anton, 'Het Narcisme van Kleine Verschillen', *Amsterdams Sociologisch Tijdschrift* 24.2 (1997), pp. 159–87.

Bourdieu, Pierre, *Distinction: A Social Critique of the Judgement of Taste*. London: Routledge & Kegan Paul (1984).

Bourdieu, Pierre, *Language and Symbolic Power*. Cambridge: Polity (1991).

Bourdieu, Pierre, Marc Fumaroli, Claude Hagège, Abram De Swaan, Immanuel Wallerstein, 'Quelle langue pour une Europe démocratique? (débat)', *Raisons* Politiques 1 (2001).

Brann, Conrad M. B., 'Democratization of Language Use in Public Domains in Nigeria', *Journal of Modern African Studies* 31.4 (1993), pp. 639–56.

Brass, Paul, *Language, Religion and Politics in North India*. Cambridge: Cambridge University Press (1974).

Brassloff, Audrey, 'Centre–Periphery Communication in Spain: The Politics of Language and the Language of Politics', in Charlotte Hoffmann (ed.), *Language, Culture and Communication in Contemporary Europe*. Clevedon/Philadelphia: Multilingual Matters (1996), pp. 111–23.

Calvet, Louis-Jean, 'The Spread of Mandingo: Military, Commercial, and Colonial Influences on a Linguistic Datum', in Robert L. Cooper (ed.), *Language Spread: Studies in Diffusion and Social Change*. Bloomington, IN: Indiana University Press (1982).

Calvet, Louis-Jean, *La Guerre des langues et les politiques linguistiques*. Paris: Payot (1987).

Calvet, Louis-Jean, 'Quel modèle sociolinguistique pour le Sénégal?', *Langage et société* 68 (June 1994), pp. 89–108.

Calvet, Louis-Jean, *Pour une écologie des langues du monde*. Paris: Plon (1999).

Calvet, Louis-Jean and François Wioland, 'L'Expansion du Wolof au Séné-gal', *Bulletin de l'IFAN* 29.3/4, series B (1967).

Carnoy, Martin, 'Whither the Nation-state?', in Martin Carnoy (ed.), *The New Global Economy in the Information Age: Reflections on Our Changing World*. University Park: Pennsylvania State University Press (1993).

Casanova, Pascale, *La République mondiale des lettres*. Paris: Éditions du Seuil (1999).

Cavalli-Sforza, Luigi Luca, *Genes, Peoples, and Languages*. New York: North Point Press (2000).

Census of India 1991 [IV, B(i), (b), C-series]. New Delhi: Registrar General of India (1999).

Cestac, Françoise, 'La Traduction et les services de la conférence à l'Organisation des Nations Unies', in Lorne Laforge (ed.), *Proceedings of the International Colloquium on Language Planning; May 25–9, 1986*. Quebec: Presses de l'Université de Laval (1987), pp. 377–93.

Chambert-Loir, Henri, 'La Démographie indonésienne', *Archipel* 51 (1996), pp. 29–34.

Chartier, Roger and Pietro Corsi (eds), *Sciences et langues en Europe*. Paris: École des Hautes Études en Sciences Sociales (1996).

Chaudenson, Robert (ed.), *Des Langues et des villes*. Paris: Didier (1990).

Chaudenson, Robert (ed.), *La Francophonie: représentations, réalités, perspectives*. Paris: Didier (1991).

Cheng, Robert L., 'Language Unification in Taiwan: Present and Future', in William C. McCormack and Stephen A. Wurm (eds), *Language and Society: Anthropological Issues*. The Hague/Paris/New York: Mouton (1979), pp. 540–78.

Church, Jeffrey and Ian King, 'Bilingualism and Network Externalities', *Canadian Journal of Economics*, 26.2 (1993), pp. 337–45.

Clayton, Thomas, 'Decentering Language in World-system Inquiry', *Language Problems and Language Planning* 23.2 (summer 1999), pp. 133–56.

Cluver, August D. de V., 'The Decline of Afrikaans', *Language Matters* 24 (1993), pp. 15–46.

Collins, Randall, *Weberian Sociological Theory*. Cambridge: Cambridge University Press (1986).

Connolly, Cyril, *Enemies of Promise*. Harmondsworth: Penguin (1961).

Conrad, Andrew W. and Joshua Fishman, 'English as a World Language: The Evidence', in Joshua L. Fishman, Robert L. Cooper and Andrew W. Conrad, *The Spread of English as an Additional Language*. Rowley, MA: Newbury House (1977).

Coulmas, Florian, 'Die Sprachenregelung in den Organen der EG', in Ulrich Ammon, Klaus J. Mattheier and Peter H. Nelde (eds), *Sociolinguistica: International Yearbook of European Sociolinguistics. Vol. 5: Focus: Status and Function of the Languages in the Political Bodies of the European Community*. Tübingen: Niemeyer (1991), pp. 24–36.

Coulmas, Florian, *Die Wirtschaft mit der Sprache: Eine Sprachsoziologische Studie*. Frankfurt: Suhrkamp (1992).

Crosby, Alfred W., *Ecological Imperialism: The Biological Expansion of Europe, 900–1900*. Cambridge: Cambridge University Press (1986).

Crozon, Ariel, 'Maneno wa Siasa, les Mots du Politique en Tanzanie', *Politique Africaine* 64.12 (1996), pp. 18–30.

Crystal, David (ed.), *The Cambridge Encyclopedia of Language*. Cambridge: Cambridge University Press (1987).

Crystal, David, *An Encyclopedic Dictionary of Language and Languages*. Oxford: Blackwell (1992).

Crystal, David, *English as a Global Language*. Cambridge: Cambridge University Press (1997).

Curtin, Philip D., *Cross-Cultural Trade in World History*. Cambridge: Cambridge University Press (1984).

Daff, Moussa, 'Sénégal', in Robert Chaudenson (ed.), *La Francophonie: représentations, réalités, perspectives*. Paris: Didier (1991), pp. 138–59.

Das Gupta, Jyotindra, *Language Conflict and National Development*. Los Angeles/London: University of California Press (1970).

De Josselin de Jong, P. E., 'Afhankelijkheid, onafhankelijkheid, vrijheid: de taalkundige situatie', *Forum der Letteren* 17. 1 (1976), p 1–22.

De Klerk, Vivian (ed.), *Vol. 15: Focus on South Africa. Varieties of English Around the World*. Amsterdam/Philadelphia: John Benjamins (1996).

De Mauro, Tullio, *Storia linguistica dell'Italia Unita*. Rome: Laterza [1963] (1983).

De Swaan, Abram, *In Care of the State: Health Care, Education and Welfare in Europe and the United States in the Modern Era*. Cambridge/New York: Polity/Oxford University Press (1988).

De Swaan, Abram, 'Kwaliteit is Klasse: De Sociale Wording en Werking van het Cultureel Smaakverschil', in *Perron Nederland*. Amsterdam: Meulenhoff (1991a), pp. 59–92.

De Swaan, Abram, 'Notes on the Emerging Global Language System: Regional, National and Supranational', *Media, Culture and Society* 13 (1991b), pp. 309–23.

De Swaan, Abram, 'The Evolving European Language System: A Theory of Communication Potential and Language Competition', *International Political Science Review* 14.3 (1993), pp. 241–57.

De Swaan, Abram, 'La Francophonie en Afrique: une vision de la sociologie et de l'économie politique de la langue', in Jean-Louis Calvet and Caroline Juillard (eds), *Les Politiques linguistiques: mythes et réalités*. Montreal: AUPELF/UREF (1996).

De Swaan, Abram, 'Widening Circles of Disidentification: On the Psycho- and Sociogenesis of the Hatred of Distant Strangers; Reflections on Rwanda', *Theory, Culture and Society* 14.2 (1997a), pp. 105–22.

De Swaan, Abram, 'Language Politics in India and Europe: A Comparison Based on a Model of Conflict of Language Interests', in Martin R. Doornbos and Sudipta Kaviraj (eds), *Dynamics of State Formation: India and Europe Compared*. New Delhi/London: Sage (1997b), pp. 125–50.

De Swaan, Abram, 'A Rejoinder to Axel van den Berg's 'Note on Rational Choice Theory, Historical Sociology and the Ceteris Paribus Assumption', *Netherlands Journal of Social Sciences* 35.2 (1999), pp. 174–6.

De Swaan, Abram, 'English in the Social Sciences', in Ulrich Ammon (ed.), *The Dominance of English as a Language of Science: Effects on Other Languages and Language Communities*. Berlin/New York: Walter de Gruyter (2001) pp. 71–85.

Deacon, Terrence W., *The Symbolic Species: The Co-evolution of Language and the Brain*. New York/London: Norton (1997).

Décsy, Gyula, *Die Linguistische Struktur Europas: Vergangenheit, Gegenwart, Zukunft*. Wiesbaden: Harassowitz (1973).

Denison, Norman, 'English in Europe, with Particular Reference to the German-speaking Area', in *Europäische Mehrsprachigkeit* [Festschrift Mario Wandruszka]. Tübingen: Niemeyer (1980).

Deutsch, Karl W., *Nationalism and Social Communication: An Inquiry into the Foundations of Nationality*. 1st edn 1953. Cambridge, MA: MIT Press (1966).

Deutsch, Karl W., 'The Trend of European Nationalism – the Language Aspect', in Joshua A. Fishman (ed.), *Readings in the Sociology of Language*. The Hague/Paris: Mouton (1968), pp. 598–606.

Dieckhoff, Alain, *L'Invention d'une nation: Israël et la modernité politique*. Paris: Gallimard (1993).

Diongue, Marietou, *Francophonie et langues africaines en Sénégal*. Dakar: École Normale Supérieure des Bibliothèques (1980).

Diouf, Makhtar, *Le Sénégal: les ethnies et la nation*. Paris: Éditions Harmattan (1994).

Doke, Clement M., *Contributions to the History of Bantu Linguistics*. Johannesburg: Witwatersrand University Press (1961).

Domínguez, Francesc, 'Toward a Language-marketing Model', *International Journal of the Sociology of Language* 134 (1998), pp. 1–14.

Dorian, Nancy (ed.), *Investigating Obsolescence: Studies in Language Contraction and Death*. Cambridge: Cambridge University Press (1989).

Dronkers, Jaap, 'The Causes of Growth of English Education in the Netherlands: Class or Internationalization?', *International Journal of Sociology* 24. 2–3 (1993), pp. 111–30.

Dua, Hans R., *Language Planning in India*. New Delhi: Harnam (1985).

Dua, Hans R., 'Formation of Linguistic States in India' [unpublished manuscript]. Mysore: Central Institute of Indian Languages (1990).

Dua, Hans R., 'Language Planning in India: Problems, Approaches and Prospects', in David Marshall (ed.), *Language Planning: Focusschrift in Honour of Joshua Fishman*. Amsterdam/Philadelphia: John Benjamins (1991), pp. 105–33.

Dua, Hans R., 'Hindi Language Spread Policy and its Implementation: Achievements and Prospects', *International Journal of the Sociology of Language* 107 (1994), pp. 115–43.

Dua, Hans R., 'The Politics of Language Conflict: Implications for Language Planning and Political Theory', *Language Problems and Language Planning* 20.1 (1996a), pp. 1–17.

Dua, Hans R., 'The Spread of English in India: Politics of Language Conflict and Language Power', in Joshua A. Fishman, Andrew W. Conrad and Alma Rubal-Lopez (eds), *Post-imperial English: Status Change in Former British and American Colonies, 1940–1990*. Berlin/New York: Mouton de Gruyter (1996b), pp. 557–88.

Dumont, P., *Le Français et les langues africaines au Sénégal*. Paris: ACCT-Karthala (1983).

Durand, Jacques, 'Linguistic Purification, the French Nation-State and the Linguist', in Charlotte Hoffmann (ed.), *Language, Culture and Communication in Contemporary Europe*. Clevedon/Philadelphia: Multilingual Matters (1996), pp. 75–92.

Dürmüller, Urs, 'Swiss Multilingualism and International Communication', in Ulrich Ammon, Klaus J. Mattheier and Peter H. Nelde (eds), *Sociolinguistica 5: Schwerpunkt: Status und Funktion der Sprachen in den Institutionen der Europäischen Gemeinschaft*. Tübingen: Niemeyer (1991), pp. 1–62.

Dwivedi, S., *Hindi on Trial*. New Delhi: Vikas (1981).

Eco, Umberto, *La Ricerca della lingua perfetta nella cultura europea*. Rome: Editori Laterza (1993).

Eisenstein, Elizabeth L., 'Some Conjectures about the Impact of Printing on Western Society and Thought: A Preliminary Report', in H. J. Graff (ed.), *Literacy and Social Development in the West: A Reader*, Cambridge: Cambridge University Press (1981).

Elias, Norbert, *What Is Sociology?*. London: Hutchinson (1978).

Encyclopaedia Britannica, http://www.britannica.com.

État de la francophonie dans le monde: rapport du Haut Conseil de la Francophonie. Paris: La Documentation Française (1986).

Étiemble, René, *Parlez-vous Franglais?* Paris: Gallimard (1973).

Eurobarometer, 'Young Europeans in 1990', European Coordination Office, no. 34.2 (1991).

Eurobarometer, 'Young Europeans', Brussels: European Commission (D. G. XXII), no. 47.2 (1997).

Eurobarometer, '25th anniversary issue', European Coordination Office, no. 50 (1999).

European Commission, *Key Data on Education in the European Union*. Luxembourg: Office for Official Publications of the European Communities (1996).

European Companion, 1993, The, ed. *Isobel Smythe-Wood*. London: D. D (1993).

Europese Commissie, *De Vijftien Lidstaten van Europa: Kerncijfers*. Luxembourg: Bureau voor Officiële Publicaties der Europese Gemeenschappen (2000).

Fabian, Johannes, *Language and Colonial Power: The Appropriation of Swahili in the Former Belgian Congo 1880–1938*. Cambridge: Cambridge University Press (1986).

Fakuade, Gbenga, 'Lingua Franca from African Sources in Nigeria: The Journey so Far', *Language Problems and Language Planning* 18.1 (1994), pp. 38–46.

Fardon, Richard and Graham Furniss (eds), *African Languages, Development and the State*. London: Routledge (1993).

Fasold, Ralph, *The Sociolinguistics of Society*. Oxford: Blackwell (1994).

Ferguson, Charles A., 'Diglossia', *Word* 15 (1959).

Finlayson, R., 'Women's Language of Respect: Isihlonipho Sabafazi', in R. Mesthrie (ed.), *Language and Social History: Studies in South African Sociolinguistics*. Cape Town: David Philip (1995), pp. 140–53.

Fishman, Joshua A., 'National Languages and Languages of Wider Communication in the Developing Nations', in Answar S. Dil (ed.), *Language in Social-Cultural Change*. Stanford, CA: Stanford University Press (1972), pp. 191–223.

Fishman, Joshua A. (ed.), *The Earliest Stage of Language Planning: The 'First Congress' Phenomenon*. Berlin: Mouton de Gruyter (1993).

Flaitz, Jeffra, *The Ideology of English: French Perceptions of English as a World Language*. Berlin: Mouton de Gruyter (1988).

Forrest, Alan, 'A New Start for Cultural Action in the European Community: Genesis and Implication of Article 128 of the Treaty on European Union', *European Journal of Cultural Policy* 1.1 (1994), pp. 11–20.

Friedrich, Carl J., *Europe: An Emergent Nation?* New York: Harper and Row (1969).

Fullante, Luis Cruz, 'The National Language Question in the Philippines, 1936 to the Present' (Diss., University of California). Los Angeles (1983).

Geertz, Clifford, 'Linguistic Etiquette', in Joshua A. Fishman (ed.), *Readings in the Sociology of Language*. The Hague/Paris: Mouton (1968), pp. 282–95.

Gehnen, Marianne, 'Die Arbeitssprachen in der Kommission der Europäischen Gemeinschaft unter besonderer Berücksichtigung des Französischen', in Ulrich Ammon, Klaus J. Mattheier and Peter H. Nelde (eds), *Sociolinguistica: International Yearbook of European Sociolinguistics. Vol. 5: Focus: Status and Function of the Languages in the Political Bodies of the European Community*. Tübingen: Niemeyer (1991), pp. 51–63.

Gensini, S., *Elementi di storia linguistica italiana*. Bergamo: Minerva (1985).

Goffin, Roger, 'Le Statut des langues et les stratégies linguistiques dans les services de traduction des Communautés Européennes', in Lorne Laforge (ed.) *Proceedings of the International Colloquium on Language Planning; May 25–29, 1986*. Quebec: Presses de l'Université de Laval (1987), pp. 365–76.

Gonzalez, Andrew and Lourdes S. Bautista, *Language Surveys in the Philippines, 1966–1984*. Manila: De la Salle University Press (1986).

Goodman, Elliot R., 'World State and World Language', in Joshua A. Fishman (ed.), *Readings in the Sociology of Language*. The Hague/Paris: Mouton (1968), pp. 717–36.

Goody, Jack, *The Logic of Writing and the Organization of Society*. London: Cambridge University Press (1986).

Goossens, Jan, 'Was ist Deutsch – und wie verhält es sich zum Niederländischen?', in J. Göschel, N. Nail and G. van der Els (eds), *Zur Theorie des Dialekts*. Wiesbaden: Steiner (1976), pp. 256–82.

Gopal, Ram, *Linguistic Affairs of India*. Bombay: Asia Publishing House (1966).

Goudsblom, Johan, 'Het Algemeen Beschaafd Nederlands', in *Taal en Sociale Werkelijkheid: Sociologische Stukken*. Amsterdam: Meulenhoff (1988), pp. 11–29.

Goudsblom, Johan, *Fire and Civilization*. London: Allen Lane (1992).

Goudsblom, Johan, Eric Jones and Stephen Mennell, *The Course of Human History: Economic Growth, Social Process, and Civilization*. Armonk, NY: Sharpe (1996).

Goyvaerts, Didier L., 'Power, Ethnicity, and the Remarkable Rise of Lingala in Bukavu, Eastern Zaire', *International Journal of the Sociology of Language* 128 (1997), pp. 25–43.

Graddol, David, *The Future of English: A Guide to Forecasting the Popularity of the English Language in the 21st Century*. London: British Council (1997).

Greenberg, Joseph H., 'The Measurement of Linguistic Diversity', *Language* 32.1 (1956), pp. 109–15.

Grin, François and François Vaillancourt, 'The Economics of Multilingualism: Overview and Analytical Framework', *Annual Review of Applied Linguistics* 17 (1997), pp. 43–65.

Groeneboer, Kees, 'Djalan ke Barat. De Weg tot het Westen; Het Nederlands in Indië 1600–1950; Een Taalpolitieke Geschiedenis' (Diss., Rijks Universiteit Leiden). Leiden (1993).

Groeneboer, Kees, 'Nederlands-Indië en het Nederlands', in Kees Groeneboer (ed.), *Koloniale Taalpolitiek in Oost en West: Nederlands-Indië, Suriname, Nederlandse Antillen en Aruba*. Amsterdam: Amsterdam University Press (1997), pp. 55–84.

Gubbins, Paul, 'Sense and Pence: An Alternative Language Policy for Europe', in Charlotte Hoffmann (ed.), *Language, Culture and Communication in Contemporary Europe*. Clevedon/Philadelphia: Multilingual Matters (1996), pp. 124–31.

Guxman, M. M., 'Some General Regularities in the Formation and Development of National Languages', in Joshua A. Fishman (ed.), *Readings in the Sociology of Language*. The Hague/Paris: Mouton (1968), pp. 766–84.

Haas, W. (ed.), *Standard Languages – Spoken and Written*. Manchester/Totown: Manchester University Press/Barnes & Noble (1982), pp. 94–122.

Hagège, Claude, *Le Français et les siècles*. Paris: Odile Jacob (1987).

Halim, Amran, 'Language Planning in Indonesia', in Lorne Laforge (ed.), *Proceedings of the International Colloquium on Language Planning; May 25–29, 1986*. Quebec: Presses de l'Université de Laval (1987), pp. 95–102.

Haselhuber, Jakob, 'Erste Ergebnisse einer empirischen Untersuchung zur Sprachensituation in der EG-Kommission', in Ulrich Ammon, Klaus J. Mattheier and Peter H. Nelde (eds), *Sociolinguistica: International Yearbook of European Sociolinguistics. Vol. 5: Focus: Status and Function of the Languages in the Political Bodies of the European Community.* Tübingen: Niemeyer (1991), pp. 37–50.

Heilbron, Johan, 'Nederlandse Vertalingen Wereldwijd: Kleine Landen en Culturele Mondialisering', in J. Heilbron, W. de Nooy and W. Tichelaar (eds), *Waarin een Klein Land...Nederlandse Cultuur in Internationaal Verband.* Amsterdam: Prometheus (1995).

Herbert, Robert K. (ed.), *Language and Society in Africa.* Johannesburg: Witwatersrand University Press (1992).

Hindley, Reg, *The Death of the Irish Language: A Qualified Obituary.* London: Routledge (1990).

Hobsbawm, Eric, *Nations and Nationalism since 1780. Programme, Myth, Reality.* Cambridge: Cambridge University Press (1990).

Hoffman, J. E., 'The Malay Language as a Force for Unity in the Indonesian Archipelago 1815–1900', *Nusantara* 4 (July 1973), pp. 19–35.

Hoffmann, Charlotte, 'Language Planning at the Crossroads: The Case of Contemporary Spain', in Charlotte Hoffmann (ed.), *Language, Culture and Communication in Contemporary Europe.* Clevedon/Philadelphia: Multilingual Matters (1996), pp. 93–110.

Hoskins, Colin and Rolf Mirus, 'Reasons for the US Dominance of the International Trade in Television Programmes', *Media, Culture and Society* 10 (1988), pp. 499–515.

India Today, State of the Nation. http://www.india-today.com/itoday/18081997/language.html.

Inglehart, Ronald F. and Margaret Woodward, 'Language Conflicts and Political Integration', *Comparative Studies in Society and History* 10 (1967), pp. 27–45.

Jablonski, Nina G. and Leslie C. Aiello (eds), *The Origin and Diversification of Language.* San Francisco: Memoirs of the California Academy of Sciences, no. 24 (1998).

Jacobs, Glenda, 'Delusions of Adequacy: Word Usage Misconceptions among First-year University Students', in *Our Multilingual Society: Supporting the Reality (Proceedings Part II of the 12th Annual Conference of the South African Applied Linguistics Association, University of Port Elizabeth, 28–30 June 1993)*, pp. 70–5.

Jaffrelot, Christophe, 'Le Multiculturalisme indien à l'épreuve: le cas des débats constitutionnels', *L'Année Sociologique* 46.1 (1996), pp. 187–210.

Jakobson, Norman, 'The Beginning of National Self-determination in Europe', in Joshua A. Fishman (ed.), *Readings in the Sociology of Language.* The Hague/Paris: Mouton (1968), pp. 585–97.

Janks, Hilary, 'Contested Terrain: English Education in South Africa 1948–1987', in I. Goodson and P. Medway (eds), *Bringing English to Order: The History and Politics of a School Subject.* London: Falmer Press (1990), pp. 242–61.

Janson, Tore and Joseph Tsonope, *Birth of a National Language: The History of Setswana.* Gaborone: Heinemann Botswana (1991).

Josselin de Jong, P. E. de, 'Afhankelijkheid, Onafhankelijkheid, Vrijheid: de Taalkundige Situatie', *Forum der Letteren* 17.1 (1976), pp. 1–22.

Kachru, Braj B., *The Alchemy of English: The Spread, Functions and Models of Non-native Englishes*. Delhi: Oxford University Press (1986).

Kashadidi, Kashala M. and Bwantsa K. Obonobon, 'Zaïre', in Robert Chaudenson (ed.), *La Francophonie: représentations, réalités, perspectives*. Paris: Didier (1991b), pp. 165–6.

Katesi, Yime-Yime K., 'Langue et identité culturelle en Afrique', *Africa* 43.2 (1988), pp. 192–212.

Katz, Michael L. and Carl Shapiro, 'Technology Adoption in the Presence of Network Externalities', *Journal of Political Economy* 94.4 (1986), pp. 822–41.

Kazadi, Ntole, *L'Afrique afro-francophone*. Paris: Didier (1991).

Khubchandani, Lachman M., 'A Demographic Typology for Hindi, Urdu, Panjabi Speakers in South Asia', in William C. McCormack and Stephen A. Wurm (eds), *Language and Society: Anthropological Issues*. The Hague/Paris/New York: Mouton (1979), pp. 183–94.

Khubchandani, Lachman M., 'Multilingual Societies: Issues of Identity and Communication', *Sociolinguistics* 16.1 (June 1986), pp. 20–34.

Kindleberger, Charles P., 'Standards as Public, Collective and Private Goods', *Kyklos* 36.3 (1983), pp. 377–96.

Kloss, Heinz and Grant D. McConnell, *The Written Languages of the World: A Survey of the Degree and Modes of Use/Les Langues écrites du monde: relevé du degré et des modes d'utilisation*, ed. Albert Verdoodt. Quebec: Presses de l'Université de Laval (1989).

Kriel, Mariana, 'Taal en Sedes: die Nasionalistiese en Religieus-morele Waardes Onderliggend aan Taalpurisme', *South African Journal of Linguistics* 15.3 (1997), pp. 75–85.

Krishnamurti, Bh., 'Problems of Language Standardization in India', in William C. McCormack and Stephen A. Wurm (eds), *Language and Society: Anthropological Issues*. The Hague/Paris/New York: Mouton (1979), pp. 673–92.

Krishnamurti, Bh., 'Problems of Standardization in Indian Languages', in Lachman M. Khubchandani (ed.), *Language in a Plural Society*. Simla: Institute for Advanced Study (1988), pp. 56–64.

Kruger, Alet, 'Translation and Interpreting in South Africa', in Victor N. Webb (ed.), *Language in South Africa: An Input into Language Planning in a Post-Apartheid South Africa*. Pretoria: LiCCA Research and Development Programme, University of Pretoria (1995), pp. 209–49.

Labrie, Normand, *La Construction linguistique de la Communauté Européenne*. Paris: Champion (1993).

Laitin, David D., 'Linguistic Conflict in Catalonia', *Language Problems and Language Planning* 11.2 (1987), pp. 129–46.

Laitin, David D., 'Language Games', *Comparative Politics* 20.3 (1988), pp. 289–302.

Laitin, David D., 'Language Policy and Political Strategy in India', *Policy Sciences* 22.3/4 (1989a), pp. 415–36.

Laitin, David D., 'Linguistic Revival: Politics and Culture in Catalonia', *Comparative Studies in Society and History* 31.3 (1989b), pp. 297–317.

Laitin, David D., *Language Repertoires and State Construction in Africa.* Cambridge: Cambridge University Press (1992).

Laitin, David D., 'The Game Theory of Language Regimes', *International Political Science Review* 14.3 (1993), pp. 227–40.

Laitin, David D., 'The Tower of Babel as a Coordination Game: Political Linguistics in Ghana', *American Political Science Review* 88 (1994), pp. 622–34.

LANGTAG, *Overview, Recommendations and Executive Summary – Part I of the Final Report of the Language Plan Task Group.* Cape Town: Ministry of Arts, Culture, Science and Technology (1996).

Laponce, Jean A., *Languages and their Territories.* Toronto: University of Toronto Press (1987).

Leibowitz, Brenda, 'Portrait of an English Student: Challenges Facing the Multilingual University', in *Our Multilingual Society: Supporting the Reality (Proceedings Part II of the 12th Annual Conference of the South African Applied Linguistics Association, University of Port Elizabeth, 28–30 June 1993)*, pp. 123–31.

Lieberman, Phillip, *The Biology an Evolution of Language.* Cambridge, MA/London: Harvard University Press (1984).

Lieberson, Stanley, 'An Extension of Greenberg's Linguistic Diversity Measures', *Language* 40.4 (1964), pp. 526–31.

Lieberson, Stanley, 'Forces Affecting Language Spread: Some Basic Propositions', in Robert L. Cooper (ed.), *Language Spread: Studies in Diffusion and Social Change.* Bloomington, IN: Indiana University Press (1982), pp. 37–62.

Makoni, Sinfree and Nkonko Kamwangamalu (eds), *Language and Institutions in Africa.* Johannesburg: Witwatersrand University Press (1998).

Mallikarjun, B., *Language Use in Administration and National Integration.* Mysore: Central Institute of Indian Languages (1986).

Mamadouh, Virginie, *De Talen in het Europese Parlement.* Amsterdam: Instituut Voor Sociale Geografie, Universiteit van Amsterdam (1995).

Mamadouh, Virginie, 'Beyond Nationalism: Three Visions of the European Union and their Implications for the Linguistic Regime of its Institutions', *GeoJournal* 48.2 (1999), pp. 133–44.

Manessy, J., *Le français en Afrique Noire: mythe, stratégies, pratiques.* Paris: Éditions l'Harmattan / IDERIC (1994).

Manorama Yearbook 1996, 'Principal Languages'. Kottayam: Malayala Manorama (1996), pp. 464–85.

Marivate, C. N., 'Language and Education, with Special Reference to the Mother-Tongue Policy in African Schools', *Language Matters* 24 (1993), pp. 91–105.

Matsela, Z. A., 'Policy Formulation for Language Use in Lesotho', in David B. Coplan, Z. A. Matsela and M. B. Mochaba, *Sesotho Language and Culture.* Rome/Lesotho: National University of Lesotho Publishing House (n.d., *c.*1992).

Mazrui, Ali A., 'Islam and the English Language in East and West Africa', in W. H. Whiteley (ed.), *Language Use and Social Change: Problems of*

Multilingualism with Special Reference to Eastern Africa. London: Oxford University Press (1971), pp. 179–97.

Mazrui, Alamin M. and Ali A. Mazrui, 'Dominant Languages in a Plural Society: English and Kiswahili in Post-colonial East Africa', *International Political Science Review* [Special Issue on the Emergent World Language System, ed. Abram de Swaan] 14.3 (July 1993), pp. 275–92.

Mazrui, Alamin M. and Ali A. Mazrui, 'A Tale of Two Englishes: The Imperial Language in Post-colonial Kenya and Uganda', in Joshua A. Fishman, Andrew W. Conrad and Alma Rubal-Lopez (eds), *Post-imperial English: Status Change in former British and American Colonies, 1940–1990.* Berlin/New York: Mouton de Gruyter (1996), pp. 271–302.

McConnell, Grant, 'Towards a Scientific Geostrategy for English', *Terminogramme* (2001).

McConnell, Grant D. and Jean-Denis Gendron (eds), *Atlas international de la vitalité linguistique/International Atlas of Language Vitality. Vol. 1: Les Langues constitutionelles de l'Inde/Constitutional Languages of India.* Quebec: Centre International d'Aménagement Linguistique/International Centre for Research on Language Planning, Université de Laval (1993).

McConnell, Grant D. and Tan Kerang, *The Written Languages of the World: A Survey of the Degree and Modes of Use. Vol. 4: China; Book 1: Written Languages; Book 2: Unwritten Languages.* Quebec: Presses de l'Université de Laval (1995).

McNeill, William H., *Plagues and Peoples.* Garden City, NJ: Anchor Press/ Doubleday (1976).

Mehrotra, Raja Ram, 'The First Congress of Hindi', in Joshua A. Fishman (ed.), *The Earliest Stage of Language Planning: The 'First Congress' Phenomenon.* Berlin: Mouton de Gruyter (1993), pp. 117–27.

Mesthrie, Rajend (ed.), *Language and Social History: Studies in South African Sociolinguistics.* Cape Town: David Philip (1995).

Mintz, Sidney W., *Sweetness and Power: The Place of Sugar in Modern History.* New York: Viking (1985).

Mintz, Stanley and Sally Price, *The Birth of African-American Culture: An Anthropological Perspective.* Boston: Beacon Press (1992).

Misra, Bal G., 'Language Movements in the Hindi Region', in E. Annamalai (ed.), *Language Movements in India.* Mysore: Central Institute of Indian Languages (1979), pp. 70–9.

Moeliono, Anton M., *Language Development and Cultivation: Alternative Approaches in Language Planning.* Canberra: Australian National University (1986).

Moeliono, Anton M., 'The First Efforts to Promote and Develop Indonesian', in Joshua A. Fishman (ed.), *The Earliest Stage of Language Planning: The 'First Congress' Phenomenon.* Berlin: Mouton de Gruyter (1993), pp. 129–42.

Moseley, Christopher and R. E. Asher (eds), *Atlas of the World's Languages.* London: Routledge (1994).

Msimang, C. T., *African Language and Language Planning in South Africa: The Nhlapo Alexander Motion of Harmonisation Revisited.* Inaugural address. Pretoria: BARD (1992).

Muth, Richard F., 'Rent', in David L. Sills (ed.), *International Encylopedia of the Social Sciences. Vol. 13.* New York/London: Macmillan/Free Press (1968), pp. 458–59.

Ndolo, Ike S., 'The Case for Promoting the Nigerian Pidgin Language', *Journal of Modern African Studies* 27 (1989), pp. 679–84.

Ngalasso, Mwatha M., 'État des langues et langues d'état au Zaïre', *Politique Africaine* 23 (1986), pp. 7–72.

Ngalasso, Mwatha M., 'Le kikongo, le français et les autres: étude de la dynamique des langues dans la ville de Kikwit (Zaire)', in Robert Chaudenson (ed.), *Des Langues et des villes.* Paris: Didier (1990), pp. 459–74.

Ngonyani, Deo, 'Language Shift and National Identity in Tanzania', *Ufahamu* 23.2 (1995), pp. 69–92.

Ngugi wa Thiong'o, *Decolonising the African Mind: The Politics of Language in African Literature.* London: Currey (1986).

Nkusi, Laurent, 'Rwanda', in Robert Chaudenson (ed.), *La Francophonie: représentations, réalités, perspectives.* Paris: Didier (1991), pp. 134–6.

Nyati-Ramahobo, Lydia, 'Language Planning in Botswana', *Language Problems and Language Planning* 22.1 (1998), pp. 48–62.

Nyunda ya Rubango, 'Le Français au Zaïre: langue "supérieure" et chances de "survie" dans un pays africain', *Language Problems and Language Planning* 10.3 (1986), pp. 253–71.

Oladejo, James, 'The National Language Question in Nigeria: Is There an Answer?', *Language Problems and Language Planning* 15.3 (1991), pp. 255–67.

Olson, Mancur, *The Logic of Collective Action: Public Goods and the Theory of Groups.* Cambridge, MA / London: Harvard University Press (1965).

Omar, Asmah Haji, 'Post-imperial English in Malaysia', in Joshua A. Fishman, Andrew W. Conrad and Alma Rubal-Lopez (eds), *Post-imperial English: Status Change in Former British and American Colonies, 1940–1990.* Berlin/New York: Mouton de Gruyter (1996), pp. 513–33.

Omar, Asmah Haji, 'Language Planning and Image Building: The Case of Malay in Malaysian Language Planning and Image Building', *International Journal of the Sociology of Language* 130 (1998), pp. 49–66.

Omotoso, Bankole Ajibabi, *Season of Migration to the South: Africa's Crises Reconsidered.* Cape Town: Tafelberg (1994).

Ong, Walter J., *Orality and Literacy: The Technologizing of the Word.* London/New York: Methuen (1982).

O'Riagáin, Pádraig, 'National and International Dimensions of Language Policy when the Minority Language is a National Language: The Case of Irish in Ireland', in Florian Coulmas (ed.), *A Language Policy for the European Community: Prospects and Quandaries.* Berlin/New York: Mouton de Gruyter (1991), pp. 255–78.

Pandit, P. B., 'Perspectives on Sociolinguistics in India', in William C. McCormack and Stephen A. Wurm, *Language and Society: Anthropological Issues.* The Hague/Paris/New York: Mouton (1979), pp. 171–82.

Parker, Ian, 'The Rise of the Vernaculars in Early Modern Europe: An Essay in the Political Economy of Language', in Bruce Bain (ed.), *The Sociogenesis of Language and Human Conduct.* New York/London: Plenum (1983), pp. 323–51.

Pennycook, Alastair, *The Cultural Politics of English as an International Language.* London/New York: Longman (1994).

Phetoana, L. T., 'Our Multilingual Society: Support and Reality; Foreign Language Medium of Instruction and the Plight of its Indigenous Users', in *Our Multilingual Society: Supporting the Reality (Proceedings Part II of the 12th Annual Conference of the Southern African Applied Linguistics Association, University of Port Elizabeth, 28–30 June, 1993)*, pp. 196–202.

Phillipson, Robert, *Linguistic Imperialism.* Oxford/New York: Oxford University Press (1992).

Pinker, Steven, *The Language Instinct: The New Science of Language and Mind.* London: Penguin (1994).

Poedjosoedarmo, Soepomo, *Javanese Influence on Indonesian.* Canberra: Australian National University (1982).

Pollock, Sheldon, 'India in the Vernacular Millennium: Literary Culture and Polity, 1000–1500', *Daedalus: Journal of the American Academy of Arts and Sciences* 127.3 (1998), pp. 41–74.

Pool, Jonathan, 'Optimal Strategies in Linguistic Games', in Joshua A. Fishman et al. (eds), *The Fergusonian Impact: In Honor of Charles A. Ferguson on the Occasion of his 65th Birthday. Vol. 2: Sociolinguistics and the Sociology of Language.* Berlin/New York/Amsterdam: Mouton de Gruyter (1986), pp. 157–72.

Pool, Jonathan, 'The Official Language Problem', *American Political Science Review* 85.2 (1991), pp. 495–514.

Pool, Jonathan, 'Optimal Language Regimes for the European Union', *International Journal of the Sociology of Language* 121 (1996), pp. 159–80.

Posner, Roland, 'Der Polyglotte Dialog: Ein Humanistengespräch über Kommunikation im mehrsprachigen Europa', *Sprachreport* 3 (1991a), pp. 6–10.

Posner, Roland, 'Society, Civilization, Mentality: Prolegomena for a Language Policy for Europe', in Florian Coulmas (ed.), *A Language Policy for the European Community.* Berlin/New York: Mouton de Gruyter (1991b), pp. 121–37.

Prah, Kwesi Kwaa (ed.), *Between Distinction and Extinction: The Harmonisation and Standardisation of African Languages.* Johannesburg: Witwatersrand University Press (1998), pp. 43–52.

Prasad, N. K., *The Language Issue in India.* New Delhi: Leeladevi (1979).

Pütz, Martin, 'Official Monolingualism in Africa: A Sociolinguistic Assessment of Linguistic and Cultural Pluralism in Africa', in M. Pütz (ed.), *Discrimination through Language in Africa: Perspectives on the Namibian Experience.* Berlin: Mouton de Gruyter (1995), pp. 155–74.

Putzel, Roger, 'Francization of Companies in Quebec: What is at Stake? Review of Les Enjeux de la Francisation des Entreprises au Québec

(1977–1984)', *International Journal of the Sociology of Language* 121 (1996), p. 199.

Rahman, Tariq, 'British Language Policies and Imperialism in India', *Language Problems and Language Planning* 20.2 (1996), pp. 91–115.

Ramaswamy, Sumathi, *Passions of the Tongue: Language Devotion in Tamil India 1891–1970*. Berkeley: University of California Press (1997).

Ramsey, S. Robert, *The Languages of China*. Princeton, NJ: Princeton University Press (1987).

Ridge, Stanley G. M., 'Language Policy in a Democratic South Africa', in Michael Herriman and Barbara Burnaby (eds), *Language Policy in English-dominant Societies*. Cleveland: Multilingual Matters (1996), pp. 15–34.

Ridge, Stanley G. M., 'Language Policy and Democratic Practice in South Africa', in Sinfree Makoni and Nkonki Kamwangamalu (eds), *Language and Institutions in Africa*. Johannesburg: Witwatersrand University Press (1998), pp. 76–102.

Ridge, Stanley G. M., 'Mixed Motives: Ideological Elements in the Support for English in South Africa' [unpublished manuscript] (*c.* 1999).

Ridge, Stanley G. M., 'Discourse Constraints and Language Policy in South Africa', *Indian Journal of Applied Linguistics* 25 (2000), pp. 116–39.

Ruhlen, Merritt, *On the Origin of Languages: Studies in Linguistic Taxonomy*. Stanford: Stanford University Press (1994).

Rwezaura, B., 'Constraining Factors to the Adoption of Kiswahili as a Language of the Law in Tanzania', *Journal of African Law* 37.1 (1993), pp. 30–45.

Ryanga, Sheila, 'Imbalances in the Modernization and Promotion of the Swahili Language in East Africa: The Case of Kenya and Tanzania', *Ufahamu* 28.3 (1990), pp. 21–34.

Samarin, William J., 'Language in the Colonization of Central Africa, 1880–1900', *Canadian Journal of African Studies* 23.2 (1989), pp. 232–49.

Schelling, Thomas C., *Micromotives and Macrobehavior*. New York: Norton (1978).

Schlossmacher, Michael, 'Die Arbeitssprachen in den Organen der Europäischen Gemeinschaft. Methoden und Ergebnisse einer Empirischen Untersuchung', in Ulrich Ammon, Klaus J. Mattheier and Peter H. Nelde (eds), *Sociolingistica: International Yearbook of European Sociolinguistics. Vol. 8: English Only? in Europe*. Tübingen: Max Niemeyer Verlag (1994), pp. 101–22.

Schuring, Gerard K., 'Sensusdata oor die Tale van Suid-Afrika in 1991'. Pretoria: Raad vor Geesteswetenskaplike Navorsing (1993a).

Schuring, Gerard K., *Language and Education in South Africa: A Policy Study*. Pretoria: Human Sciences Research Council (1993b).

Schwartzberg, Joseph E., 'Factors in the Linguistic Reorganization of Indian States', in P. Wallace (ed.), *Region and Nation in India*. New Delhi: Oxford University Press (1985), pp. 155–82.

Scotton, Carol Myers M., 'Lingua Francas and Socioeconomic Integration: Evidence from Africa', in Robert L. Cooper (ed.), *Language Spread:*

Studies in Diffusion and Social Change. Bloomington, IN: Indiana University Press (1982), pp. 63–94.

Sibayan, Bonifacio P., 'Pilipino and the Filipino's Renewed Search for a Linguistic Symbol of Unity and Identity', in Joshua A. Fishman et al. (eds), *The Fergusonian Impact: In Honour of Charles A. Ferguson on the Occasion of his 65th Birthday. Vol. 2: Sociolinguistics and the Sociology of Language*. Berlin/New York/Amsterdam: Mouton de Gruyter (1986), pp. 351–60.

Siegel, James T., *Solo in the New Order: Language and Hierarchy in an Indonesian City*. Princeton, NJ: Princeton University Press (n. d., 1993), pp. 1–30.

Skutnabb-Kangas, Tove and Robert Phillipson (eds), *Linguistic Human Rights: Overcoming Linguistic Discrimination*. Berlin/New York: Mouton de Gruyter (1994).

Sridhar, S. N., 'Language Variation, Attitudes, and Rivalry: The Spread of Hindi in India', in Peter H. Lowenberg (ed.), *Language Spread and Language Policy: Issues, Implications and Case Studies*. Washington, DC: Georgetown University Press (1987), pp. 300–19.

Srivastava, R. N., 'Language Movements against Hindi as an Official Language', in E. Annamalai (ed.), *Language Movements in India*. Mysore: Central Institute of Indian Languages (1979), pp. 80–90.

Steinhauer, Hein, 'The Indonesian Linguistic Scene : 500 Languages Now, 50 in the Next Century?' in Sudaporn Luksaneeyanawin (ed.), *Pan-Asiatic Linguistics, Proceedings of the Third International Symposium on Language and Linguistics*. Vol. III. Bangkok: Chlalongkorn University Printing House (1993), pp. 1463–77.

Steinhauer, Hein, 'The Indonesian Language Situation and Linguistics: Prospects and Possibilties', *Bijdragen tot de Taal-, Land- en Volkenkunde* 150 (1994), pp. 755–84.

Steinhauer, Hein, *Endangered Languages in Southeast Asia*. Leiden: Koninklijk Instituut voor Taal-, Land- en Volkenkunde (1997).

Steinhauer, Hein, *Indonesisch en Indonesische Streektalen*. Inaugural Address, Catholic University of Nijmegen, 14 January (2000).

Strevens, Peter, 'The Spread of English and the Decline of French: A Paradox for Canada', in Lorne Laforge (ed.), *Proceedings of the International Colloquium on Language Planning; May 25–29, 1986*. Quebec: Presses de l'Université Laval (1987), pp. 349–56.

Swigart, Leigh, 'Wolof, langue ou ethnie: le dévelopement d'une identité nationale', in Robert Chaudenson (ed.), *Des Langues et des Villes*. Paris: Didier (1990), pp. 545–52.

Thompson, Leonard, *A History of South Africa*. New Haven, CT, and London: Yale University Press (1995).

Titlestad, Peter, 'English, the Constitution and South Africa's Language Future', in Vivian de Klerk (ed.), *Varieties of English around the World. Vol. 15: Focus on South Africa*. Amsterdam/Philadelphia: John Benjamins (1996), pp. 163–73.

Truchot, Claude, 'Les Langues européennes des territoires nationaux aux espaces globalisés. Observations sur les effets linguistiques de la mondialisation en Europe'. *Terminogramme* (2001).

Uhlenbeck, E. M., 'The Threat of Rapid Language Death: A Recently Acknowledged Global Problem', in *The Low Countries: Arts and Society in Flanders and the Netherlands. Vol. 1: 1993–1994*. Rekkem: Stichting Ons Erfdeel (1994), pp. 25–31.

Vaillancourt, François, 'Language and Socioeconomic Status in Quebec: Measurement, Findings, Determinants and Policy Costs', *International Journal of the Sociology of Language* 121 (1996), pp. 69–92.

Van Binsbergen, Wim, 'Minority Language, Ethnicity and the State in Two African Situations: The Nkoya of Zambia and the Kalanga of Botswana', in Richard Fardon and Graham Furniss (eds), *African Languages, Development and the State*. London/New York: Routledge (1994), pp. 142–90.

Van Bruggen, Carry, *Hedendaagsch Fetischisme*. Amsterdam: Querido (1925).

Van Calcar, Co and Jan Karel Koppen, *Cultureel Kapitaal: Op Weg naar een Instrument*. Amsterdam: St Kohnstamm Fonds (1984).

Van der Plank, Pieter, 'Taalassimilatie van Europese Taalminderheden: Een Inventariserende en Hypothesevormende Studie naar Assimilatieverschijnselen onder Europese Taalgroepen' (Diss., University of Utrecht). Rotterdam (1971).

Van Doorn, J. A. A., *De Laatste Eeuw van Indië: Ontwikkeling en Ondergang van een Koloniaal Project*. Amsterdam: Bert Bakker (1994).

Van Parijs, Philippe, 'The Ground Floor of the World: On the Socioeconomic Consequences of Linguistic Globalization', *International Political Science Review* 21.2 (2000) pp. 217–33.

Van Rensburg, Christo (ed.), *Afrikaans in Afrika*. Pretoria: Van Schaik (1997).

Van Woerden, *Moenie Kyknie*. Amsterdam: Nijgh & Van Ditmar (1993).

Varis, Tapio, 'The International Flow of Television Programs', *Journal of Communication* 34.2 (1984), pp. 143–52.

Veltman, Calvin, 'The English Language in Quebec 1940–1990', in Joshua A. Fishman, Andrew W. Conrad and Alma Rubal-Lopez (eds), *Post-imperial English: Status Change in Former British and American Colonies, 1940–1990*. Berlin: Mouton de Gruyter (1996), pp. 205–40.

Venter, Dawid, 'The Democratization of Language in South Africa? A World System Perspective', paper presented at the ISA-SASA conference at Stellenbosch/Belville, 27–8 January (1999).

Venter, Dawid, *The Political Sociology of Language*. In press.

Verdoodt, A., 'Social and Linguistic Structures of Burundi, a Typical "Unimodal" Country', in William C. McCormack and Stephen A. Wurm (eds), *Language and Society: Anthropological Issues*. The Hague/Paris/New York: Mouton (1979), pp. 509–31.

Vermes, G. and J. Boutet (eds), *France, pays multilingue. Tome I: Les langues en France, un enjeu historique et social*. Paris: Éditions l'Harmattan (1987).

Vogel, Ann, 'Über Mangel, Verlust und Verleugnung von Fremdsprachkompetenz: Eine Analyse des Russischunterrichts in der DDR als Beitrag zur Untersuchung der europäischen Fremdsprachensituation' [unpublished MA thesis]. Amsterdam: ACCESS, University of Amsterdam (1994).

Wallerstein, Immanuel, *The Modern World System: Capitalist Agriculture and the Origins of the European World-economy in the Sixteenth Century.* San Francisco: Academic Press (1974).

Wardhaugh, Ronald, *Languages in Competition: Dominance, Diversity and Decline.* Oxford/London: Blackwell/Deutsch (1987).

Webb, Vic, René Dirven and Elma Kock, 'Afrikaans: Feite en Interpretaties', in V. N. Webb (ed.), *Afrikaans ná Apartheid.* Pretoria: Van Schaik (1992), pp. 27–67.

Webb, Vic, 'English and Language Planning in South Africa: The Flip-side', in Vivian de Klerk (ed.), *Focus on South Africa.* Amsterdam/Philadelphia: John Benjamins (1996), pp. 175–90.

Weber, Nico, 'Machine Translation, Evaluation and Translation Quality Assessment', in Nico Weber (ed.), *Machine Translation: Theory, Applications and Evaluation; an Assessment of the State-of-the-art.* St Augustin: Gardez! (1998), pp. 47–84.

Weenink, Don, 'Socializing an International Elite? Proposal for a Study of Dutch–English Bilingual Classes' [unpublished paper]. Amsterdam School for Social Science Research (2000).

Weindling, Paul, 'The League of Nations and International Medical Communication in Europe between the First and Second World Wars', in Roger Chartier and Pietro Corsi (eds), *Sciences et langues en Europe.* Paris: École des Hautes Études en Sciences Sociales (1996), pp. 209–19.

Wesseling, H. L. (ed.), *Expansion and Reaction.* Leiden: Leiden University Press (1978).

Whiteley, Wilfred, *Swahili, the Rise of a National Language.* London: Methuen (1969).

Whiteley, Wilfred (ed.), *Language Use and Social Change: Problems of Multilingualism with Special Reference to Eastern Africa.* London: Oxford University Press (1971).

Wilkes, Arnet, 'The Black Languages', in Victor N. Webb (ed.), *Language in South Africa: An Input into Language Planning for a Post-Apartheid South Africa.* Pretoria: LiCCA Research and Development Programme, University of Pretoria (1995).

Wright, Sue, *Community and Communication: The Role of Language in Nation State Building and European Integration.* Cleveland: Multilingual Matters (2000).

Wurm, Stephen, Peter Mühlhäusler and Darrell Tyron (eds), *Atlas of Languages of International Communication in the Pacific, Asia and the Americas.* Berlin: Mouton de Gruyter (1996).

Yahya-Othman, Saida and Herman Batibo, 'The Swinging Pendulum: English in Tanzania 1940–1990', in Joshua A. Fishman, Andrew W. Conrad and Alma Rubal-Lopez (eds), *Post-imperial English: Status Change in Former British and American Colonies 1940–1990.* Berlin/New York: Mouton de Gruyter (1996), pp. 373–400.

Zapp, Franz-Josef, *La Politique des langues étrangéres en Europe – une esquisse du problème.* Brussels: European Cooperation Fund (1979).

Zolberg, Aristide, 'Why Islam is like Spanish', *Politics and Society* 27.1 (1999), pp. 5–38.

Index